BY GEORGE

BY GEORGE

The Autobiography of George Foreman

GEORGE FOREMAN
and Joel Engel

VILLARD BOOKS
NEW YORK
1995

A leatherbound, signed first edition of this book
has been published by the Easton Press.

Grateful acknowledgment is made to Dwarf Music for permission
to reprint four lines from "Rainy Day Women 12 and 35" by Bob Dylan.
Copyright © 1966 by Dwarf Music. Reprinted by permission.

Library of Congress Cataloging-in-Publication Data

Foreman, George
By George : the autobiography of George Foreman /
by George Foreman and Joel Engel.
p.   cm.
ISBN 0-679-44394-0 (alk. paper)
1. Foreman, George—Biography. 2. Boxers (Sports)—United
States—Biography. I. Engel, Joel. II. Title.
GV1132.F65A3   1995
796.8'3'092—dc20
[B]   95-7693

Manufactured in the United States of America on acid-free paper

24689753

FIRST TRADE EDITION

Book design by Carole Lowenstein

To my wife, Joan, who was the answer to my prayers.
She came along when I needed her
and gave me the best reason of all to live—and to love life.

—George Foreman

To my father-in-law, Joe Blindman,
who on November 5 celebrated his first birthday away from us
by cheering from a ringside seat in heaven.

—Joel Engel

Acknowledgments

Sincere thanks to the following people, whose invaluable assistance made this book possible:

Mary Ellen Strote, for her keen insights and excellent taste.

Mort Sharnik, for generously sharing his encyclopedic knowledge.

Ilene Arenberg, for her helpful transcriptions.

Pat Rizzo, for finding the shortest distance between two points.

Catherine Peck, for knowing whom to call and how to get there.

Fran and Maggie Engel, for their endless patience.

David Rosenthal, for his grace under fire.

Henry Holmes, for at least thirty-five reasons—which is why I gave him the glove that knocked out Michael Moorer and regained for me the heavyweight championship.

Harve Bennett, for being the catalyst this book needed.

And to the following people, my deepest gratitude for helping to make me who I am today:

Jim Brown, who was the first to tell me that I could get a second chance. Seldom does a hero on the field also turn out to be a hero in real life. Many thanks, Jimmy, for being that hero.

Lyndon Baines Johnson, the politician who went beyond politics to compassion. His creation of the Job Corps rescued me from the gutter. I was, and always will be, proud to wear my LBJ Stetson in his honor.

Charles "Doc" Broadus, who saw something in me that no one else could see. Thank you for having faith in me—even when I didn't—and for helping so many others.

Larry King, whose radio show kept me in touch with the world during the years when I didn't have a television. Thank you for the voice of one crying in the wilderness.

My sister Willie Mae, who, year after year, does the hard work of a family. Thank you for being what I couldn't be. Thank you on behalf of all our family.

Barney Oldfield, for a lifetime of friendship, devotion, counsel, and wisdom. The world would be a far better place if everyone were lucky enough to have a friend like you.

And, oh yeah. Thank you, Jesus.

Introduction

Before reading this book, you should know a few facts about me.

One: I never use foul language. As a young man I could swear with the best of them. But I left that behind long ago. I've since found other words to express my thoughts. When necessary in these pages, I like to substitute "blankety-blank" for words that aren't in my family dictionary.

Two: I never make references to a human being's color. As I did with bad language, I've eliminated from my vocabulary words that distinguish between people. They're irrelevant to me, and their use only divides us from each other. I know from my own life that the issue of prejudice is much broader than the frame into which people usually try to squeeze it. What separates us is not color but behavior. I once came across some words by Victor Frankl, a man who'd survived terrible atrocities in a Nazi concentration camp at the hands of men who, after all, were the same color as he: "There are only two races of people in the world, the decent and the indecent." So when reading this book, if you find yourself guessing or wondering about one person or another's color, please ask yourself why you need to know.

Three: I have a good memory and have written the events described here just as they happened. But my life has taken shape along its own course, and it's not a course anyone else I know has followed. So some of the terrain may look unfamiliar, and some of the decisions I've made probably wouldn't be the ones you would have made in my shoes. As the guy who wore those size 14s, even I can't always explain reasons for this or that. All I can do is tell my story, and hope it makes sense to you.

And I pray you take away something important from the reading.

BY GEORGE

Chapter One

I'M NOT MUCH OF A SLEEPER. Haven't been since I was a kid and needed to keep one eye open all night to shoo away the rats and mice. Now, after reading into the wee hours, I doze off at five or six. Then I sleep late, so I'm usually not any help getting the kids ready for school.

One morning in 1984, I was awakened shortly after falling asleep by the angry voice of my oldest son, George—"Little George," we call him—who was ten. "No," he screamed. "I'm not going to wear those. I don't want to look poor."

This sounded interesting. On my way to investigate, I heard my wife arguing with him. "There's nothing wrong with those pants," Joan said. "They're clean, they're pressed, and you're going to wear them."

Neither Joan nor Little George noticed me standing in the doorway to Little George's room. On the bed was the item in dispute, a pair of faded blue jeans that Joan had chosen to go with the checked shirt he already had on. "What's wrong here?" I asked. But I already knew: Living in a nice house in a good neighborhood (Humble, a suburb of Houston), going to a fine school, my boy had no idea what poor really meant (he'd even pronounced the word "poor" instead of "po' "); I'd never bothered to explain to him where I'd come from.

That night, I took Little George for a ride through Houston's Fifth Ward, an area cursed by poverty and despair. Nothing in his experience jibed with what he saw there. He'd never known these mean streets—let alone believed they existed a few miles from home. And he'd certainly not suspected that his own father had grown up there. He sat in silence as I pointed out my life's landmarks. For a time, I think, he had to decide whether he even considered himself my kin.

I understood his reaction. At his age, I couldn't imagine life outside my little neighborhood. The places I saw on television and in movies seemed imaginary. Watching how people lived on film was my version of an opium den.

Almost from the time I was born, on January 10, 1949, anger and hunger shaped my youth. There was always more than enough fury in my house and never enough food. My mom, the former Nancy Ree Nelson, had given birth to seven mouths—mine, the fifth, being the biggest—more than she could feed well on her income as a cook, even holding two jobs and working seven days a week. She had grown up on a sharecropping farm outside of Marshall, Texas, one of nine sisters and a brother. People would come from miles away to see those girls, rags on their heads, working the plow mules, digging stumps, and picking cotton. Her dad relied on everybody to pull their weight. And when her only brother got in trouble with the law and had to leave town, the sisters pulled his weight, too. Mom could only dream of going to school.

She moved the family to Houston soon after having me, a baby who didn't look much like his four older brothers and sisters: Robert, Willie Mae, Gloria, and Mary Alice. The reason she moved was both to avoid gossip about my father and to improve her economic chances. Houston was to be our shot at big wages and indoor toilets. That the move didn't work out as planned had little to do with Mom's abilities or perseverance. She was a powerful lady, and a leader by example. We didn't know we were poor, because in our house you just didn't hear that sort of talk. I was aware that some people had more to eat and different clothes to wear every day, and I could see that others treated them better. But I never measured what they had against what I didn't. The haves inspired me to believe that we, too, would one day have enough.

The optimism came from my mother. Our dad, J. D. Foreman, was absent much more than he was there. Mom couldn't count on him for anything. Unless she found him early on a Friday night, he drank away most of his railroad worker's salary. We lived mainly on the nickels and dimes she made. When I think of the pain Mom had to overcome in order to put on a happy face, and when I imagine being in her position and having to do the same, I cry in gratitude and admiration. What does it feel like to know that you're doing everything you can, and still your kids are hungry? (Is it possible that only I was feeling hungry all the time?)

Though I loved them all, Aunt Leola was my favorite of Mom's sisters, and I think I was hers. A bit older than my mother and with two girls and no boys, she treated me like her own. That carried over to her daughters, from whom I usually got more affection than from my own sisters. When Leola invited me for dinner, I'd eat all of mine, then start acting sad. "You want some?" my cousin Linda would ask. I'd nod my head and she'd give me the rest of hers. Her sister Alma would say, "Uh-uh, I'm eating *my* food."

Linda would say, "Well, you know he's going to get that sad face, so give it to him before he starts." And she would.

My sisters weren't as easy. They'd warn, "Don't you start snatching anyone's food now. Mama, he's getting ready to snatch food."

Between the seven of us, there was never enough for me. A good breakfast was a bowl of cornflakes, some evaporated milk diluted with water, and a little sugar. By the time I went back for a second bowl, only crumbs would remain. I'd dilute the remaining drops of milk, then hopelessly shake the sugar bowl to get out a few more grains.

Every other Sunday Mom made pancakes—or what passed for pancakes, given that she didn't have baking powder to make them rise—and bacon. Each of us got one strip. As much as I loved to inhale it, the smell of the bacon made that lonely piece into a tease. After finishing mine, I'd look longingly at Mom's ration. "Sure, baby," she'd say. "Come on over here and get you some."

Though she was expected to cook hundreds of meals a day at the O.S.T. Café, my mom was seldom permitted to eat the food they served there. She often bought inexpensive cans of sardines to take to work for her lunch or dinner. (Naturally, if I was in the kitchen early, staring at them, she would offer them to me.) On Fridays, she'd bring home a single hamburger and break it into eight pieces. Everybody got a taste. I remember thinking, *Boy, that's rich man's food, a hamburger.* That mustard's tang is still in my mouth.

Most of my friends weren't quite as strapped. Even so, if I dropped by as lunchtime approached, it usually meant being invited to "run along home now" while they ate. Once in a while, they'd just usher me into another room. Smelling their food and hearing the tinkle of forks was torture. On some nights, I stood in the dark on neighbors' porches, looking into their kitchens, amazed that families (most with fewer than seven kids, I guess) had leftovers at each meal, even pieces of meat. I always hoped they would find me and ask me in.

For school lunches, Mom sometimes came up with a paper-thin slice of luncheon meat; more often, I got a mayonnaise sandwich. When I had nothing at all, I pretended to carry a big lunch by blowing up a brown paper sack to make it look full. Sometimes I'd rub the bag in grease and crumple it to make it look used. Since I would never ask for any food outside the family, my pride made me pretend that I wasn't hungry. I spent a lot of time fantasizing about those little cartons of milk that cost six cents.

Somehow, though, my mother kept us from starving. She was an artist, turning a few skimpy ingredients into a masterwork. And oh, what magic she could perform on a hambone. The bone came from a hog that my aunts would buy together from a farm outside town and have butchered. The only one of the sisters with more than two mouths to feed, my mother was naturally the poorest. Once or twice she had enough to buy the intestines, which became chitlins. But usually she'd get only the bones. Necessity being my mother's best friend, she didn't waste an inch. Working it and working it, she could extract enough fat to make hot-water corn bread that tasted especially good because it had been fried to taste like pork. She also scraped the bones for tiny flecks of meat she added to beans—a meal by itself. And when there was nothing left to do to the bone, she'd roast it until the marrow was soft and delicious. To this day, I love houses small enough to smell from every room just what's cooking in the kitchen.

It was Aunt Leola who named me George Edward. And besides a name, she gave me my first dose of confidence. When I was little she'd tell me, "Go up there and screw in that lightbulb for your Aunt Leola. You're so tall. You are such a big little man." I'd get down off that ladder thinking I was a giant. I loved her so much, not least because in her house my anger didn't burn so brightly.

At home, I usually had a bad case of mean temper. My older brother and sisters teased me terribly, calling me "Mo-head." I didn't know what "Mo-head" meant or where that nickname came from (and wouldn't for many years), only that I didn't like it. Even as a tiny boy, I'd warn them to get away and I'd hit back. Sometimes they said, "You're not really our brother." And though I never considered the words anything other than a mean joke, I hated that tease most of all. "I am *too* your brother," I'd say, trying to beat on them as punishment. "I *am* your brother."

They thought that was funny, this little kid refusing to be bullied. I'd pop anyone in the eye. To them I was the puppy who by nature is more belligerent than the others in the litter. You pet him in the wrong spot, and he growls. For fun, you might even pick that spot on purpose, just to get a reaction.

Once my brothers and sisters found my hot buttons—and there were rows of them—they kept pushing. I fought them and fought them and fought them. No matter how much bigger they were, or how badly they were beating me, I kept fighting. I never quit. Eventually they'd get too tired to keep at it, but I never did. Even before I outgrew them, which I did at an early age, they learned that the fun of teasing me wasn't worth the consequences. Once they'd turned up my fire, nobody could turn it down. So instead of "Mo-head," which earned instant retaliation, they began just calling me "Monk," for monkey. This, I felt, wasn't a slur but a term of endearment. (It stayed with me for years and got passed along to my second son.)

What I didn't learn until much later was that my siblings blamed me for the trouble between my parents that drove my father out of the house. After I was born and they'd moved to Houston, Dad began his worst drinking, and my parents escalated their ferocious fights. Now they're back together; now they're broken up again.

Whatever problems my folks had together, it didn't affect my father's faith in me. He believed from the time I was an infant that I was going to be a champion. He loved me. He'd never seen my kind of fire in any kid. Like the others, he pushed my buttons just to get a rise. Sure enough, I'd go off, popping him in the eye. "Heavyweight champion of the world," he'd shout, raising my arm after I'd tried to beat up someone four times my size. "Stronger than Jack Johnson. Hits like Jack Dempsey." I didn't recognize those names, didn't even understand what heavyweight champion of the world was. But I enjoyed his pleasure in my antics.

My mother wanted me to stay away from athletics. Recognizing that I was more hot-headed than her other children, she worried that a terrible fate awaited me, especially if I played some competitive game and lost my temper. In those days in Fifth Ward, most boys who had fire and no fear died. The "Bloody Fifth," we called it. Every weekend someone got killed in a knife fight. And if your enemies didn't get you, the police would. They didn't bother the good, law-abiding people, but would make examples of the bad element, most of whom hung out at the ice house, where the ice trucks brought their ice to load into iceboxes. The aim of the police was to tame you, to break your spirit: to turn a wild stallion into a stable horse. I remember one courageous boy, filled with too much liquor and the boxing skills he'd learned in prison, standing up to the police. After he opened his mouth a little too loud, they got him down and delivered so many savage kicks that doctors had to reconstruct his torso without some of the tendons and ribs. Another boy was beat so badly that he never talked again before dying in his twenties. Sooner or later, all the tough guys got beaten by the police.

Mom knew that I would never cry mercy to the police or anyone, that they—or someone else—would have to kill me to stop me or shut me up. That's why *she* beat on me, often and hard—crucial beatings, strategic and tactical, administered completely out of love and concern. She was not trying to instill the fear of God, but the fear of *her*. She wanted me more afraid of what she would do to me if I disobeyed her than of any trouble I might get into in the streets. "I'm going to *kill* you," her voice would boom.

One day, while she was at work, I snuck off to a local swimming pool that she'd warned me time and again to stay away from. It was a place where the lifeguards didn't have to pass a swimming test; they may not even have been able to swim. Kids drowned there. But I wanted to swim and figured I'd get away with it because I'd get home and dried off long before she came back from her job. I didn't count on someone spying me at the pool and tattling, nor on the distinctive smell of chlorine soaked into my skin. I'll never forget the fury in her eyes: I was in for a whipping. She took a belt and began lashing my chest and head. I backed away from her, trying to protect myself from the blows. It was no use to call for my brothers and sisters, so I screamed bloody murder to the neighbors: "Help. She's killing me." When no one came, I grabbed the belt away from her. Now what was she going to do? Cursing my disobedience, she climbed on me like a wrestler and pounded me with her fists.

Mom's technique worked. Being more afraid of her than of drowning, I never went to that pool again. Nothing else would have kept me away.

I was thirteen when she struck me for the last time. I'd come home one Saturday just as my sister finished washing the last of the dinner dishes, and having missed the meal, I was hungry. I checked the refrigerator and saw a rare sight: food. I grabbed the leftovers and started to make a big sandwich. My sister pointed out that the kitchen had closed, and she didn't want any more mess to clean up.

"Get out of here," she said.

"Get out of here yourself," I yelled.

"You get out of here," she insisted.

When I wouldn't, she began yelling for Mom, who came in carrying a full head of steam.

"I'm not bothering her," I explained. "I'm just making something to eat."

"You better get out of here," Mom said.

"I told you, I'm hungry and I want something to eat. I'm not bothering her."

"I mean it, young man, you get out of here right now. And don't you talk back to me. You hear?"

That's when she picked up her sturdy shoe.

I felt she was being unreasonable—taking my sister's side in an argument that didn't need to be an argument. I was a hungry kid. What more mattered? You bet I was going to leave, and not just the kitchen. As I stormed past her, she took a swing at me with the shoe, landing a blow on my back. Just as it hit, I bumped against her by accident. By that age, I already towered over my mother, and the impact sent her reeling against the counter. I walked out of the house and went to Aunt Leola's, intending never to come back. Mom and Leola discussed the situation, and after a couple of cooling-off days, I went home. To my way of thinking, this had been blown out of proportion; I didn't need to apologize.

Mom played it right. She warned me, "If you live in this house, you have to obey." She meant that she couldn't control me any longer, but still demanded respect. Unsaid was something we both already knew, that she wouldn't fight me anymore; she was done using force.

By then, she didn't have to. Whether I knew it or not, I'd gotten her point.

. . .

School and George Foreman mixed as well as fire and ice, no matter which one I attended, and there were many as we moved around the area. Failing every subject and every grade, I must have impressed the teachers as being a boy going nowhere fast—except to jail or an early grave. My one good memory of a teacher came, oddly enough, as a result of punishment for misbehaving: I stayed late after class to clean the blackboard. "Georgie, Porgie, puddin' 'n' pie, kissed the girls and made them cry," the teacher chanted. It had such a nice ring to it, I actually thanked her; years passed until I recognized the words as a nursery rhyme.

In Fifth Ward schools, teachers couldn't afford to throw good time after bad students. The easiest and quickest way to judge a child's potential was through his appearance. Based, I assume, on experience, they'd predetermined that the clothes we wore—new or old, clean or dirty—reflected our potential for success, and they rationed their efforts accordingly. Clean clothes and creased pants were more important than brains. And by that yardstick, I was fated to fulfill their expectations.

Most families had more money than the Foremans. To us, the "good" jobs were longshoreman and nurse, and "well-to-do" students were those who lived in homes where both parents worked. Kids from these homes could occasionally afford new clothes. We were clothed from sacks of used garments donated by the people at Mom's restaurant. My brothers and sisters and I would pull pants, shirts, whatever out of the sack, searching for anything that fit. Finding something we actually liked was not a realistic priority. I used to hope against hope that I'd happen on a pair of sneakers, but I never did. We mended holes in our shoes with cardboard and hid the holes in our socks by pulling the ankles down low. Once when the restaurant owner's wife cleaned out her closet and found a bunch of dresses from the Roaring Twenties, my sisters went off to school in purple and green, looking like flappers.

I began fourth grade intending to fool and impress my new teacher. After washing and bleaching the two pairs of beat-up white pants I'd just gotten from the restaurant sack, I smoothed the legs into razor-sharp creases, then placed them on the gas water heater to dry. Though stiff at first, they didn't need ironing. (We did own an iron, but it was the kind you heated in a fire. It came in handy because we often didn't have electricity.)

For a while, the teacher probably took me for a longshoreman's son, maybe even a doctor's. She treated me relatively well, which is to say that she included me with her eyes during lessons and called on me when I raised my hand. Soon, though, she caught on to my charade. Noticing my same clothes every day, and that these clothes got progressively less splendid, she pegged me as a ne'er-do-well. It must not have occurred to her that any kid going to all that trouble must care a great deal about learning—or at least about making a decent impression.

With other teachers I tried different schemes; some even worked temporarily. I would befriend a boy in whom, I could see, they had hope: someone who dressed well; someone with two working parents. I'd offer him protection and friendship in exchange for being seen with me, figuring some of his charm might rub off and that teachers would reconsider their appraisal of me based on the company I kept.

They didn't.

My disappointments made me stop trying in class. Except for the disruptions I regularly caused, I might've been considered dead at my desk.

So, I became a champion at playing hooky. Pretending to go off to school like everyone else, I devised a complete route that led me back home after Mom left for work. I crawled through the window and slept most of the morning. In the afternoon, I reversed tracks to make it look like I was walking out of school with the rest of my classmates. But one day, while sneaking in through the window, I got busted by my cousin Rita; she was staying with us while she looked for a job. Seeing her surprised me—she wasn't supposed to be there, either. I tried to act as if I'd forgotten something.

"Come on," she said. "You know you weren't going to school."

"Yes I was," I insisted. "Really, I forgot something."

"It doesn't matter. Nobody in this family is ever going to be anything anyway," she said, naming each of my family members. "You might as well forget it."

"That's a lie," I said. "I'm going to *be* something."

"Monk," she said sadly, "you may as well go back to bed."

I couldn't believe her words. I was determined to succeed, somehow, at *something*. It hurt that she would write me off so early. Not that I had done anything to show her otherwise. But until then, I honestly had no sense at all that someone might consider me a failure. Why—for not going to school? Everyone else was doing that too. That's why I jumped on Rita when she invited me to give up. I didn't know that not going to school might mess up my life. No one had ever talked to me about the future, and how school might fit into it. And besides, at that age, the future didn't exist anyway.

By sixth grade, I was noticeably bigger than the other kids. That made sense, since I was older than most, having repeated more than one year. My teacher struggled to educate me, but I didn't learn. The only reason they promoted a few of us was our age.

"Some of you are not going to make it," my teacher said before graduation from grade school. "Look at you. You've spent all these years just getting to this point. You're bound to spend the rest of your time in junior high." I felt crushed. At thirteen, with a working vocabulary of about a hundred words, I abandoned any remaining hopes I may have harbored about learning. It would take years to shed that discouragement.

I didn't care about my lessons. But that fall I discovered sports. Junior high was about nothing but football.

Knowing my mother would never agree to let me play, I forged her name on the consent form. By the time she found out, it was too late to stop me. Besides, she took some satisfaction from knowing that football kept me from dropping out.

Coach Bryant called me "Hardnose," because nobody was tougher or more determined. We called him "Bear," in honor of the famous coach at the University of Alabama, Paul "Bear" Bryant. A mean, gruff, and unforgiving man, our Bear had an almost sadistic penchant for using a paddle whenever he felt displeased with a performance. But he taught me pride. And playing to please him did wonders for my self respect. A big, strong defensive lineman, I could sack a quarterback and tackle runners better than anyone. I loved the competition, the success, the winning, the team spirit, and Coach's high standards. He sometimes positioned the linemen across a chalk stripe on the field, then sent the fastest halfback to try to run through us. If he made it, the whole line got whacked with the paddle.

We all feared him, though I was especially afraid because of an absolute edict he had against smoking. He'd lecture us over and over about how smoking reduced your wind and undermined your skills. When he caught someone smoking, a heavy hand administered the law of the paddle, and by the time he got through, the cigarette wasn't the only thing smoking.

Sad to say, I had already developed a serious nicotine habit. It started with stealing smokes from my parents—coughing and laughing, getting dizzy on purpose—and continued as a growing addiction. Mom knew I smoked, and my friends smoked with me. The only person I hid my cigarettes from was Coach Bryant. And when he caught me one day in the ninth grade, everything changed.

It happened like this: After practice, we always went to a soda fountain in the back of a drugstore on Lyons Avenue, Fifth Ward's main drag. If we had enough money, we'd get a soda. If not, we'd buy or bum cigarettes. As I walked out of the drugstore one day, a smoke in my mouth, there was the last person I expected to see—Coach, sitting behind the wheel of his car. Since this was at least two hours after practice, he should have been home already.

"Hey, George," he yelled through his open window. "I see that cigarette."

I froze. Yes, I was afraid of being paddled. But I was more ashamed that this man whom I admired and who, I thought, respected me, should catch me doing something he abhorred, condemned, and forbade. To escape that shame, I never went back to football practice. And without football I stayed out of school completely; it had nothing to offer me.

My mom began getting calls from the principal's office, telling her that I'd been playing hooky every day. She pleaded with me, but nothing she said could make me go. Finally, the authorities told her that I was old enough to quit school legally. And if I didn't actually drop out, they explained, they would pursue me as a truant. It was an easy call, and Mom couldn't resist anymore. I ended my formal education without earning even a junior high school diploma.

We moved a lot when I was a kid. Mom brought home about twenty-six bucks a week, and we often had to balance rent and groceries; sometimes rent had to give. We'd pack up quickly and go from one place to the next. Though we never escaped Fifth Ward, I was always meeting new kids in different schools and neighborhoods.

One constant was visiting Aunt Leola. I loved that she let me watch television all night, something I couldn't do at home because we couldn't afford a TV. Roy Rogers was my favorite, and my role model. I tried to imitate his facial expressions, posture, and swagger. Watching him, I felt transported out of my life. It was only when he and his cowboy pals sat down to a big camp-fire meal that I got jolted back to reality, realizing that I wouldn't feel full after their pork and beans.

I also liked *The Donna Reed Show* and *Leave It to Beaver*, and all of the other sitcoms about families. I remember wondering what it would be like to have my own bed, like Beaver and Wally; or to be able to shut off the reading lamp next to the bed. That was the image—reaching up from bed to turn off the light—that stuck in my brain; it seemed the height of luxury. Meanwhile, we were lucky to have a bare, hanging lightbulb in our room—that is, if the house had electricity.

All of the houses we lived in shared the same characteristics. They were small. They were dark. They were rat-infested. The house I liked more than the others was in a neighborhood in which most of the kids lived with two working parents. To me, they were affluent.

One night, three older boys from that neighborhood and I took off to the park after dinner. We played ball for a while, then headed for home, passing houses and other buildings on the way. As I watched, they each picked up a handful of rocks and began throwing them at windows. It soon became a contest to see who could break the most glass. I joined in. It was the first time I'd ever done anything that might be called juvenile delinquency. My love for Mom, my respect for her, my fear of her, had always held me in check. Now, new friends took over her role as an influence on me.

My life of crime escalated quickly. Two buddies and I were out one night when we saw a guy walking alone in the dark across the park. "Let's get him," someone said. It was more a dare than a command. We argued about it, but then summoned the nerve to use our numbers against him. Two of us held him down without hurting him, the other got his wallet. Then we ran, joining up later to split the loot.

This was easy money, and I kept earning it this way for a couple of years. I used the cash to pay for cigarettes, food, carfare to visit my girlfriend across town, clothes to wear when I saw her, and cheap wine, which I had begun putting away in impressive amounts. You need a good drink to mug a guy right, I guess to quell your conscience. It was a cycle; I stole money to buy drink, and I got drunk to steal more money.

Now, this may be hard to believe, but I can truthfully claim that I didn't understand how serious a crime it was to take someone's money; it seemed the same as picking apples off a tree that didn't belong to you. It wasn't arrogance, but ignorance, kind of like my son's thinking faded blue jeans meant poverty. For me in those days, the law was the law of the jungle, where the end justified the means. *Survival.*

What might have straightened me out was church. Realizing that her power to influence my actions had all but vanished, Mom urged me constantly to read the Bible and go to services, which, working seven days and nights a week, she was too busy to attend herself. My older siblings were already believers; at home, I often found them on their knees praying, and I teased them. When they dragged me to churches where people showed the spirit alive in them by playing tambourines and dancing, I'd mock them by doing some jitterbug dance out front.

I'd go through the motions to please my mother, but religion seemed like hokum. Only weak people took religion seriously. Miserable people. Broken people. Hopeless people. Each time one of those fiery boys in my neighborhood had the fire kicked out of him—broken, like a wild stallion—he turned to religion. You could predict the next kid to find God by checking to see who got a steel plate in his head. Men who couldn't hit back anymore, women beaten by life—they bought religion. Nobody I looked up to.

So I didn't learn the lessons that Scripture might have taught me about good and evil. I used my size (by age sixteen I would be six foot one and weigh one hundred eighty-five pounds), my fists, and my strength to take what I needed, and even considered myself a good kid, not a villain. I remember one night out with my friend Nicholas, needing some money to see my girlfriend. We spotted a lone figure in the darkness and, as usual, tackled him to the ground. I held him down as Nicholas searched his pockets. Nothing. His waistband. Nothing again. Then Nicholas took off his right shoe, convinced that the turnip hid blood. *Still* nothing. When Nicholas took off the left shoe, the guy kicked him. That infuriated Nicholas. He took out of his pocket something I'd never seen him use, an icepick, ready to stab our mark. He would have, too, if I hadn't gotten in his way and helped the guy fight him off. In my mind, that made me a good kid, which is how my self-image remained until not long after.

Nicholas, my friend Charles, and I mugged a guy who had the nerve to be appalled at what we'd done. "Come back here," he kept screaming as we walked away calmly, counting the money. He called the police—a pretty unusual response in a neighborhood that considered most muggings part of the cost of living—which brought out a dragnet. Cop cars, sirens blaring, were everywhere. When we saw the police chasing us—us?—we began running, at different speeds and in different directions. I ended up hiding in the short crawl space beneath a house.

As I lay there waiting and wondering why the police were interested in us, I began thinking about the big white German shepherds that sometimes rode in the patrol cars. I knew that the policemen themselves couldn't find me, but thought that the dogs might be able to sniff me out. That's when I noticed a large puddle beneath a sewer pipe at the back of the house and remembered a television show about an escaped convict running from bloodhounds. To throw them off the scent, he sloshed through a stream. Deciding to do the same, I used the water and dirt to make mud, which I then covered myself in, head to toe; every part of me dripped with it. No way could those dogs sniff me through that stuff. Wearing my new camouflage uniform, I'd wait it out until it was safe to go home.

All of a sudden it hit me. I realized that I was like that criminal on television. He ran from dogs; I'd run from dogs. He hid his scent in water; I'd rolled in slop. Both of us were bad guys. Feeling sick and ashamed, I heard the echo of my cousin Rita's words: "You may as well go back to bed, Monk. Nobody in this family's going to be anything."

"Oh my God," I said out loud. "I'm a criminal." A fifteen-year-old criminal.

I kept hiding for another hour or so, until full darkness. Then I crawled out from under the house. Some kids coming back from a party were laughing and joking. "Hey, y'all seen the cops?" I asked, the mud dripping off me.

They looked at me like I was the creature from the black lagoon, and said the cops hadn't been around for a while.

At home, I ignored questions about where I'd gotten so filthy. I couldn't say that I'd been on the journey of a lifetime.

Later, when everyone was asleep, I cried. My life as a professional criminal ended that night. Though I still wanted to be a thug and a tough guy, I would never steal again.

From the time I was six, possibly even before, I wanted to fight. Anyone.

Other kids would dare me, "Betcha can't beat him."

"Betcha I can," I'd reply.

I'd provoke two or three guys; I didn't care. I just wanted to mix it up. I never lost.

By junior high the violence had become second nature. Everyone knew my reputation, and they knew it was a reputation I cultivated.

Walking home from school one day, a boy I barely knew approached me. "Hey, Monk," he said, pointing to a fellow about our age, a good-looking boy and a sharp dresser. "I want you to punch that guy."

"Okay," I said.

I walked up to the kid and, without warning, busted his face, putting him on the ground as quickly as if he'd been shot. I did it because I'd been asked, no other reason. (Later, I found out that the first guy's girlfriend had taken a shine to this boy, and he wanted his rival undone.)

Other people started using me as an enforcer. Unlike some toughs, though, I never took money for it. Nor did I ever use a knife. I figured knives were for cowards. You could be cut or stabbed and not even realize it till you saw the blood. Using my fist, I got the satisfaction of seeing my man fall. I considered it a win when he stayed down, not when his clothes turned red from an open wound.

When I got to be someone with a bit of standing among other Fifth Ward thugs, I met Hilton Murdoch, who came from a well-to-do family of two working parents; he was a bona fide killer. Not much good with his fists, he'd act as though he wanted to fight, then pull out a carpet layer's knife and slash his opponent to shreds. He also had an especially ugly henchman we called Ickyboo, who hid in the shadows carrying either a wooden plank or a heavy stick that he'd wield on command. My introduction to them came after a particularly vicious attack of theirs. A kid named Thomas, a nice-looking, hard-working boy, crossed their path walking home from school one day. Surly and already annoyed by anyone who looked like he was going to accomplish something in life, Murdoch challenged him to fight. Thomas knew that if he backed down, Murdoch would own him, so he fought; in fact, he won Round 1. With Murdoch on the ground, apparently beaten, Round 2 began when a plank of wood smashed Thomas's skull from behind, knocking him out and doing severe brain damage. As Ickyboo stood watching, Murdoch carved up Thomas unmercifully with his knife. When Thomas was finally discharged from the hospital, he needed someone to dress and feed him, and could only stare ahead.

Murdoch liked me, and the higher I rose in the ranks of the Fifth Ward thugs, the more he wanted to be around me. I considered him a friend, though one I kept at a distance. I did not feel about him the way I felt about my buddy Charles Miller, whom I loved. Charles and I were blood brothers. If he had a shirt, I had a shirt. If I had shoes, he had shoes. Murdoch could see how much Charles meant to me. When I was around, he treated Charles with respect. Otherwise, he would have preferred to see him dead. The sentiment was mutual.

One day Murdoch walked up to Charles at the park. "Hey, man," he said. "Let's box."

Murdoch would never have done that had I been around. Charles knew enough to look around for Ickyboo. Seeing that they were apparently alone, he accepted the challenge. Charles was tough—tougher, he thought, than Murdoch.

In a fair fight, I'd have bet Charles. But Murdoch took out some brass knuckles and swung at Charles's head, opening a cut above his eyes that gushed blood. Charles cried out. A passerby saw the blood and yelled that he was going to get the police. Charles scrambled. He found me and, crying, told me what happened.

I had to avenge Charles. Walking up and down Lyons Avenue, I asked everywhere after Murdoch until long past dark. He was hiding, nowhere to be found.

That night I went to a party. After drinking my fair share, I stood alone outside, getting some air. In a shadow was a face that looked like an executioner's mask. I knew it was Ickyboo and that he was holding a piece of wood. That meant Murdoch was close. Very close, in fact. He stepped out of another shadow, his knife blade, visible in the street light, thrust inches from my belly.

"Hey, man, you looking for me?" he asked. "I heard you were looking for me."

I didn't answer.

"You looking for me?" he repeated.

I agonized over which way to go. Saying yes, I'd likely be battered and bleeding to death in a matter of moments. Saying no, I'd have to live with the terrible shame of knowing I backed down, of knowing that he got the better of me. And I wasn't sure which was worse.

"No," I finally said.

"Good," he muttered, pulling the knife back. "I'll see ya." He and Ickyboo walked away.

I suffered instantly. For the first time in my life, I knew cowardice—and now I preferred death. How could I live this down? I wasn't supposed to be afraid of two hundred people, let alone two. Just like that, my identity had disappeared.

I even knew why I'd done it: my mother. All those years of her beating on me, molding me, trying to straighten me out. She used to tell me, "It's better to say, 'There he goes' than 'There he lays.' " That night, I had heard her voice as my conscience. But it had cost me my manhood. I felt castrated.

Taking a deep breath, I went back inside and told my friends most of the story—leaving out the part where I backed down. Several of us went looking for Murdoch and Ickyboo. Two blocks away, we found and surrounded them. There'd be no escape now.

"Fight me fair and square," I demanded. "Put your knife down and use your fists."

"I'm not going to fight that big man," Murdoch said. "No way. I can't whip him."

Even then, after he had refused the challenge in front of half a dozen witnesses, I thought I could see him sniggling at me: He knew that he'd already won.

To my friends I was a hero. And though Murdoch never told anyone else about what had happened at the party, I couldn't

escape my self-hatred. To compensate, I turned vicious and savage, picking fights in school, on the street, at pickup basketball
games—anyone, anytime, anywhere; sometimes two or three a
day. I wanted to overcome any man in my path. When I walked,
I saw people afraid of me. That, I believed, was as it should be.

One day I went to the drugstore on Lyons Avenue and heard
someone say, "Cool down, everyone, Big George is here."

Then someone else: "Hey, Big Monk."

And Murdoch: "There he is. You don't want any trouble with
that man." His voice conveyed respect, not sarcasm.

This was my coronation. They'd named me King of the Jungle.

A decade later, as heavyweight champ, I went back to the old
neighborhood and saw Murdoch again. He was sitting on a
bench in front of a gas station. Next to him was Thomas, the boy
he'd turned into a vegetable, whose father owned the station.
Both stared straight ahead, one brain-damaged, one a dope
fiend. It was hard to tell which was which. Next time I heard
about Murdoch, he'd died of an overdose.

Chapter Two

AFTER QUITTING SCHOOL, I washed dishes for a few weeks in the restaurant where my mother worked, then left for a real job and real money: $1.25 an hour moving furniture at Wald Transfer and Storage with my older brother Robert. We called him Sonny and I idolized him. Ten years older than I, Sonny was already a hard-working family man, making good wages and living in a decent house with his wife and two children. He got me the job on a temporary basis. If I proved myself to the bosses, they would hire me on full time, up my salary, and, best of all, give me a pair of overalls with my name embroidered in a little circle above the pocket.

A single assignment of moving an office from one location to another, with all the heavy furniture, files, and business equipment, could take weeks. I'd wake at six to be there at eight, and sometimes stay until midnight. The money I made—fifty dollars, say, for fifty hours; I never saw that extra quarter—I used to help Mom buy groceries, and to have a little fun myself.

I worked hard to impress the bosses. With my strength and stamina, I believed I had a decent future in the moving business. And I made new friends. The guys on the crew would get a bottle after work and share a few snorts; they were responsible for shifting my taste in alcohol from cheap wine to cheap gin. One night I drank too much and was picked up for public drunkenness. Because I was a minor, Mom had to get me out of jail. For days afterward, I was too embarrassed to face her.

One Monday, the boss told us that we'd been hired for an emergency job, and would have to work from eight in the morning until midnight every day until completion. I was worn out by Wednesday. On Thursday, we took a dinner break at five with instructions to return in an hour. Instead of eating, I went home to rest and slept through to the next day. Too ashamed to go back, I was willing to forfeit the back pay they owed me.

Sonny told me the following week that the other guys had laughed and called me lazy. He said, "Look, George, they're hiring a lot of people. If you go and tell the man that you have an explanation, I think he'll take you back, and I think you'll get the job full time. You're strong and you're hard-working. They like that. Anyone can make a mistake. Just apologize and make up a good explanation."

Explanation. I wasn't sure I'd ever heard the word before, and could barely remember it; to let it roll off my tongue seemed impossible. But I had to try if I wanted the job back. Without it, I had nothing.

My tail between my legs, I went to see the foreman, a tough, authoritative guy who'd started out as a mover about twenty years earlier. "Mr. Grimes," I said, "I'd like to talk to you, because I'd like to work again, to get my job back."

"You walked off," he said brusquely while doing paperwork, refusing even to glance toward me.

"I know I did, sir. But I have a, a, a"—the word wouldn't come—"a *esclanation.*"

He looked me dead in the eye. "Listen, Foreman," he said, throwing my pay envelope at me. "Don't you ever come out here again. If I see you out here I'll call the cops. We don't want your kind. Take your money and your *esclanation* and get lost."

I felt humiliated, like a failure. How could I tell Mom? I didn't. Instead, I let my actions speak for me. For about a month I just hung around the house, doing nothing. I *was* a nothing—but I hated her knowing that about me. I hated disappointing her.

My sister Mary Alice, bless her, had read or heard about the Great Society program formulated by President Lyndon Johnson in his new War on Poverty. The employment office, she said, would enroll me in a program that allowed you to earn while learning a decent trade—laundry worker, for instance. The next afternoon I applied in person and was told that you had to be at least eighteen. Reading the disappointment on my face, the man at the office suggested an alternative: the Job Corps, which was intended to provide kids like me "a second chance to become productive members of society" through schooling and job skills. The clerk explained that they would send me out of state to live at a Corps training center, feed me three meals a day, teach me what my own school hadn't, give me thirty dollars a month spending money, and stow away fifty dollars a month that would be mine to keep after completing the two-year course.

I might not otherwise have taken the application, but I'd already heard about the Job Corps in the pool hall. Anyone who wasted as many hours as I did there, watching sports on the wall-mounted television, had to have seen the public-service ads for the Job Corps starring the Baltimore Colts quarterback Johnny Unitas and the great Cleveland Browns running back Jim Brown. "You can get a second chance," they, too, had said. These were my heroes—Brown especially—so the words "Job Corps" resonated. I took an application and went home to talk to Mom.

"Jim Brown says that if I join, I can get a second chance," I told her. "But I have to leave home, Mom. And I hate to leave you. What do you think?" As excited as I was, part of me—a big part—wanted her to say no. I was only sixteen, and despite all the trouble I'd gotten into, the thought of leaving home—home being wherever my mother was—made me tremble.

"Son," she said. "If you leave, I'll be happy for you. Getting away from this element could change your life. That's your second chance right there."

I put the papers down in front of her. "You have to sign," I said.

She picked up a pen and looked at me. "I'll sign if you want to do it,'' she said. Swallowing hard, I nodded. Before signing, she swallowed hard too.

My friend Roy Harrison joined with me on the buddy plan. The Job Corps was sending us together to the Fort Vanney Training Center outside Grants Pass, Oregon. It might as well have been Afghanistan for all we knew. I had to ask where Oregon was.

Mom told me later that she shut herself in the bathroom and cried when I left. I cried, too, all the way down Lyons Avenue, in the back of Roy's mother's car heading downtown. Staring out at my old haunts, I thought about my mom and my friends, how they were getting to stay and have a wonderful time in our own Fifth Ward. Why did I have to go?

Roy's mother dropped us at the Rice Hotel, where Job Corps officials had a van waiting to take us to the airport; they also checked us in at the terminal and got us on the plane. Neither Roy nor I had ever been within miles of an airplane. The stewardesses were friendly and patient. They showed us how to tighten our seatbelts, lower the tray tables to eat (I loved the food; had two lunches), lock the lavatory door, clear our air pressure–plugged ears. Everything new and strange had to be taught or learned. Like a baby being born, I was leaving one world and entering another. In the world I'd left, everyone looked like me. In this one, no one but Roy did.

We landed in San Francisco, where another Job Corps aide was waiting to escort us to the flight for Medford, Oregon. She walked us from one side of the airport to the other. I wanted to spend a year there, watching the people, all of them looking important, walking hurriedly to or from somewhere I'd never been. I had no idea that this existed beyond Fifth Ward. It was a dizzying thought. What else was out here?

If anything, the crew on the second flight were nicer than on the first (though, to my colossal disappointment, no meal was served). After we landed we were driven to Grants Pass. Only in movies and picture books had I seen such beautiful places, and never did I anticipate that I would actually find myself in one. Green hills, winding streams. And oh, that fresh, sweet air.

Breathing deeply, I could smell every cowboy campfire Roy Rogers ever lit; could imagine Beaver and Wally on a Boy Scout outing. This was the place of my heroes and fantasies. And where I now lived.

But, as I learned, you can't take Fifth Ward out of the boy. I picked fights with almost every young man in my dormitory, just to let them know, in case they were wondering, that you couldn't push George Foreman around; soon I earned a reputation as the center's bully. Looking at me sideways or any which way—just looking at me, period—earned you a knuckle sandwich with relish. This was not, I admit, the smartest way to make friends. And I didn't for a long time.

Even in the cafeteria, my house of worship, I continued my reign of terror. I was lucky I wasn't kicked out in the first few weeks. The people running the Job Corps set and insisted on high standards of behavior for their Corpsmen; that was the purpose of the program, to teach the self-discipline needed to seize opportunity. Thank God they knew that kids like me were no altar boys. Not that all of us had raging fists; in fact, I was in a small minority. But all of us, obviously, faced some kind of trouble that made us leave home at a tender age. So a little leniency was the rule. Besides, the counselors working with us hadn't taken the job to get rich. They believed that society ought to offer a hand to its poor, and they weren't inclined to withdraw that open hand too quickly.

It was in the cafeteria that I met the woman who became my surrogate mother, Mrs. Moon, the cook. In her late forties or so, Mrs. Moon seemed to single me out to receive the comfort of her attention. She smiled at me, and when I passed by her on line with my tray, she somehow knew to scoop on a little extra this or that, something more than the others got. She'd see me pick on another kid and then scold me without anger—even one time when I smashed a dinner tray over someone's head. "Now George," she'd say, "you've got to control that temper."

"Yes, ma'am." I wasn't about to argue with the woman who decided how much I got to eat.

Not long afterward Mrs. Moon dropped a bombshell.

"George," she said, "I'm going to bring you home with me one weekend." I didn't know what to say. I just felt lucky and a little confused.

A few weeks later, she picked me up in her truck and drove me almost an hour on roads that wound in circles through green hills covered in wildflowers. Her husband was the friendly type you'd think would be married to someone like Mrs. Moon. Though older and a bit frail, he welcomed me before I got out of the truck. Inside was their son, as sweet a boy as ever lived. Mr. Moon sat with me while Mrs. Moon cooked. He asked me about myself and told me about himself.

Dinner was like a drug. Pot roast with gravy, potatoes, vegetables, and thick slices of bread with which to sop it all up. Not only was it delicious in the way that only moms can make it, but Mrs. Moon knew the magic words: "George, would you like some more?"

Yes, ma'am.

She gave me all I wanted, and I wanted a lot. "I made this special for you," she said. Meaning, she must have bought three pot roasts, because I ran out of room before she ran out of food. I doubt that that had ever happened before.

After dinner, I took her son outside to play, teasing him like a little brother.

"Now remember," Mrs. Moon said before her husband drove me home, "you watch that temper. I'll see you on Monday, and we'll have you back here again next month."

I asked Mr. Moon whether they brought home a different Job Corpsman every weekend. He said that this was the first time. I was astounded. I hadn't made any particular moves in order to be treated well. Mrs. Moon just made me feel that I was special. She liked me for me. And as it turned out, I was the only boy she ever invited to dinner; I went at least once a month for the six months I was in Oregon. Her words echoed in my ears: "You watch that temper." The way she said it, smiling and cheerful, I believed she knew something I didn't. And I wanted to do as she said. Most of all, I wanted to please her.

But I couldn't stop myself from bullying. It was the one thing I did well. In every other way I was ordinary, I believed, and I was afraid no one would think me special unless I beat them up. I even concocted reasons for cold-cocking someone. "What'd you say to me?" "Nothing." "Yes you did, I heard you." *Wham!* Or, "What're you lookin' at?" *Wham!* It didn't matter that this was the least threatening place I'd ever been. I wasn't fighting to live, I was living to fight.

Except for Mrs. Moon, I felt truly alone. Even my friend Roy had enough of me. Plus, there was no social life. Grants Pass was lucky to get a new movie twice a month, and the only other recreation was ice skating, an activity for which I had no talent. At home in Houston, I drank and fought. Here, being too young to visit bars, I just fought.

Since people often ran when they saw me coming, finding places to be alone and cry from a terrible homesickness wasn't difficult. "Man," Roy said, "you're always talking about old times at home. I don't want to hear about that. This is now." Roy cut me loose, too. I guess I wasn't cool enough for him.

I wrote letters to Mom, lying that the Job Corps didn't live up to its advertising and saying I wanted to come back to Houston and be like Sonny—to get a job and take care of a family. I wanted her sympathy. But Mom wrote back, "Son, *nothing* is like they say it is. And as for Sonny, you just try to be yourself. Be George."

Finally I made a friend, and through him found a whole world. Richard Kibble was a down-and-out hippie kid from Tacoma, Washington, without a crumb of aggression in his soul. Good thing, too, because under his long hair and beard he was a scrawny wisp without a muscle anywhere. And yet, he was fearless. Which is how we met. Coming into the barracks one night, loud as usual, I must have disturbed his reading. "Hey," he yelled. "Quiet. Stop making noise." (We had so little privacy. The sixteen beds located at each end of the barracks were arranged in four groups of four, each group separated only by some lockers.)

I stopped to see who'd challenged me. "Come on, man," I said, striding menacingly toward him. "I'll fight you. I'll fight you right now."

Richard didn't take the bait. Sitting cross-legged on his bed, the book on his lap, he seemed so serene. "That's all you *can* do is fight," he said. "Don't you have any brains to talk? Why don't you try fighting with your mouth?"

A new concept for me. "What're you talking about?"

"Sit down," he said. "I want you to listen to something."

I did as I was told as he reached over to his phonograph and put the needle on a record. Sounding scratchy, a rock-and-roll song came on. I said, "Man, get out of there with this," and started to leave.

"Listen," he insisted.

I did: "Well, they'll stone ya when you're trying to be so good / They'll stone you just a-like they said they would. . . . But I would not feel so all alone / Everybody must get stoned."

I listened to that whole Bob Dylan song and the one after that and the whole first side of that album. We talked about Dylan, his lyrics, and the philosophies of life explained in rock songs. This was strange to me, but appealing too; talking about ideas, about what things mean.

Richard was twenty-one, the upper age limit for Job Corps, which meant that he'd be out in a year no matter what. He said he'd had a lot of problems at home and figured this program would be a good place "to get my head together." I'd never heard the phrase before but understood what he meant. There was something about him, the way he spoke, the words he used, that I liked.

Walking by once when I was bullying someone, he continued without stopping, as if I were less than nothing—which is what he said as he passed, contemptuous of me for playing the fool. The message struck home. He never laid a glove on me, but I felt whipped—mentally. That was the first time I'd ever been impressed by strength from a mind instead of a muscle.

My respect for him grew; I started calling him Richard Kimble for the character in *The Fugitive*. We spent weeks' worth of hours listening to the music he chose, especially Dylan. I grew familiar with every song Richard played. I increasingly understood and related to them. So began the real education of George Foreman.

Being Richard's friend allowed me to meet other guys (females stayed in a different area code). Most of them I'd beaten up. I suppose that gave us a shared experience. One time when we were in the day room listening on radio to Cassius Clay fight Floyd Patterson, someone yelled out, "Hey, George. You're always picking on people. If you think you're so bad, why don't you become a boxer?"

I heard the tease as a dare. It reminded me of when Murdoch had asked me whether I was looking for him. This time, I wouldn't back down. "All right, I will," I said. "I'll become a boxer. I'll show you." I don't think any of the guys took me seriously.

Soon I began joining their all-night bull sessions. With no drugs or alcohol allowed, all we had was talk. I listened to stories from and about the different places everyone grew up. Being a proud Texan, but lacking the words to describe what that meant to me, I told my mother to use some of the money I'd been sending her to buy an LBJ Stetson, which was the kind of cowboy hat President Johnson used to favor. Since it had been all the rage when I left, I planned to show my new friends how to really style. When it arrived, they made fun of me.

"Don't wear that," Richard warned me. "They'll think you're country."

"Hey, Tex," someone yelled.

"What're you talking about, man?" I said. "This here is an LBJ Stetson."

I couldn't wear it without being called Tex, and I hated that, so I hardly did. The lesson—one of many—was that styles don't always travel well.

For some reason (or maybe obvious reasons), a good number of these guys were from New York, where, judging by them, you got away with insulting someone's family. In Houston, you couldn't say the words "your mother" without risking your life. Richard and the others used that phrase to try to make me lighten up.

Their taunts weren't clever, but at first I could barely restrain myself from wanting to rip their throats out. Eventually, after noticing I'd be the only one upset, I got to tolerate the slurs; they were, after all, trying to help me.

"How's your mama?" they'd ask.

"Fine."

"Well, tell her I want her back. Your daddy wants her."

"Yeah, and I'm *your* daddy," I'd say. Then we'd all laugh and agree that I was getting better. Afterward, I'd go outside and hyperventilate. I couldn't let them know I wanted to kill them. Still, this was progress.

School at the center was a revelation. The instructors insisted that Job Corpsmen master basic educational tools. This really was my "second chance." Simple concepts, the difference between nouns and pronouns, turned me on. Even handwriting got attention. I practiced and practiced. "Hey, George, that looks pretty good," my teacher said. "Keep it up."

They gave me books to read. I'd never read a book before. At first I pretended, just moving my eyes across the words, then I couldn't stop. Short stories, like "The Lottery," by Shirley Jackson. I'd run up to the teacher all excited, telling him my insights. He encouraged me and offered more food for thought, like: "If the lottery was only a symbol, a metaphor, how was Jackson using it to represent the real world?" I loved lying there with my book, thinking up answers. Symbols and metaphors were wonderful, a universe unlocked. The more I read, the more alive the characters became. Scenes seemed so real, I found myself reenacting them.

Words. Words transformed thinking into magic. I read sometimes in order to discover words I'd never seen. I'd look in the dictionary, repeat the words and their definitions, then construct my own sentences. And oh, the dictionary. I believed dictionaries contained all knowledge. One word connected to another, and to another, an endless chain. Books began to seem like meals. I devoured them, looking for answers. When I graduated to biographies and histories, *The Autobiography of Malcolm X* thrilled me because of his long journey of change and redemption. Letters to my mother became sagas of my exciting reading encounters, or lists of wonderful new words that I knew she'd be excited to see.

Meanwhile, as I learned more practical lessons, like fence building and carpentry, it crossed my mind that these teachers, one and all, may only have been pretending to like me or care about me. It may have been insecurity making me think this way, but so what? Even if they were fooling, what did it matter? I could have benefited from my elementary school teachers faking it that way, too. For the first time, George Foreman stood firmly on his own feet. I'd suffered a lot of grief—and not only in school—in order to survive daily life. Here, none of that applied. It was enough simply to be George Foreman.

We took day trips to fish and hike. I stood in a stream with hip waders on, the sky blue, air brisk, water babbling, remembering my fourth-grade picture book titled *The Road to Everywhere*. Since I'd been nowhere, I'd stared intently at the photos of places like this, burning the image onto my brain. Then I'd closed my eyes and pictured myself in that image. And now, *this* was the stream I used to see behind my closed eyes.

Still, though, I continued bullying and fighting. Look at me wrong, even smile at me the wrong way, and you were in trouble. It disgusted me. And Richard, too. He couldn't understand the aggression, or why I didn't control it.

After four months, he announced that he was leaving the program either to return home or to hitchhike anywhere. He was nearly twenty-two, he said, and wanted to get on with life rather than prepare for it.

Before leaving he called me to his bunk. "Here, I want you to have this," he said, handing me Dylan's *Blonde on Blonde*.

"Are you kidding?" I asked, as though he were presenting me with a priceless heirloom.

"You have got to stop fighting with your hands and use your mind," he said.

Only in movies do moments like that lead directly to happy endings. I treasured that album, and the gesture, but I ignored Richard's warning.

At the six-month mark, I was transferred to the Parks Job Corps Center outside Pleasanton, California. I chose that site for my vocational training because I'd read in the Job Corps newsletter that Parks had first-rate phys ed facilities, including a bona fide boxing program. That challenge from my buddies to become a boxer had stuck, and I was determined to show them—even if we never saw one another again.

The Parks Center was operated by Litton Industries, one of seven large corporations that had contracted with the government to provide vocational training to Corpsmen. A major defense contractor, Litton designed and built, among other high-tech equipment, advanced air navigational systems. Our training was considerably less sophisticated. We learned skilled, assembly-line tasks that could help us find decent jobs.

I was standing in the camp's processing center when someone pointed out Charles Broadus, a short but muscular man who was head of the base's security, as well as chief cook and bottle washer. He was the guy who tried to straighten kids out when they had problems, and the one to see for anything having to do with the site's athletic activities. Everybody called him Doc.

"I want to be a boxer," I said nervously. "You think I can?"

He looked me up and down, a sneer on his face. "You're big enough," he said. "And you're ugly enough. Come on down to the gym." With that, he walked on.

I visited the gym. Not seeing Doc, I introduced myself to the boxing coach. All around were guys working out, sparring, hitting the bag, jumping rope. They looked like pros. "Doc Broadus told me to come down here and take up boxing," I said.

"You ever boxed before?" he asked.

"Only on the street."

"The street, huh?" He paused, took a deep breath. "Look around you. You see these guys? They all know how to box. They're training, and I have to work with them. You don't know anything. So the fact is, I won't be able to give you enough time to learn. Sorry."

Later, I ran into Doc Broadus. "Hey," he said. "I thought I told you to come down to the gym." When I related what had happened, he arranged a time for us to meet there.

He didn't say anything as he watched me hit the bag and throw shadow punches. "You want to be a boxer," he said, "you've got to box." Then he pointed out a skinny guy across the room. "I'm going to put you in the ring against that boy." I wanted to laugh, thinking I could snap that young man like a twig.

Confident and excited, I told the guys from my dorm to come as witnesses. "I'm going to be a boxer," I declared, imagining that I'd do what I'd always done on the streets. I hoped they'd be there when I beat that boy up.

Doc laced my gloves on and I climbed in the ring with this guy who was maybe three quarters my size. He circled around me. I went right after him, throwing punch after punch with instant knockout in mind. Not one punch landed. Missing, my momentum carried me off-balance and made me fall. This was new. In street fights, I'd always swung from the heels but never missed. I couldn't even touch this young man unless I charged him like a wrestler. And when I did, he'd jab, causing me to lose my balance and fall again. Everybody laughed, some holding their stomachs, appreciating this spectacle: the bully getting his comeuppance. No one was more aware of that than the bully.

Embarrassed and ashamed of believing that street fighting could be compared to boxing, I didn't go back to the gym. Later I saw Doc Broadus. "Why haven't you been down?" he asked. "Scared?"

"No."

"Then why?"

"I don't have any shoes—boxing shoes," I said. It was a good line.

"Sit right down here on the curb and wait for me," he said. "I'll be right back."

A few minutes later he came back from his office with a new pair of boxing shoes. Without an excuse, I went through the motions of working out with him. But when he suggested another match, I again stopped going.

None of my dorm mates dared mention the short boxing career of George Foreman—at least, not when I was around. My reputation for ferocity had been established in Pleasanton, just as it had in Grants Pass. I'd wanted my fellow Corpsmen—two thousand of them—to respect and fear me. And most of them did. That's why they wouldn't mess with me. They knew that if I had overheard them making fun of me, I might beat the stuffing out of them.

But I might not have, too. Mr. and Mrs. Moon, bless their hearts, had driven all the way from Oregon—at least an eight-hour drive—just to check on me, to make sure that I'd settled in to my new home. They took me to a home-cooking restaurant, where Mrs. Moon again said in that smiling way she had, "Now, George, I want you to watch your temper." Letting down Mrs. Moon was like letting down my mother.

And I was letting her down because rage still remained in George Foreman. But in almost every other way, I felt myself changed and changing daily. Books and learning had done that. Beginning to think for myself, I even abandoned any last pretext of religion. My reading and questioning had led me to believe religion was only for poor people. What religious people did I know who weren't poor? Who sang songs like "Amazing Grace" who wasn't poor? No one. The Bible, what was that? Just some sheepherder's handbook. I wanted *real* knowledge.

I loved my classes and my teachers. In math, they took time to explain the skills I'd missed years before. Each skill led to another, like rungs on a ladder. When I began to understand algebra, I asked for but didn't receive glasses; my eyes tested perfect. Too bad; people who wore glasses looked so smart.

I was introduced to anthropology and history. I even took a Latin class. Its sole purpose was to teach English word roots. Learning to define a word through its parts thrilled me. I was insatiable. One of the center's part-time counselors, George Gale, was also an opera singer in San Francisco. When I expressed curiosity, he took me to rehearsals and performances. "You're something," he said to me, "the way you're interested in everything."

He was right. I'd been reborn.

That first Christmas I went home to visit Mom, bringing with me books and lists of words I wanted her to learn. I showed her the transistor radio I'd built myself in electronics assembly class. Is that my son? she wanted to know. I barely recognized myself.

That's why, I think, the bully clung to me. As my identity changed, I needed something—anything—to ground me. My violence, readiness to fight, connected me to my past.

It surfaced again while I was walking up the dorm stairs soon after New Year's. Coming down the stairs was another boy, and on his feet I saw my Chuck Taylor tennis shoes that had been stolen from the dryer two months before. "Those are mine," I told him.

"Oh," he said. "Sure. Here." He slipped them off and walked on in his socks.

I took the shoes and headed for my room, then began thinking, *This guy stole my new tennis shoes. Now they're all worn out.* I turned around and found him minutes later. "I can't let you get away with that," I said.

"What are you talking ab—" he started to ask before I beat him mercilessly.

He filed a complaint.

The first center official to see me was George Gale, tears in his eyes. "I don't understand," he said. "I just don't understand." He couldn't reconcile the young man he'd befriended with the thug. Which was the real George?

Knowing that I'd disappointed Mr. Gale was a terrible punishment. I hated doing that, as I'd hated disappointing Mrs. Moon, as I'd hated disappointing my mother. All that disappointment was taking a toll.

While George and I slowly drew close again, the relationship was never altogether the same. Once he'd seen the thug George, he couldn't quite trust the model student George. I understood.

Meanwhile, the Corps's local sponsor, Litton, began to discuss throwing me out of the program as an incorrigible. That I was allowed to remain can be seen as an act of Providence, one of many that run through my life like the dots on a connect-the-dots drawing. Stephen Uslan, the site director and one of the prime movers behind the Job Corps, stood against most of his center staff in wanting to give me another chance.

I nearly blew that one, too.

My dorm and two others were taken on a half-day boat trip

and picnic. On the bus on the way back to the center, everyone grabbed some leftover boxes of food to take to their dorms. I had mine in my arms when I stepped off the bus. Another boy, who was waiting there, threw a punch that landed flush on my chin. "Give my back my cookies," he demanded.

A bit woozy, I dropped the boxes and went for him. He hit me again. By the time I got my arms around him, two officials separated us.

Walking back to my dorm, I tried to forget about what happened. But just like the stolen sneakers, it burned a hole in my personal morality: I'd been shown up. I told some of my pals and worked myself into a frenzy. With no moderating voice like Richard Kibble's, revenge dominated.

We found out which dorm and room the cookie boy occupied, and a bunch of us headed there. I knocked on the door.

"Who is it?" a voice inside called.

Well, I couldn't very well say it was a hit squad. "Open the door," I growled.

"Who is it?"

"You know who it is."

With that, I slammed my right fist into the door—and was as surprised as anyone that it went clean through to the other side. Unlocking and opening the door, I saw several guys jump through the window. Good thing they lived on the first floor.

My old friend Roy, who'd been transferred to Pleasanton with me, grabbed and held one of them. I didn't beat him too severely, since he wasn't the kid who'd sucker-punched me, and I went home pleased that at least *someone* had been made to pay.

The real surprise came the next day: The police arrived to question me. Somebody said I'd broken through their door with a gun, which I then waved in their faces. The cops didn't believe the accusation, though my standing as a Job Corpsman dropped badly—and it hadn't far to fall. My expulsion was nearly certain, with even director Uslan wavering in favor of kicking me out.

But Doc Broadus told the powers-that-be that I had the makings of a champion boxer. Anyone who'd seen my only bout would have been suspicious of Doc's claim. Fortunately, I had someone else in my corner.

Gordon Stanford, a San Francisco psychologist, was, like George Gale, a part-time counselor at the center. Also like George, he took me under his wing and into his confidence. It was a mutual-admiration society. He spoke with an English accent and smoked cigarettes through a long, slender holder. For me, this man was sophistication. When word got around that I'd probably have to pack up, I took the bus to his office in San Francisco. Gordon may have been surprised to hear how sorry I was and how desperately I wanted to stay in the program (though wanting to seem cool, I also pretended not to care what happened to me). For as long as I'd known him, I'd been a broken record of complaints: the food, facilities, social life, dorm mates, and who knows what else. But maybe, being a psychologist, he wasn't shocked to hear that deep down I loved the Job Corps, that I wanted to do something with my life—make my mother and myself proud.

Gordon drove me to his home, where his wife cooked us a huge dinner. Even amid this crisis, my appetite didn't fail me. We talked more about my dreams, and then he took me back to the base with a promise to write a letter in my behalf.

For a few days I lived in limbo, not knowing my fate. Then word came down that I was being offered a final shot to redeem myself. Gordon's letter had tipped the scale. He later showed me a copy. Though I'd gotten into plenty of trouble, he wrote, "there's something special about George. . . . It would be in the best interests of both George and the Job Corps to keep him with us."

As with all "last chances," there was a catch: that I give myself over to Doc Broadus for organized boxing as a way to channel my rage. It seemed reasonable, at least at first. "I'll do anything, Doc," I said. "I won't miss practice." So I started to box.

Doc Broadus worked me to exhaustion, draining off every drop of energy that might have gone to extracurricular hostilities. I sparred and learned the distinctions between boxing and street fighting. One of them was strategy—I'd never had one on the street, where the bigger, tougher guy usually wins. In boxing, skill, not brute strength, determines the winner.

Though on a scale of 1 to 10, my skills were about ½, Doc had incredible faith in my talent and progress. He entered me in a Diamond Belt competition the Job Corps sponsored at the center. I thought he was rushing things a bit, and frankly was worried about being embarrassed. Rather than refusing to go, I just didn't show up. He called me late that night.

"It's a good thing you didn't come," he said cannily. "They didn't have a match for you. You would have gotten a trophy for doing nothing." Some years, he explained, pickings among fighters in a particular class are slim or none. "There's another tournament in a few weeks."

He must have figured out that I wanted a trophy more than anything—something to show the boys in Fifth Ward as the spoils of a champion. He was right. When I saw the trophies some of the other guys had won—some for doing nothing—I was envious. All I had to do next time, I decided, was show up and pick up my heavyweight trophy. So a few weeks later I did go—and found myself in the ring against a tough, good-looking boy from the Navy. To get that trophy, I'd have to fight.

I was nervous, but by now I had a fair command of the basics (up to a 1 on that 1-to-10 scale) to back up my innate strength and talent. I knocked my opponent out in the first round, then jumped around the ring screaming as if I'd won the world championship. This was a lot more fun than anticipated.

Climbing out of the ring, I noticed several members of the Job Corps who'd been sitting near ringside. One of them was the boy whose door I'd punched. "Good fight, man," he said with sincerity. "You're going to be a hell of a boxer."

"Thank you," I replied, hoping I sounded just as gracious.

That single exchange is frozen in memory for me, as vivid as if it had happened today. In that moment, I saw the world turned upside down and recognized that I'd been standing on my head all along. My enemy complimented me, and I'd thanked him. Now he wasn't my enemy anymore. He stood for all my "enemies." I could stop fighting him, and I could stop fighting all the others. I didn't have to prove myself to the guy in the next room or the next desk or the next aisle or the next block. For the first time since I was six years old, my need to harm others softened; in fact, it ceased.

I changed that night. It was now clear to me that my destiny would not be grim. Boxing may or may not have figured in; I couldn't see that far and anyway had no preference for boxing over anything else. I didn't know where I'd be going, only that I was going somewhere and I was going to be somebody.

And that's all I'd ever fought for.

Chapter Three

OVERNIGHT I became a poster boy for the Job Corps: I'd gone from being a junior high dropout to a young man who now devoured books; from unemployable teenager to skilled factory worker; from thug to humanitarian. Well, not quite humanitarian, but as I dedicated myself to the "sweet science," I discovered more compassion for others.

Wherever Doc took me to fight, which was just about everywhere, the story ended the same way. At the opening bell, I'd rush my opponent and pummel him ferociously, swinging from all angles until the punches either took their toll—usually in a couple of minutes—or accidentally found the bull's-eye. I developed a reputation on the Golden Gloves circuit as a hitter, not a boxer. Deservedly so. I didn't practice my skills the way Doc would have preferred. Why bother? I'd learned the basics and couldn't have been more successful, anyway. And since it never occurred to me to become a professional boxer, technical proficiency wasn't necessary.

My father's brother-in-law, Judge Simpson, came to one fight. I'd never known him well; in fact, he didn't live in Houston, he lived right there in the San Francisco Bay area. Since I'd become friends with his grandson, a boy almost my age, he wanted to see what I was made of. I won the fight. A few days later, he took me aside. "Look, I don't want you hanging out with his kind," he said of his own grandson. "You look like you really want to work for something. That boy doesn't. You can be something, George, but he's going nowhere. Stay away." It stunned me to hear praise like that from a member of my family.

My San Francisco win had been as a junior. For my premiere as a senior, Doc took me to a Golden Gloves tournament in Las Vegas. Winning that qualified me for the national Golden Gloves tournament in Milwaukee. As usual, I went after my opponent with a vengeance, trying to finish him in a hurry. But he was skillful and had been coached well to bob and weave at the on-slaught. I kept missing with big, roundhouse shots intended to end the fight, and I lost my balance and stumbled. (It didn't help that the canvas shoes we wore in those days became slippery on the rosin-covered mat a few bouts into the night.) The judges ruled one of my stumbles a knockdown. Though neither of us did any damage, I lost because of that "knockdown."

I wasn't the only member of my team to be eliminated. Of our original eleven, only Jesse Valdez, a 139-pounder, remained. Be-cause of that, we couldn't go back to the hotel; we had to hang around and watch him fight until he won it all or was eliminated. While we were waiting, I saw a minute or two of the sandy-haired kid who would win the tournament's heavyweight divi-sion. Clay Hodges stood about six feet four inches and was pretty flashy. He would soon prove important in my life.

Though I'd lost for the first time, I didn't take it badly. Boxing had already been very, very good to me. I thought I'd gotten out of it everything it had to offer. With Job Corps graduation com-ing up, I could go home and get on with my life.

That's where Doc and I diverged. In me, a powerful heavy-weight with raw talent to spare, he saw visions of champion-ships. All I wanted was to go back to Houston with a sack full of trophies to show off to my buddies, and find an electronics-assembly job so that I could take care of Mom and my family the way Sonny did. Everyone would respect me.

Doc said, "Listen, man. Don't go. If you want to turn pro after graduating the Job Corps, there's a group of guys who'll back you. You'll get salary and expenses. All you'll have to worry about is boxing." (The partnership would have been modeled on the conglomerate that managed Joe Frazier after he won the 1964 Olympic heavyweight gold medal.) "Or, if you want to go to the Olympics, we'll work on that."

As far as I was concerned, there was nothing to work on. I knew almost nothing about the Olympics—had never followed them nor heard much discussion of them—and didn't want to know more. Even after failing in the Golden Gloves nationals, I felt no need to chase victory. I figured I'd already walked the length of boxing's glory road. Thanks, but no thanks, I told Doc.

Graduation from the Job Corps wasn't marked by any special ceremony. We filled out some papers, got our discharges and certificates validating our electronics skills, and picked up a check for about twelve hundred dollars. I so badly wanted to get home with my booty that I left without saying good-bye to Doc. The dread of having to debate him again over my future was more powerful than my sense of gratitude—and I owed him a lot. Some months before, he had arranged for me to take my Army induction tests through the draft board in Oakland, from where, he believed, I was less likely to be chosen for duty in Vietnam. At the time, I was prepared and ready—and I expected—to do my military duty. But Doc must have been right, because after my second physical I received a status lower than 1-A and never heard from the draft board; I still have no idea exactly why I was overlooked.

I arrived in Houston with a swelled chest and head, having left as a boy and returned as a man. I had money to give to Mom, money to buy clothes, and money to show around. Mom was proud of her baby who'd changed for the better, and I believed that my troubled days were dead and buried. As for my friends and acquaintances, most of them were preparing for induction and probable service in Vietnam. Me, I'd been on an adventure, and they treated me as a conquering hero. Life had never tasted so sweet.

First item on the agenda was to pass the G.E.D. test. Nervous about getting through it, I designed my own refresher course. But I came to see that the Job Corps education had taught me more than I realized. As soon as I saw the questions, I knew I would pass. And I did.

Next up: finding a job. Houston had several factories where my new skills could be used. Not all of them, however, advertised their willingness to be what was now officially called an Equal Opportunity Employer. I applied to those places displaying the sign. At those that did, I eagerly filled out applications and sat back to wait for offers.

Unfortunately, I sat back more than I waited—drinking some beers and a few bottles of wine and a pint or three of gin. For two years I'd had almost no alcohol, not because I'd sworn off the sauce but because Job Corps sites were dry. Thank God they were; otherwise I'd never have graduated. The more I drank, the more motivation I lost, the more belligerent I became. I remember a party where I started flirting with another guy's girlfriend. Unwanted advances. The boyfriend warned me away. When I dared him to step outside, someone quietly convinced him not to go. "All right, forget it," he said, walking out. His girlfriend followed. After sobering up, I felt ashamed.

Alcohol transformed me into a monster without a conscience. At a friend's house one night, I saw a pretty young lady accompanied by her date and his brother. Under the influence, I sidled up next to her. "I've got company," she said. Then her boyfriend came over, his brother behind him. "She's with me," the boyfriend said.

I beat up both brothers.

The next day I didn't remember a thing. My only reminders were my sore knuckles. A day after that I received an arrest warrant in the mail; the brothers had filed charges. As instructed I took the warrant to the police station. "We should lock you up," the desk sergeant told me. "But here's the choice: a hundred-dollar fine or do time."

"I don't know what happened," I told my mom. I was distraught and depressed. With no effort, I'd undone two years of work and study, and was falling back into the snakepit.

"Son," she said, "it's clear what has to be. You just have to get out of here."

She was right, of course. But where could I go? By then I'd

squandered the twelve hundred dollars. Mom borrowed the money from somewhere to pay the fine and keep me out of jail.

Soon thereafter, fate came calling: Doc Broadus tracked me down. He and I had still not spoken since my leaving, so I imagined his call was meant mainly as a lesson in courtesy and manners. But Mom got on the line before me and made a decision that shocked me, especially because she considered boxing a short step removed from street brawling.

"Mr. Broadus," she said. "Can you help my son? Please. Take him and do something with him. Just get him out of here."

I wish I could have seen Doc's face. Whatever his surprise, he certainly came on board. He evidently cashed his paycheck and—angering his wife ("You did *what*? For *who*?")—bought me a one-way airplane ticket to Oakland. Meanwhile, Mom again tapped her credit sources and scrounged together a few dollars to put in my pocket. This time, her tears good-bye were from gratitude. There was much to be thankful for.

Doc drove me from the airport back to Pleasanton, where he'd landed me work at the Job Corps center, plus room and board. A dishwasher and floor mopper, I attacked the job, intending to become the best dishwasher and floor mopper in California. I always finished my work quickly and then helped other workers finish theirs. If I saw someone carrying something heavy, I grabbed it. If the cook had a big job to do, I volunteered. I was beginning to appreciate what I had—work and food—and where I was.

At the camp's gym, Doc trained me rigorously. Whatever he said to do, I did. (Except for one thing: smoking. I hid it from Doc, as I had from Coach Bryant in school. Mine was a cruel, unbreakable habit. I often tried to quit, throwing cigarettes away, only to later pick through ashtrays and light smashed butts.) Wherever Doc said to fight, I fought. I owed this man who'd sacrificed for me and demonstrated such faith in me. What, exactly, I owed him and why I was doing this were not yet clear to me. I just hoped that the reason would appear in time. And it soon did.

Doc explained that he wanted me to prepare for the 1968 Mexico City Olympics, less than a year away. Muhammad Ali, Doc explained, had won a gold medal in the 1960 Olympics, Joe Frazier at the 1964 Games. Both had ended up rich and famous. And if I won, I would find my pot of gold waiting at the end of the rainbow. Problem was, I saw little evidence that I could even make the Olympic team, let alone win the heavyweight class. But Doc believed I could, and anyway, his plan was the only plan of any kind I had. Boxing was my best opportunity to buy a decent life for my mother. That's all I cared about. In fact, I cared so much that I even managed to quit smoking.

And soon, on my nineteenth birthday—January 10, 1968—I gave up drinking, too. At a party for me, I had more than one too many. The next day, I asked a friend where he'd gotten his black eye and other bruises. He answered that I'd beaten him. His crime had been gently telling me to cool down. "Who're you talking to?" I'd asked before pummeling him.

With tears in my eyes, I apologized and I promised that I would never take another drink. I've kept that promise for more than twenty-five years.

Despite my hard work and training, my skills weren't all they should have been. Doc preached the importance of speed and finesse, and I learned all the moves he taught. But I did so without any heart. I stood six foot one, and weighed about two hundred pounds. My years of street schooling made it difficult to give up on power, pure and simple, as my main weapon. I led with my strong suit, believing that it couldn't be topped.

Of all the boxers trying to make the Olympic team, I'd fought the least—maybe five fights. And since experience is the best teacher, Doc set out to change that. I beat three guys within a month, putting them all down quickly. Then Doc hooked up with a promoter named Henry Winston, who worked for Dick Sadler. Sadler managed a top welterweight, Charley Shipes, who'd recently fought for the title against the champion, Curtis Cokes. In early February 1968, hoping for another title shot, Shipes was to headline a card at a club in downtown Oakland.

Doc and Winston pressed Sadler to showcase me on the same card. They argued that my knockout punch might get me out of Palookaville, straight to the pros without stopping at the Olympics. Sadler, dreaming of deep-pocket investors attracted by a knockout artist, went along. He even suggested that they plaster posters all over Oakland announcing the local club debut of "amateur heavyweight sensation" George Foreman. (In those days, pros and amateurs were allowed to fight on the same bill, so long as the amateur bouts were followed by an intermission.)

I spent the day of the fight walking a picket line with my fellow workers at the Job Corps center. I didn't completely understand what they were demonstrating for, but I instinctively believed that, as labor, I ought to be with them. Later, they'd be coming to see me fight. On the other hand, I owed management. Since becoming a full-time boxer, I'd handed over the mopping and dishes to someone who could be there during the day—when the chores needed to be done—and taken a position they'd created especially for me: closing down the Corpsmen's rec rooms whenever I got home, usually after the last bus. (Later, when I traveled frequently, I became a paid boxing instructor.) They'd also moved me into the center's bachelor's quarters. It was a sweet deal. I enjoyed privacy, all I could eat, and enough money for bus fare and essentials. So I owed allegiance to both camps, but I walked the picket line with my friends.

"George, you should rest," they said.

"I'm staying," I insisted. At nineteen, rest was an alien concept. Besides, I enjoyed sharing the anticipation and excitement with those who were coming to see me fight. Someone brought a copy of the *Oakland Tribune* and we all had a laugh over the photo of me with the caption HEAVYWEIGHT SENSATION. It reminded me of my father's words: "The future heavyweight champ of the world. Stronger than Jack Johnson. Hits like Jack Dempsey."

My opponent was Clay Hodges, the tall, flashy blond I'd seen win the national Golden Gloves in Milwaukee the previous year. (I didn't know then that he'd also been the runner-up to Joe Frazier at the 1964 Olympic trials.) Feeling confident, I still figured that no amount of flash could protect him from my barrage of punches. At the opening bell I charged and within seconds threw a right that landed on his chin and dropped him to the canvas. He got up by eight, and for the remainder of the round backed away from the blizzard of punches—maybe two hundred—using his jab to keep me off-balance.

Amateur fights are three three-minute rounds, if the fighters go the distance. The better boxer in each round, decided by the judges, scores a point. The victory goes to the boxer who wins at least two rounds, or knocks out his opponent. Since every one of my fights had ended in knockout, that was my whole program. I never expected to see Clay get up after taking that kind of shot, so I didn't really know what to do next.

And I hadn't paced myself. A minute through the second round, I was spent, and barely threw a punch for the rest of the fight. Nearly wheezing from exhaustion, I called on all the skills Doc had taught me (and that I hadn't practiced well enough) to defend myself from his stinging jabs and short hooks; more landed than I could block. It turned out to be the easiest fight in the world to score.

Bill Caplan, whom I would later know well, was the ring announcer. "The winner," he bellowed, "two rounds to one, Clay Hodges." Afterward, I sat for a long time on the rubbing table, contemplating my failure. At the intermission before the pro card began, Bill came in and patted me on the back. "Don't worry, George," he said, "you're going to be a good boxer." His words meant a lot to me, especially because I believed I'd let everyone down. All my friends. The Job Corps. Doc. Myself.

Several of us, including the doctor from the Job Corps, Dr. Trent, had a late supper afterward. My face and eyes had begun to swell. "Maybe, George," Dr. Trent said, "just maybe, you should forget about boxing and go to college."

"Not a chance," Doc said. "He learned a lot in this fight. Didn't you, George?"

"Yeah."

"He'll be back better than ever," Doc said.

That started a round of encouragement. "Yeah, sure he will." I nodded bravely, wishing that they hadn't come to see me. I wished that I hadn't bragged about being the heavyweight champ. I wished that I was in the gym at that moment, training.

Doc was right. I had learned some important lessons, and best of all, I'd learned them without getting hurt. The new and improving George Foreman listened to his trainer with both ears and an open mind. *It's good I lost. That's right. It was coming too easy before. I realize now I've got to work. This isn't Lyons Avenue in Houston. This is the big leagues I'm trying. I'm going to pace myself. Learn defense. I'll always have the big punch; old faithful. But I'll have something else, too.*

Doc loved the change. I'd been a stubborn piece of clay, but now the shaping was easier, and I could see his happiness. That was a shock. Given the expectations he'd had before the fight, he should have been the second most disappointed man in the club; maybe even the first. Would I fight again? Did I really have the talent? Or was he guilty of wishful thinking? We both wanted answers.

My next fight would be crucial if I had any hope of making the Olympic team: the San Francisco Golden Gloves. Winning automatically qualified you for either the national Golden Gloves tournament or the national AAUs; and winning either of those qualified you to be one of eight (in each weight category) competing in the Olympic trials. My winning the previous year had meant zilch; I'd done it as a junior. The seniors, particularly in an Olympic year, promised to be much tougher. The good news: Only I and another senior heavyweight had applied; one fight, winner take all. The bad news: My opponent was a young man who'd mowed down everyone in his path. Until me, that is. I won sensationally, in a knockout. I was on my way to Toledo for the AAUs.

But Doc insisted that I have a tune-up first. He wanted me to enter another Golden Gloves regional tournament, this one in Las Vegas. Protesting that I'd already qualified, I reminded myself that father knew best. Or did he?

My first-round opponent turned out to be Clay Hodges, who needed a tournament win in order to qualify for the nationals.

I'd like to say that since *I'd* already qualified, I let up. The truth is that our second fight quickly turned into the first fight's twin. I came out swinging and knocked him down. And sure enough, he got up. I swung and swung until I was exhausted. Then he pecked and pecked. "The winner, two rounds to one, Clay Hodges." Two losses—my *only* two losses—within two months. The same guy.

I'd never been so discouraged. *I just cannot beat this young man. How can I ever beat him? And if I can't beat him, I can't go to the Olympics. And even if I go straight to the pros, what's the point if there's always going to be a guy around who can always beat me? I can't whip him. I'll never be champ. And if you're not champ, you can't make the real money. What's the point?* In my mind, I had two opponents: Clay Hodges and everyone else. And everyone else I could beat.

When the national AAUs arrived, I nervously searched the entrants for that blond head. My goodness, he wasn't there! The joy, the relief, was profound. Clay Hodges must have lost that tournament in Las Vegas. Since I hadn't stuck around to see his next round, it had never occurred to me that he might get beat, and that he wouldn't be there to peck at me. With knockout ease, I won the national AAU tournament.

Only later did I learn that Clay *had* indeed won that Las Vegas tournament—taking the finals, in fact, with a knockout that sent the loser into unconsciousness. He hadn't competed at the AAU tournament because his reserve unit of the Army National Guard, in which he was a second lieutenant, was on duty that weekend. During Vietnam, I suppose, special deals, particularly for officers, were a tough sell. If Clay hadn't been on duty—well, it's something I often wonder about. Maybe he does, too.

Before the Olympic trials began, the AAU organizers took their winners to Germany; they wanted us to get some international competition, which they insisted was a horse of a different color. They were right. The international rules had one purpose: to prevent Americans from winning. Rule Number 1: Cheat the American boxer. Rule Number 2: American boxer, don't feel bad when they cheat you.

My first bout was in Hanover against a left-hander who kept

bending down; that was his style, I suppose. But every time I hit him, the referee issued a warning for low blows. What else could I do? Finally, they disqualified me. When we moved on to Berlin, I knocked down my opponent so many times in the first round that the referee stopped the fight.

Germany itself was wonderful. This being my first time out of the United States, I was overwhelmed by the clean streets, the flower gardens on every corner, the remarkable old buildings. I was the stranger in a strange land made to feel welcome, and the Germans could not do enough to please us. They invited us into their homes for dinner and lodging. They dragged us to discos for entertainment. Back in Houston and California, I was the last guy to hit the dance floor. Here, they couldn't believe my moves. "Oh, show us that new dance, George," they'd say. I'd be crippled if I boogied like that now.

The trip home was as exciting as my time in Europe. Because as appealing as Germany had been, I got goose bumps when I heard the captain say that we'd soon be landing at Kennedy Airport in New York City, United States of America. Everyone on the plane cheered. It wasn't until that moment, with everyone on the plane cheering, that I realized how truly American I feel. A shiver ran up my spine.

The Olympic trials consisted of eight competitors for each weight class—the national AAU winner, the national Golden Gloves winner, the winners from the far East and far West, and each of the four military service champs (the Army, Navy, Air Force, and Marines). The favorite among the heavyweights was the Army champ, whose size (bigger than me), straight-up style (preferred in international competition), punching power (he'd K.O.'d all comers), and international experience (extensive) also made him the Olympic coaches' choice. I sensed them rooting against me, not because they didn't like me, but because they wanted to send the boxer with the best chance to bring home the Gold. In their estimation, I was not that man.

On my way to the finals I knocked out a giant from Washington, D.C., and a southpaw with a great left hook. Then I faced the all-Army champ, who was equally tough. Our match was an old-fashioned brawl, two big fellas pounding each other. After taking and dishing out a lot of punishment, I finally just shut my eyes, reached back, and swung as if my right arm was a baseball bat. I think when he saw it coming he froze, like a deer in headlights. It caught him in the solar plexus. His eyes bugged out as he doubled over, trying to get his breath. I stormed across the ring at him. End of fight. But because he was the runner-up, the rules said we had to face each other again in the finals. And the finals turned out to be a replay of the first time. Same punch; same reaction. This time, I won it all.

Whether the Olympic coaches wanted me or not, I, the least experienced boxer in the tournament, was now the American heavyweight representative to Mexico City.

Before checking into the Olympic training center in New Mexico, where we were expected to stay until the Games began, the entire team went to Denver for outfitting. A well-dressed stranger approached me there and identified himself as a campaign representative for Richard Nixon, who'd just won the Republican nomination for President. "You're a winner," the guy said, "and we think we've got us a winner, too. We'd like you to come out to some of our events and campaign for Nixon." What I knew about politics could fit on the head of a pin. I told him that I was flattered, which I was, but that I didn't have enough time. This was my first exposure to the power of sports and celebrity.

In New Mexico, I took my instructions now not from Doc, but from the team's coach, Pappy Gault. His workouts were severe and endless, because he wanted to make us experts in the pure boxing skills that won international fights. One of my only breaks from these workouts came during calls home to Mom. We talked about the weather, my brothers and sisters, the Job Corps—anything but boxing; the word refused to cross her lips. I knew she'd reconciled herself to boxing as a mixed blessing. As long as I didn't get killed and kept my nose clean, she could endure the bargain with the devil.

"You're okay?" she'd ask.

"Yeah, Mom, I'm fine. They're feeding me plenty."

"You're not in trouble?"

"No, Mom. I'm staying out of trouble."

"That's good, George, that's good. That's all I need to hear."

My mother's attitude reminded me of that famous prayer asking for courage to change what can be, serenity to accept what can't, and wisdom to know the difference. I was doing this for her, and she knew that, too. But she didn't have to like it.

A *Sports Illustrated* reporter came to New Mexico to do a feature story on America's boxers. As the team's heavyweight, usually the glamour division, I became a focus of the article. But that wasn't the only reason. There was also my mouth, which had begun working overtime since my fists now spoke only in the ring. I'd gotten over being a bully; now, I got my kicks from teasing and practical jokes. Combine that with confidence in my right hand, and no wonder the *S.I.* reporter was intrigued by this inexperienced fighter who'd stunned everyone at the trials and was now predicting gold for himself and America. My timing was right; boxing existed in Muhammad Ali's shadow a year after he'd been stripped of his title for refusing to be inducted into the Army. His personality dominated the sport. Not only did boxers believe they wouldn't be noticed without some showmanship, reporters were desperate for anyone who could fill that void.

Like Ali, I invented and narrated rhymes: "George is nimble / George is quick / Watch me / I can really stick." Or, "I'll move to your right / Stick all night / Move to your left / Cause your death." I also took off on one of Muhammad's infamous taunts, the one from his fight against Ernie Terrell, who'd refused to accept his name change from Cassius Clay. "What's my name?" he'd asked Terrell after each stinging punch.

"Let's talk about a fighter of yesterday / Everybody remembers old Cassius Clay / If he got me in the ring and asked *my* name / Why, that poor boy would die of shame."

Despite the publicity, I was generally ignored. That's because athletics wasn't the big story of the 1968 Olympics.

The Boycott—whether America's top athletes would protest against the United States by staying out of the Games—was Topic

Number 1. Leading the boycott charge was Harry Edwards, a sociology professor at San Jose State who was also a member of the Panther party. "It don't matter if you run or jump or shuffle," he'd say. "If you do it for the man, they're all the same."

Edwards and the other boycott leaders mainly recruited star athletes whose absence would be newsworthy—like Kareem Abdul-Jabbar. The leaders came to our New Mexico camp, took a look around the boxing team, and made speeches. But because they didn't see any big-name stars (maybe they should have spoken to Nixon's man in Denver), they passed us by the way a freight train would a hobo. None of us was asked to join the boycott.

Fact is, their pitch was most successful with guys like Kareem, who were used to radical messages because they attended college on campuses already hot with protests about the war in Vietnam. College is a world of youth, exuberance, and talk—not reality. Whether the students' anger was righteous, I don't know. I knew only that their world wasn't the one I saw. Maybe I was ignorant, but even at its most desperate and violent, the world I'd grown up in hadn't made me mad. I'd never, not for a day, felt inferior to anything or anyone. Yes, I'd been hungry. But I always believed I would develop skills and earn a living for me and my family. How could I protest against "the establishment," when that establishment had created the Job Corps for guys like me? I'd been lifted by an airplane out of poverty into a place where for the first time I ate three hot meals a day and learned everything I needed to begin learning on my own. Besides, I'd experienced prejudice in a way that Harry Edwards and his colleagues maybe had not. Remember, my family and teachers in grade school had shared my physical characteristics. But that hadn't prevented them from prejudging me and the type of man I might become. Those memories are why I've eliminated from my vocabulary adjectives that distinguish between people.

The Mexico City Olympic Village was like a cocoon. Unless we went out of our way to get the news from home (and I didn't) the athletes weren't even aware of the violent riots taking place in town between police and students. Television wasn't inter-preting our own experiences, as it did for viewers everywhere else. So when I heard that Tommie Smith and John Carlos were being expelled from the Village for raising clenched fists on the victory stand after finishing first and third in the 200-meter dash, I felt bewildered, then sickened. I'd never actually talked to ei-ther man, but when I jogged at the stadium I'd seen them work-ing out or stretching on the grass, letting tourists take snapshots of them. Sprinters are the marquee stars of any track meet, and from a distance they seemed arrogant—like strutting peacocks.

Instead of boycotting, Tommie and John had made a political statement. They knew the eyes of the world would be focused on them. What they didn't know, because they were young and immature, was how badly their protest would ricochet.

My first clue that the outside world had intruded on us in the Village was when I saw reporters and cameramen circling John like buzzards. Then someone told me that he and Tommie were being expelled. When I got closer to John, I saw that he looked sad—sadder than sad, as though he'd lost his mother. I won-dered if others saw this too. Probably not. Since I was a kid I'd been zeroing in on the emotion hidden in someone's face; was it fear or confidence? John's shattered face showed me grief and, I guessed, regret. I felt like crying for him.

Without headlines and the evening news to "explain" and magnify what they'd done, I considered John's and Tommie's protest to be a faddish statement of the times—like wearing a dashiki, long hair, faded blue jeans, an Afro. Expelling them from our family seemed an injustice. *Why do they have to go? How can they do that? It's not fair.*

That night, I still couldn't erase John's face from my mind. I found myself saying to some friends, "I'm not fighting any-more."

At the time, I'd won three bouts. (My first fight, which went the distance, was against a Polish boxer, Lucjan Trela. He squat-ted down real low and kept jabbing me in the middle. He was tough. Tougher still was my third-round opponent, Giorgio Bambini. He was a big Italian southpaw who hit me with a straight left that set off a siren in my head and made me go a little wacky. I waved my arms to fight off the flashing lights and whirring, and when he stopped to see what was wrong, I woke up and knocked him out.) Only the finals were left to go. I was this far from my goal, but the anger blotted out everything else. Saying the words made them real. Yes, I would stage my own protest against the people and forces who'd caused John Carlos so much pain.

"I'm not fighting," I repeated.

Word spread at the speed of sound that George Foreman wasn't fighting anymore. Soon I began hearing from dozens of people, in person and by telephone, trying to change my mind. Doc and other athletes pointed out that I would be throwing away my future. "George," Doc said, "this is what you've been working for."

"Did you see his face?" I asked. "Did you see it?" I was nearly crying.

The more everyone talked, the more bullheaded I became. This protest took on a life of its own. But explaining it was like the game of telephone. By the time the news reached American officials, they believed I was joining the organized boycott, not staging my own.

One of those who came to see me was Barney Oldfield, who worked for Litton Industries in public relations, community affairs, and special projects as an aide to Litton chairman Tex Thornton. Barney arranged for me to visit a Litton factory outside Mexico City that made parts for computers. All of the workers were women, and most of them had never been so close to a "celebrity" before—and an American at that. Their excited reaction helped me to realize how the rest of the world viewed Olympic athletes, and reminded me how far I'd really traveled. This was the mirror image of John and Tommie. Like them, I had been operating in a vacuum. It was a revelation to see these women look up to me. No one ever had.

Back at the Village that night, someone said that he'd talked to John Carlos. "John says for you to just go on out there and do your thing," he told me. "You go ahead and win the gold."

"Is that what he said?" I asked.

"Yeah, he doesn't want you to quit. He's pulling for you. You have to go out there."

A little older and wiser now, I think it's highly doubtful that John Carlos actually passed along this message. I never got a chance to ask. (The only other time I saw him was at the 1984 Olympics in Los Angeles. There he sat, cheering for Carl Lewis, who was waving the American flag during a victory lap after winning a gold medal.)

In any event, the tactic worked. I soon found myself in the dressing room with the other two American finalists, preparing to fight a big Russian, Ionas Chepulis. I wanted to win and hoped I would, but he had the international experience everyone talked about. This was 1968, the height of the Cold War. All the terrible images of Soviet athletes flooded my mind—robots exercising in hip-deep snow; guys with nuclear fists. To beat them, you needed James Bond and a magic briefcase, like *From Russia, with Love*. If I was going to win, I would have to knock him out. No way was an American going to get a decision. The judges would find a way to deny us victory. Everyone knew it.

Sure enough, Albert Robinson, a featherweight we considered America's best chance for boxing gold, burst through the door in tears. He'd been disqualified—just seconds, he claimed, before knocking the other guy out.

I called my mother. "Even if I lose," I said, "I'll still get a medal." I was already preparing myself. I'd seen Bob Beamon's medal hanging around his neck (he'd long-jumped past twenty-nine feet, two feet farther than anyone ever had). It was so mysteriously beautiful to me that I couldn't think straight about getting one myself; I wanted it too much.

Mom didn't care about any medal. "Just hurry home and eat," she said. End of discussion.

It was comforting to know that the best part of the world didn't depend on my winning. There'd always be Mom, loving me no matter what, ready with comfort and ham hocks.

Ronny Harris, a lightweight, came in smiling. He'd defied the odds and won on points. "Nothin' to it," he declared.

My bones shook as I tried to remember everything Pappy

Gault had stressed. "You've got to use the jab," he'd said. "Jab, jab, jab." It's the punch that's easiest to fire off and the one closest to your opponent. When he starts a combination, it forces him back to square one. And it builds up points.

Before going to the ring, I filled my robe pocket with some beads a girlfriend had given me and a small American flag one of the assistant coaches had given me for luck.

By lucky coincidence, the fighter whom Chepulis had beaten in the previous round was a hometown boy, Joaquín Rocha. That meant the Mexican fans would have rooted for Jack the Ripper against him. I'd never received such an enthusiastic ovation. It seemed the entire country was in my corner.

Pappy's coaching didn't desert me. Whenever Chepulis came forward, I stuck out the left jab. He kept charging me and running into it. The funny thing was, I felt so scared of getting hit that I closed my eyes each time. The jab knocked him so far backward that I didn't have an opportunity to use the right. My only worry was whether they'd find some reason to disqualify me. Finally, when I opened my eyes and began landing the right, the referee stopped the fight.

I'd won. The fans' screams were for me, the heavyweight gold medalist.

To express good sportsmanship and humility, the champion is expected to bow to the judges and spectators in the ring's four directions. Before doing that, I snatched the small flag from my robe pocket. Despite the later press reports and most people's interpretation, my waving the flag wasn't exactly the gesture of patriotism it appeared to be. Nor was it a counterdemonstration to Tommie Smith and John Carlos. The truth is less simple.

For the weeks I'd been in Olympic Village, I'd seen hundreds of young men who could have been my brothers. "Hey, how're ya doin', homeboy?" I'd say to a fellow coming back from a workout. But instead of responding in English, he'd speak some language that sounded about as intelligible as gargling. I soon learned that your flag and your colors were what identified you. But once I'd won and was in the ring, I didn't think that the letters u.s.a. on the chest of my shirt were enough.

The flag.

"You see," I meant the waving to say, "this is an American who won this medal."

So, yes, there was a big element of patriotism in what I did; being in the Olympics, you couldn't help but love your country more than before. But I meant it in a way that was much bigger than ordinary patriotism. It was about identity. An American—that's who I was. I was waving the flag as much for myself as for my country. I was letting everyone know who I was and at the same time saying that I was proud to be an American. (I also considered my Olympic uniform to take the place of the military uniform I'd never gotten to wear.)

At the time I couldn't imagine that anyone would misinterpret. But the next day, in a campaign speech in Madison Square Garden, Richard Nixon referred to "that young man at the Olympics who made us all so proud. He wasn't afraid to show his patriotism." (Later I received a letter from someone in the Midwest that read, "You returned honor and dignity to the country after what Jacqueline Kennedy just did." For the longest time I wondered what Jackie Kennedy had to do with boxing. I didn't understand the reference to her marrying Aristotle Onassis.)

I got a call from Hubert Humphrey's staff asking if I would go out on the campaign trail. Still ignorant of the whole political ballgame (to say the least), I knew nothing about Humphrey. Then someone mentioned that he was LBJ's Vice President; if he won, the Job Corps would probably be continued; if Nixon won, the program might be axed. That was a good enough reason for me to make some whistle stops with the Humphrey campaign, though I have to admit that if Nixon had called, I'd probably have gone out with him, too. The best part of the campaigning was meeting other celebrities—guys like Rafer Johnson, Chubby Checker, Lee Majors. They knew my name.

The actor Gene Barry walked up to me out of the blue. "Hey, George," he said, "how ya' doin'?"

Imagine—being recognized by Bat Masterson. I called my mother to tell her.

Humphrey lost. But I met his outgoing boss, President Johnson, a few weeks later. I was the only Olympian to do so. He agreed to the meeting because of the Job Corps connection. Before going to the White House, it struck me that in ceremonies like this the President was always handing out an award to someone else. I thought he deserved one, too, so I presented him with a plaque that read:

> *To President Lyndon Baines Johnson*
> *from George Foreman*
> *1968 Olympic Heavyweight Gold Medal Winner*
> *In appreciation for fathering the Job Corps program*
> *which gave young Americans like me*
> *hope, dignity, and self-respect.*

That same weekend someone introduced me to Coach Vince Lombardi, whose Green Bay Packers were in Washington to play the Redskins. Lombardi was the man who'd devised the motto "Winning isn't everything, it's the only thing." He came over to my table at a restaurant but he didn't say a word to me after our introduction. He just stared at me, like he was studying me. I could tell he liked what he saw, but it was strange. Finally he told me how proud I'd made him at the Olympics, that I was a good American. Before leaving, he asked for my address. A few weeks later, he sent me a photo of himself and a long letter about achievement and winning. He approved of me, he said. He made me begin to realize what I had accomplished.

At home, though, happiness became unhappiness. One of the elementary schools I attended, Atherton, held an awards ceremony for the Olympic winner. As with LBJ, I turned the tables by presenting them with my Olympic wreath. It was intended as a reminder to treat every child—apparently well-off and apparently poor—the same. "Because you just never know what's going to happen," I said.

I wore the gold medal everywhere so that Fifth Ward could share in the victory. But I guess a lot of people didn't see it exactly as a victory. I visited homes decorated with giant posters of Smith and Carlos that showed them with their heads down, clenched fists in the air. It was pretty clear that I didn't fit in.

Speaking at schools and community get-togethers, I often ran into Panthers who shot me strange looks; their faces said that I'd betrayed the cause. But I didn't really understand the cause. We were in different armies. My uniform was a pair of trunks. And until winning the gold medal, I'd always felt a little guilty and a little sorry for not being a real soldier.

I began to feel that I didn't belong anywhere. That feeling was salted the night I ran into a "friend" I hadn't seen since the Olympics.

"Hey, man," I said. "What's goin' on?" As usual I had the medal around my neck. Seeing it, his face hardened.

"Man," he said, his voice slow and pained, "how could you lift up the flag that way when the brothers were doing their thing?" He was speaking the words everyone else thought. They hit me like a hammer. It was true; I really didn't belong.

What a homecoming. Imagine—the Olympic heavyweight champion, an outcast. There was no place to escape but into myself. That's when I began withdrawing. It wasn't long before I became the kind of man it was easy to root against.

Chapter Four

WHILE DECIDING where to go and what to do with my life, I moved into the ramshackle house Mom rented on Dan Street. Its three tiny rooms were already crowded with my two younger brothers, Roy and Kenneth, and my older sister Gloria, who was getting back on her feet after having a baby. Mom was still struggling, more since I wasn't sending my Job Corps pay. But she didn't mind feeding an extra mouth, even such a big one. She loved having her boy at home for a spell—as long as he stayed out of trouble.

As magazine writers and newspaper reporters came from all over the world, promoters and managers began romancing me to turn pro. One of them was Fred Hofheinz, the son of Roy Hofheinz, who built the Astrodome. Fred had just gone into business with Mike Mannix and Bob Arum to promote boxing and show the bouts on closed-circuit television. He showed me around the Astrodome and told me that if I signed with them they'd hire Angelo Dundee, the trainer who helped make Muhammad Ali great.

Fred gave me a ride home. A mile from the house, I said that I wanted to walk the rest of the way. He insisted on going all the way to my door, but I claimed to need exercise and fresh air. The truth is that I was ashamed of Mom's house and afraid that if he saw it he'd think that I'd jump at a few dimes. Of course, he didn't have to see the house to know I needed the money. All he had to see was the neighborhood. Even so, I was trying to preserve my dignity.

Hearing how well I spoke of my mother, some of these guys must have figured that the way to me went through her. Jimmy Iselin, who managed Buster Mathis and whose father was president of the New York Jets, picked her up one Sunday in a limousine and took her to the Oilers-Jets game at the Astrodome. She sat in the visiting team's owner's box, and was treated royally, with fancy food and fine service. Afterward he brought her home, walked her inside, and explained what they were prepared "to do for George." Then he put a pile of cash on the table—more than my mother had ever seen in one place.

"That's for starters," he added.

"Listen," Mom said, "you can put ten million up here, it won't make a bit of difference. First of all, I don't want George to box. Second, that boy's going to do whatever he's going to do anyway. I don't make decisions for him. He makes up his own mind, and when he does, you'll know."

I hadn't decided anything, except that I no longer belonged in Houston. When Laney Junior College in Oakland offered me a football scholarship, I leaned toward getting an education. Then I realized that college couldn't help me buy my mother a new dress, let alone a house and car, and that without new and bigger fights, strangers would soon stop asking for my autograph, celebrities wouldn't recognize me, and *The Dating Game* and other shows would stop booking me. It wasn't like today, when an Olympic medal can mean millions in promotions and endorsements; in the sixties, a gold medallion around your neck didn't in and of itself put a nickel in your pocket.

After a couple of months, I returned to my job teaching boxing at the Job Corps center in Pleasanton. Doc Broadus organized a homecoming welcome and parade in my honor, and arranged to have a helicopter fly me in from the Oakland Airport. He and I both knew that much of the credit for my gold medal went to him.

"I got some promoters interested in you," Doc said. "Let's talk about that."

I knew what he wanted to talk about, and I didn't want to face it. Two years before, Doc had drawn up a contract giving him half of my future earnings in exchange for his management. Feeling beholden, I'd played along and signed. Only once, when the boxing coach at Lackland Air Force Base had come to the Job Corps to meet me, had this "contract" even been mentioned. The coach, Bill Ross, had seen me fight in San Francisco and invited me to join the Air Force on a sweet deal.

"All you'll do is box," he'd promised. "You'll have plenty of sparring partners and the best training. You can prepare full time for the Olympic trials. And you won't go to Vietnam."

I had intended to consider Bill's offer seriously. But Doc had blown a gasket when he found out I might accept. Waving the contract and screaming theft, he'd run Bill out of the gym.

I laughed at the time. Now, though, the game was real. My gold medal and the attention it brought me was forcing Doc and me to settle this thorny issue.

"Doc," I said, "I've talked to a number of promoters already. I don't have any idea what I'm doing yet."

"Well, I've got a contract," he said. "I'm enforcing it."

"There's no contract, Doc. That contract's no good. You can't sign a contract with a seventeen-year-old kid. I'm sorry."

I *was* sorry, too, for what that misunderstanding did to our friendship—what was left of it, anyway. More, I was hurt and disappointed that he'd resurrected the contract and assumed he could be my manager for life. I saw his attempt as an effort to exploit an unsophisticated boy.

A few months later, returning from a Houston visit, I ran into Dick Sadler at the Oakland Airport. He was training Sonny Liston, the surly ex-champ who'd lost his title to Cassius Clay in 1964. Now, at age thirty-seven, Liston was again among the top-ranked heavyweights and looking for a title shot. Dick remembered me from the previous spring, when Doc Broadus had taken me to his gym in Oakland to spar with Sonny before his fight against Henry Clark. Sonny had needed sparring partners and I'd needed the work against big guys like Sonny for my Olympic training.

On impulse I said, "Hey, Dick. Maybe you can help me. I need to learn a bit more about boxing. Maybe I could do some exhibitions—you know, take advantage of my medal. Can you help?"

"Sure, son," he said.

"Just some exhibitions." In other words, proceed with caution.

"Exhibitions it is. You can travel around with Sonny, fight on some of the same cards. We'll spread your name and fame."

As I prepared to begin working out with Sonny and Dick during my hours away from work, word came that the Job Corps center was soon to close. Richard Nixon had just taken office and was cutting back or eliminating some of LBJ's programs. Even though I stood out as the program's most conspicuous success story (my boxing robe said GEORGE FOREMAN, THE FIGHTING CORPSMAN on the back), I lost my home and my job. But that wasn't as difficult as seeing a worthwhile program being undermined.

Dick Sadler helped me rent a small apartment in Hayward, near the boxing gym he used in Oakland. I didn't have a car, so except for the times Sadler picked me up in his limo, I walked everywhere. Other people would see me on the street and ask if I needed a ride.

"No thanks," I'd say. "Need the exercise." I was ashamed that the Olympic heavyweight gold medalist was too poor to afford a car. After all, I was famous; I'd been all over television. And even my friends with ordinary jobs owned cars. I wanted people to think that I was without wheels by choice.

I trained full time with Sonny. Everything he did, I did. We often ate dinner together and afterward took a walk. To say that Sonny Liston was a man of few words is to say that the sun is warm. Normally, he just glared. So when he suddenly began talking about himself on one of our walks, I hung on to every syllable.

He talked about the 1964 fight against Cassius Clay in Miami Beach, when he lost the title that he'd taken two years before from Floyd Patterson. Some people still point to that Clay fight as proof that boxing is, or was, fixed. But the Sonny Liston I got to know was too mean and too proud—and had come from too far behind—to throw the championship away on purpose.

He explained to me that after he beat Patterson, the fans treated him like dirt. Not Clay himself, but the fans' dislike for him, was, he believed, what had robbed his punch of its sting. Furthermore, their love for Clay had less to do with Clay than with their rejection of him. To hear him tell it, he was a beaten man before he even stepped into the ring. The man had a king-sized chip on his shoulder.

"When I won the championship from Patterson," he said in his sandpaper voice, "everyone acted like I stole it: 'What're you doing as heavyweight champion? What's someone like you doing with the belt?' "

Patterson was considered a gentleman and was beloved by fans throughout his career. After winning the 1952 Olympic middleweight gold medal, he'd turned pro as a heavyweight. Four years later, just shy of his twenty-second birthday, he beat Archie Moore and became the youngest heavyweight champ to date. In 1959, he lost the title to Ingemar Johansson, then won it back in a rematch. In 1962, Liston knocked him out in Round 1, and did the same a year later in a fight that lasted seven seconds longer than the first.

In contrast to Patterson's charm and grace, Liston was an ornery creature. An ex-con who'd served time for armed robbery, he liked few people and felt that fewer still liked him; and he trusted no one completely. Soon after winning the title, Attorney General Robert Kennedy's task force on organized crime investigated him for alleged underworld ties; Sonny was said to have been a mob enforcer. (The Kennedy people had begged Patterson not to fight Liston. When Patterson insisted, they rooted openly against Liston.) Unindicted but tainted, Sonny considered the investigation further evidence of universal forces aligned against him.

He told me, "When I was champ, I used to hear people say that I didn't deserve the title. Then when I lost to Clay, the same people told me I should have won. I know I should have.

I should have. I could have. But they all acted like they didn't want me to."

It may be hard to believe that heavyweight champs can feel so hurt by a lack of appreciation; people consider top boxers to be immune to that sort of thing. But I understood immediately—his words struck home. They reached a faraway place in me, where I kept the memories of elementary school and the teachers who wondered why I was there. I interpreted Sonny's words as a sort of admission that he'd unconsciously sacrificed his title to satisfy the fans who said he was unworthy and undeserving. Now, older and more bitter, he was on a quest to regain it—and this time to keep it.

Sonny and I sparred constantly, which was about the best training I could have had. He stood his ground and refused to submit to my superior strength and two-inch height advantage. I empathized with him, looked up to him, wanted his approval and friendship. When I heard him tell Dick Sadler, "You tell that big blankety-blank to come in here and get my bag," I felt accepted. But I rarely heard another word from him on any subject until one day in the dressing room.

"Hey, George," he said. I nearly jumped at the sound of his voice calling my name. "So you want to be heavyweight champ of the world, huh?"

"Yeah, Sonny, I do," I said. I was like a little puppy. "You think I can do it? What do you think?" I leaned in close, waiting to receive some good advice.

"Well," he said, "when you get to be heavyweight champ, you spit on the sidewalk and they write about it in the paper." He stopped and stared ahead for a moment. "Me, all I care about is the dough-re-me."

Those were the last words he spoke to me for three months— until the day he brought in a copy of a prominent magazine that featured a long profile of him.

"Here," he said, throwing it at me. "Dirty writer, saying I'm running around yelling 'Mammy, Mammy, Mammy' all the time. Liar!"

I wondered what he was talking about as I searched the table of contents. When I found the article, I read it.

"Hey, Sonny," I said. "This is great. He's saying that you belong up there on Mount Rushmore with all those presidents. I wish someone would write something like that about me."

"Oh, give me that." He snatched the magazine and walked away, mumbling, "Mammy, Mammy, Mammy."

I still didn't know what he meant.

A few days later we were in the back of Sadler's limousine on the way to Sonny's appointment with the chiropractor. I'd brought a book on horoscopes to read while waiting for him. I knew nothing about astrology, but I'd heard fascinating talk and wanted to investigate. As I read about my sign, Capricorn, every description seemed to fit.

"Wow," I said, "this horoscope stuff is true. It's *true*. Hey, Sonny, when were you born?"

"Come on, man," he said, "don't believe that stuff. Bunch of lies."

"No, Sonny, I'm telling you. Here, read this." I handed the book to him.

"Get that blankety-blank book out of my face," he said, slapping it away.

I sat back, the wind sucked out of me. Why would my friend do that?

Sonny got out of the limo for his appointment, and Sadler noticed my hurt. "Don't get upset, George," he said. "The big man can't read."

I guess I should have figured that out. When we'd been together in public, people would ask for our autographs. I'd sign ten for his every one. His pen moved deliberately across the paper, as if he were forging a signature someone had taught him to memorize.

"He thought you knew," Sadler said. "And in case you didn't, he didn't want you to find out. He doesn't like anyone to know."

A few months later, Sonny and I were to fight on the same card in Las Vegas, I against Bob Hazelton, Sonny against Leotis Martin for the vacant North American Boxing Federation title. If he won, his next fight might be for the big title against Jimmy Ellis. Since we'd barely grunted a word toward each other since that day in the limo, it was a surprise when Sonny called me up to his hotel room.

"Come here, George. I want to talk to you, boy."

"Yeah?"

"Read this." He handed me his contract.

"You're supposed to get fifty percent—"

"Are you sure that's what it says?"

"Yeah, fifty percent."

"That's what I thought."

Sonny's trusting me to verify the terms of his contract was, to me, the ultimate compliment. Whatever anger I still felt for his slapping the book away instantly disappeared. Something else happened, too. Forgiving him helped me to understand the cruelty of illiteracy—how it could distort a proud man. I saw in him what might have happened to me had fate been less kind.

That night, I knocked out Hazelton in the first round. Sonny was winning his fight, too, when Martin suddenly knocked him out.

Later, I went to his home for a little gathering his wife had planned. It turned into a condolence call. The depression wore on Sonny like a straitjacket. He sat in the backyard, staring ahead, a dog on his lap. He'd told me that he cared only about the "dough-re-me," but now I saw that must have been a lie. Here he was, next to his swimming pool in the backyard of his mansion, knowing he'd never have to work again—and hurting badly inside. His wife told me that he'd been like that, quiet and still, since coming home. I brought him a soda and squatted down next to him. He barely acknowledged me. His wife began sobbing.

"What you guys gotta understand is that sometimes you lose," she said. "You can't win them all. Nobody wins them all. You hear that, George? You lose. Everybody loses. But you can't just die."

I never saw Sonny Liston again. A year later, he died under mysterious circumstances at age thirty-eight.

. . .

Dick Sadler arranged an exhibition for me in Arizona, then one in Houston on a card headlined by Joe Frazier. He'd been right when he said the media would spread my fame.

Out of nowhere he declared, "You need to turn pro." All right. "I got you your first fight in Madison Square Garden. Frazier's the main event. You'll get five grand in cash." All right. "After a couple fights, you can fight for the title."

The title?

Those words had a sweet ring to them; still, they didn't sound possible. I knew Sadler was right, that I had to turn pro sooner or later. And five thousand dollars—that was all the money in the world. But any mention of my fighting anytime soon for the title was just fast-talk; you'd have to be a fool not to see that. Even so, there were worse lies to believe.

"All right," I said.

When we got to New York the week before the fight, someone handed me a boilerplate manager-fighter contract. Dick and I had shaken hands, but without a written agreement between us, Madison Square Garden would forbid me from fighting. I looked over the contract with suspicion. It was one thing to fight in Sadler's stable. It was another to formalize our arrangement. Sadler would have an exclusive for three and a half years, and I would get two thirds of the purse and he one third—standard, everyone said. Maybe a little better than standard. Some boxers—and I remembered Liston's deal—split fifty-fifty.

I didn't know where to turn. I trusted only Mom, but in this matter she couldn't help. I could imagine her saying, "George, you're a big boy. You do what you think is right."

I weighed the situation: Sadler had been paying my expenses anyway; I owed him for that. If I signed with him, I'd get to continue training with Liston. If not, I'd have to pack my bag and go elsewhere, and end up signing with someone sometime. But where and with whom? Compared to other managers who'd approached me, Sadler's game was easier to swallow. With him, I'd at least have a say in who my opponents would be. Joe Frazier (who would be fighting Jerry Quarry at the Garden to defend the

New York World Heavyweight title) and other boxers managed by corporations, had little or no say in whom they fought.

I signed. But since New York considered twenty-year-olds too young to enter into contracts, I had to send it to Houston for my mother's signature. I had a manager.

On June 23, 1969, in Madison Square Garden, I knocked out Don Waldheim in the third round. Before, I'd thought that I was entitled to press hoopla just because I was the Olympic gold medalist. But I guess professional boxing was littered with plenty of gold medal busts. That's where Sadler really knew the game and earned his money. My Waldheim bout caught the spillover attention from the Frazier-Quarry fight. That made it easier for Sadler to find me other fights—a lot of them.

As it turned out, though, Madison Square Garden was about the only arena offering a decent purse. Every time I fought there I made good money, while places like Scranton and Lake Geneva paid me four hundred dollars, six hundred dollars, two hundred. Even bigger cities like Seattle and Miami Beach wouldn't make me much more. Though Sadler was supposed to get only a third of my earnings, he took half. That seemed fair, and I didn't challenge him on it, because his expenses far outweighed my income. I fought several bouts that barely covered my hotel phone bill (calls to Mom). What mattered was winning—and that I did, almost always by knockout. I trained hard and with determination. Each step I took closer to the top made me want to go higher.

In those days, conventional wisdom held that athletes in training ought to refrain from consorting with women. "Bad for the wind, bad for the legs," they said. Joe Louis himself told me that he always avoided female contact for at least a month before a fight. He thought it made you weak. But one time, ten days before a fight, some friends came to camp and kidnapped him for a night on the town. The next day, he said, he ran farther and hit the bag harder than ever.

"What are you doing, man?" his trainer asked.

"Nothing," Louis snapped. "Just want to get in shape."

Guilty and worried, he trained with equal ferocity over the next nine days.

When the bell rang for the fight, Louis ran out to center ring and unleashed a vicious assault. Back in his corner between rounds, his trainer asked what in the heck he was doing.

"Just fighting," he said.

But he was really trying to end the bout in a hurry, he said—before his legs and strength gave way from reduced stamina.

Definitely not wanting to lose my strength, either, I kept Joe's story in mind. For the most part it wasn't hard to avoid female companionship. Not only was I without a car, I felt unwelcome at the parties where you'd normally meet the opposite sex. In the East Bay, the hometown of Huey Newton and the Panthers, the walls of most houses I visited were decorated with posters of Tommie Smith and John Carlos on the victory stand; flag-waving George Foreman was not exactly every girl's flavor of the month. Also, I was shy.

Only one time did I give in to temptation. Fifteen days before a fight against Mel Turnbow, I was with a girl—a beautiful girl—I'd met through a friend. But afterward I was almost sick with regret and terrified of the consequences to my life; after all, if I lost, my career would probably be over before it really started. And to lose for something so stupid was, well, stupid.

The next day, like Joe Louis, I attacked my training with a vengeance. Out running in the hills with Charley Shipes, who was to fight on the same card, I lost my footing on a curve. *It's happening*, I thought. *It's true. My legs are gone. What happened to Joe Louis is happening to me.* Charley glanced over, to see if I was all right. *He knows. He knows.*

Panic, pure and simple. No boxer ever punched the bag harder or jumped rope longer than I did over the next two weeks. Every few seconds, it seemed, I would check my wind—*Am I breathing too hard?*—and test my leg strength. The worry was far more exhausting than the workout. Turnbow was a giant of a man and a skillful boxer who often sparred with Muhammad Ali. I cursed myself. Why had I risked everything? Why had I given in? *I need another two weeks.*

In the ring before the fight, Sadler reiterated words of wisdom. "Take your time," he said. "Go out there and plant your jabs, set him up. Beat him in the body. Make him weak. Don't try to knock him out until then." I nodded. Yes, that had been the game plan, and an excellent one—but not for someone in a weakened condition. *I'm gonna lose my wind. He doesn't know I spent the night with that girl.*

At the opening bell, I rushed Turnbow like a comet racing across the sky. *Wham, boom, wham, boom, wham, wham, boom, boom, boom, wham, wham!* He went down and I backed up into a neutral corner, gasping for breath. I heard Sadler in the corner.

"Hey, man," he said, worried and annoyed, "what the blankety-blank are you doing? Take your time. You understand. Just take your time. You're going to get into it, you're going to get into it."

I nodded. "Okay."

When Turnbow stood, I charged him like a stone flung from a slingshot, out of control—and bumped my cheek into his. The collision instantly raised a bump over the bone. I could feel it. But no matter. *Wham, boom, wham, boom, boom, wham, wham, wham, boom.* I knew Sadler was beside himself. A minute later, *wham!* I knocked Turnbow out, completely out.

Today, where that bump was raised remains a tiny dent. A reminder of a lesson learned, it's the only visible physical evidence of my boxing life.

Over the next three years, I fought on average more than once a month, so my love life was a low-scoring event. As the last of the barnstorming, ballyhooing promoters, Dick Sadler would take his stable on the road for three- or four-state tours lasting five weeks. Of all his boxers, I could fight most often because my knockout punch usually ended the action in a hurry: July 1, 1969, Fred Askew, first-round K.O.; July 14, Sylvester Dullaire, first-round K.O.; August 18, Chuck Wepner, third-round K.O.; September 18, John Carroll, first-round K.O.; and on and on. I fought three times in December alone, the third time only two days after winning a ten-round decision.

It wasn't for money that I fought so often; our income depended on gate receipts and often didn't cover expenses. What I was fighting for was experience to become a complete boxer. Since a fighter usually has only one chance to climb to the top of the heavyweight ladder, he'd better bring everything with him to every rung. Because the higher he goes, the harder it gets.

By February 16, 1970, when I appeared in Madison Square Garden on another Joe Frazier card, I'd fought and won fourteen pro bouts. Frazier, who would that night win the world heavyweight title against Jimmy Ellis, hadn't fought once in that stretch. Only twice had any of my fights gone the distance; all but one of the rest finished in fewer than five rounds. Unfortunately, I took ten that night to beat Gregorio Peralta. Given the small army of reporters present to witness Frazier's fight, I would have jumped a few rungs on that ladder with a more typical display.

A little upset afterward, I felt I'd missed a chance. But Sadler convinced me that we were on schedule. "You're not going to make much money now," he said. "But you're learning the sport, and that's what counts. The money will come later. Lots of it. But you've gotta know the sport."

I knew the sport well enough by August to score a third-round knockout of George Chuvalo, who'd beaten and/or gone the distance against every top heavyweight and never been knocked down.

Sadler and I had an understanding. He'd tell me everything he knew, and I'd try to learn it. He'd tell me everything to do, and I'd try to do it. I thought of Sadler as General Bradley on the road to Berlin.

Sadler called me "son." The word had a soothing sound, especially because I'd kind of put my mother on the shelf; she was just another distraction I needed to avoid. What I didn't know then was that Sadler called everyone "son." Anyway, it wouldn't have mattered, even if I had known. I willingly made him my master, and was glad to soak up whatever he had to offer outside the ring as well. With the most naive and dedicated pupil he'd ever had sitting at his feet, he doled out all of his philosophy about a boxer's life. In Sadler's world, boxers were to beware of women. I heard a hundred stories about guys who'd lost their mind and money to them.

"Each town has its own girls," he said. "You're supposed to meet 'em and leave 'em."

And you're not supposed to brush up against failure. He

pointed to another hundred sad and cautionary tales to be learned in the gym—boxers who'd squandered chances and money, or talent and time. Every man past his best days who'd hadn't quite made the top—state champs, participants in championship fights, contenders who never got the chance—had the kind of problems you could see without looking hard. At least ninety percent were alcoholics. I didn't need Sadler to scare me about avoiding their fates. I worried that if I even talked to them, I'd catch whatever bad luck they were carrying.

It's painful to remember how I isolated myself. I was like the bubble boy, kept beneath a plastic cover to avoid disease. I hid from people like that "friend" in Houston who'd questioned my flag waving; I wouldn't let anyone get close enough to talk to me about that again. I hid from women who would zap my strength. I hid from the streets, where Cleveland Williams was drunk-driving when the police shot him. I hid from those I thought wanted a piece of my future. I hid from anyone who might have pulled out a marijuana cigarette in front of me—during this era, that was almost everyone. I had to protect what I'd already won and wanted still to win.

I trained. I boxed. I talked to Sadler. And I read—a thousand books. I traveled with a briefcase full of them. History. Philosophy. Adventure stories. Even legal books. *Law Made Simple.*

Sadler believed that I'd given over my life to him because of his power. He didn't understand that it was just my devotion. The truth surfaced when (as the song always says) a woman came between us. What's ironic is that Sadler introduced her to me.

In late 1970, we went to Minneapolis so that he could investigate "a business opportunity." Sadler was like Ralph Kramden in *The Honeymooners*—always brewing some get-rich-quick scheme. He and a partner planned to buy a microfilm company, put minorities to work using federal retraining funds, then go public. For seven thousand dollars, I would be part owner and see my name on the company's letterhead. The truth was that he included me only to use my name as a calling card; it bought credibility. He would take the Olympic gold medalist and "future heavyweight champion" around town as a draw for investment bankers.

Worried that I would get bored holed up in Minnesota and go back to California, he wanted to introduce me to a young lady. When I wasn't interested, he engineered a blind date. She turned out to be a beautiful young woman who dressed and wore her hair like Angela Davis.

"Wow," I said. This woman was worth a long vacation from my plastic bubble. Her name was Adrienne Calhoun.

We went dancing. Wow, again. I'd never seen anyone move quite that way. I asked her to spend the night with me. "Nah," she said. Disappointed, relieved, and intrigued, I asked to see her the next night. She said yes. And the next night. She said yes then, too. Good thing I didn't have a fight scheduled.

Sadler soon started to worry about this infatuation. He repeated his lessons about a woman's place in a boxer's life. I didn't need to hear that from him, and thought he would have realized that by now. Since he still couldn't leave it alone, he did the one thing that would put some physical distance between Adrienne and me: In February of 1971, he set up a fight in St. Paul with a boxer named Charlie Boston, whom I knocked out in the first round.

A month later Adrienne and I met in New York for the first Joe Frazier–Muhammad Ali fight. The ring announcer introduced me at ringside as "the next top contender." My record was twenty-six wins in twenty-six professional fights, twenty-three of them by knockout.

After the fight, Sadler knocked at my hotel-room door. I opened it and, stepping aside so he could see Adrienne, asked if he remembered her. Looking unhappy, he at first pretended not to, then admitted, "Oh, yeah." The ring announcer's introduction must have echoed in his ear. "Well, top contender, you've got to train tomorrow."

I took his meaning. In fact, those words were so effective that he used the line or some variation of it whenever he saw Adrienne and me together. He wanted to do everything in his power to put a wedge between us.

I fought only six more times the rest of the year. When possible I flew into Minneapolis to visit Adrienne. Sometimes she met me in Hayward or other cities, but only after a fight—and only if another one wasn't scheduled.

As we drew closer, I made clear to her that boxing was my wife. That was obvious. She understood, and made it clear that she liked her office job and wouldn't quit. We probably spent more hours on the telephone than in person; we talked every day.

I can't say for sure that I would have married Adrienne if not for Sadler. I may have married just to show him that I held my own leash.

"You meet women on the street, you leave it on the street," he'd say. "You don't need this woman. She's just after your money."

I'd listen and listen to his stories of boxers with steel chins and glass hearts who ended up in the home for the pathetic. "They had it made until they met their women, who took their money and left them broke."

I listened until I knew the words by heart. I didn't buy what he was selling. In my mind, any woman worth the time deserved to be treated as I'd have liked my mother to be treated. I had to make Sadler know that I wasn't just running around with a gold digger, that she was a woman—and that I was a man—of substance.

Besides, Adrienne had given me an ultimatum. "Look," she said, "this isn't going anywhere. I'm not coming to see you anymore unless you marry me."

We married in December 1971 at the Baptist church Mom attended. It drove Sadler crazy. (Mom, too; she cried. And since she was one of only three other guests at the wedding—including Adrienne's aunt and niece—her unhappiness was conspicuous.) Of course, he would have been more crazed if Adrienne had actually left Minneapolis and moved to Hayward with me. Maybe he saw her staying in the Midwest as proof of his authority over me. If he did, he was mistaken. What he didn't know was that it was only my willingness to listen that made him a good teacher. And there was never a moment when I considered marriage more sacred than the heavyweight championship.

. . .

Before the Ali-Frazier fight, some promoters took me to a jazz spot in Harlem that everyone said was the place to go. We were shown a good table. I looked around the room. This was sure enough the place. There sat Walt Frazier, super guard of the Knicks, six months after his first N.B.A. championship win. He was Mr. Smooth on the court, maybe the best guard of his day. I went over and introduced myself.

"Oh, yeah," he said with cool detachment. "I've seen you do your thing, you've seen me do mine."

That was it. Dismissed.

I felt hurt that Walt Frazier hadn't taken me as seriously as I thought I deserved. But I'd learned something anyway. *So that's how it's done*—that's how you handle stardom. I filed the lesson away for use when necessary—say, after I became champ.

An hour or so later I saw Jim Brown at another table. I was like a little kid inside. How could I not go over to him? Maybe I'd get a chance to sit and explain how important a role he'd played in my life; that if he hadn't inspired me to join the Job Corps, I'd probably be dead or in jail. How would I thank him? I could show him my sideburns modeled on his in the movie *100 Rifles*. I'd mention how many push-ups and sit-ups I'd done to look like Jim Brown, or explain that I'd spent hours in front of the mirror, practicing walking like him.

Turned out, Jim Brown wanted nothing to do with a young up-and-coming fighter. I got from him only a polite smile and limp handshake. Not even eye contact.

So that's really how it's done.

These were the days when I was sculpting George Foreman. I shaped the clay to match what Sadler taught; manipulated it to resemble characters in books and movies; and squeezed it to copy heroes—whether or not they met my expectations. Any way that Jim Brown and Walt Frazier acted I would have interpreted as the "right" way. If they'd been warm and respectful, I'd have modeled myself after that. So when they were just the opposite, that's what I took as my mold. Ego doesn't say, "They ought to have treated me better." Ego says, "So that's how it's done." The Brown-Frazier version of George Foreman made his debut the next night, at the Ali-Frazier fight.

To earn my title shot, I had to look, even in street clothes, like I deserved that title more than Frazier, who was defending it, or Ali, who just might recapture it after four years. It seemed pretty obvious that my road to the title went through at least one of the two—which is a lot like finally getting on *Jeopardy* and having to play against a four-time champ who has already won $84,000. I wanted the championship but honestly didn't want anything to do with either of them.

Frazier took the fight in fifteen brutal rounds. Watching him did nothing to lessen my fear. I'd been in fights all my life with tough guys; tough guys generally couldn't fight. But Frazier was as tough a boxer as ever wore the championship belt. While most fighters were like walls that had holes in them here and there, Joe Frazier was a brick wall with no cracks. He had a certain rhythm in the ring. He rolled with the hard shots, like Pac-Man eating them up. If you hurt him, he liked it. And if you missed, he got mad. Sometimes he'd pop up from a crouch and take you down with one to the chin. Then there was the left. There were no holes, no weaknesses I could see.

Ours must have been a mutual-admiration society. Frazier apparently hoped that I'd lose to someone else, and therefore my place as a contender, because over the next two years he rejected me time and again as an opponent. At both of his title defenses after Ali, I dogged him at ringside.

"Fight me, Joe," I'd demand.

"Your time'll come, son," he said the first time.

"Anytime, kid," he said the second.

But he didn't mean it.

Sadler said, "The way to get Frazier is to beat Ali. Then he'll have to come to us."

That sounded wrong to me—unnecessarily risky. I didn't want to have to beat both Ali and Frazier. My hope was that both of them would retire.

None of my seven fights that year went the distance. Two ended in the first round, two in the second, one each in the third and fourth, and one—against Gregorio Peralta again—went ten. The next year, 1972, all five fights ended in the second round. I fought in February, March, April, and May, and then not again until October.

All the while, Sadler devoted himself to engineering a championship fight. Without asking me, he aligned us with Marty Erlichman, Barbra Streisand's manager; Sadler said he had a lot of corporate contacts. When I wondered what corporate contacts had to do with getting me a title shot, he explained that Erlichman was trying to broker a deal for me to become Ford's commercial spokesman, much as Coke had signed Muhammad Ali. In theory, my increased visibility on the tube would translate into a wider fan base. The more fans I had, the louder they'd clamor for me to fight Frazier, which for Frazier meant a payday he couldn't refuse. I couldn't argue the logic, but I still recognized it as a bunch of hooey. Even then I knew that nobody gets any endorsements without first being champ; they were arguing the cart before the horse, and selling pie in the sky to Sadler, who was trying to sell it to me.

My gut feeling was not to sign. We'd come this far without anyone breaking off a piece of me or buying the right to meddle. Sadler argued in favor. I think he was frustrated by Frazier's refusals, and was willing to stir the pot to see if anything changed. And no doubt, the baseline cash in his pocket that would arrive regardless of whether I won or lost played a part in his thinking. In exchange for half of all ancillary revenues from my fights (including commercial fees and closed-circuit showings), Erlichman's group was to pay me a substantial annual salary for ten years.

The money was attractive to me, too. I had my mother to think of. And my wife. And our soon-to-be-born baby, who evidently had been conceived during a three-day trip I took to Minneapolis in March, right after one fight and five weeks before another.

Holding my nose, I signed the contract.

When the pie refused to come down out of the sky, Erlichman sold the contract to a group of East Coast businessmen. Insisting that we were still to the good, Sadler likened the sale to one bank buying your mortgage from another bank. He said, "What difference does it make where the check comes from?"

I didn't appear in any commercials or enjoy any public relations bonanzas. But by October we heard that the W.B.A. (World Boxing Association) was pressuring Frazier not to ignore the Number 1 contender any longer.

Soon to fight against Terry Sorrels in Salt Lake City, I trained for the week beforehand at the local Job Corps center, where Doc Broadus had been transferred after the Pleasanton center's closure. We'd barely spoken for three years, since our falling out over that bogus contract. Seeing him, I realized not only how far I'd come in such a short time, but how much I cared for this man. I decided that if I got to be champ, I'd bring him with me.

By the time I stepped in to the ring against Sorrels, I'd been off for five months. The outcome was typical, though—second-round K.O. After the fight, Sadler called me into a corner.

"We didn't draw many people tonight," he said, "but you did make some money." Looking around to be sure we were alone, he started counting out twenty-dollar bills. "One, two, three, four, one hundred. One, two, three, four, two hundred."

As he counted, I suddenly felt sick to my stomach. Here was my partner, my manager, my trainer, wearing a Dick Tracy fedora with the front brim turned up, divvying up the spoils as though we'd just rolled some mark on the street. I felt sleazy, like this wasn't legitimate. It was at that moment that my whole relationship with him seemed sick and the corporate contract sinister. *How could he have gotten me into this deal? I'm never working with him again.*

Of course, we were still contractually bound—but only for another few months; after that I'd be free of Sadler forever. So when Joe Frazier finally said yes, I buried my unhappiness in order to train for the fight on January 22, 1973, in Kingston, Jamaica. I had only two months and a few days to get ready for the toughest guy around.

Try as I might, train as I might, I just couldn't feel comfortable with Sadler. I needed someone as savvy and tough as he, but someone I trusted. Even before I appeared on *The Tonight Show* to hype the fight, negative thoughts about him were sticking to me like flypaper. It was a distraction I didn't need.

Then I saw the man I needed.

Waiting in the green room before the show was James Brown's all-in-one manager, road manager, friend, and adviser; James was also appearing on the show.

I'd first met Mr. Moore, as I respectfully called him until his death, in mid-1969 when I fought in Las Vegas on the undercard to Sonny Liston's main event. James Brown had been playing the Hilton, a historic event for Vegas. Every day I'd see Mr. Moore holding court in the hotel restaurant. He knew everybody—celebrities especially. I'd sit and joke with him. He didn't seem to mind, though he didn't take particular notice of me, either. He'd continue laughing and joking, no matter who was or wasn't there. With his constant companion, an expensive Nikon camera, he'd taken enough pictures of whatever and whoever to fill a dozen scrapbooks.

"Hey, Mr. Moore," I said. I didn't even know his first name. "Remember me? George Foreman. The Olympic gold medalist. Remember? We met in Vegas a few years ago."

"Yeah, yeah," he said. Big, fat fellow. In his fifties. Weary and wise. "How you doin', George?"

"Good. Listen. I want to talk with you because I'm going to be champion of the world."

"Yeah, okay." He sounded as though he'd heard lines like that more than once. "Call me when you get to be champ."

"I'll do that," I said. "I'll call you next month, after I'm champ."

I admired this man. Why? I didn't exactly know; it was an instinctive feel. My life needed a force like him.

Meanwhile, as the Frazier fight drew near, I grew more unhappy and disenchanted with the corporate contract. Studying the fine print and doing some arithmetic, I discovered that these guys back East were going to take home a greater share of the proceeds than I would; at best I'd make a hundred grand. My rage stewed, then reached the boiling point. What drove me over the edge was that Sadler had dared to say yes to this agreement; he hadn't looked out for me.

I hired some New York lawyers. In the middle of the promoters' negotiations with Prime Minister Michael Manley of Jamaica, who was pushing the fight as a showcase for his country, I announced I wouldn't get into the ring with Frazier. I decided I'd rather walk away, even now, when I was so close to my goal, than benefit these people who hadn't been there at five-thirty every morning doing roadwork. As crazy as it sounds, I made the decision to quit boxing.

That meant I'd need a job.

I called my friend and sometime adviser Barney Oldfield, hoping that he'd get me work at Litton Industries. Barney pointed out that I'd come a long way from Mexico City, let alone Fifth Ward, and had worked too hard to throw away an opportunity that probably comes only once.

"Yeah," I said, "but I can't let those guys get away with this. I'm not going to be another bad Joe Louis story, fighting for years and having nothing to show for it. I'd rather not fight at all."

"Well," Barney said, "it seems to me that what you should do is go down there and win the title. You knock Joe Frazier out. Then come back here and fight it out in court. I can't see any judge in the land ruling against you."

Barney may have detected a pattern of behavior. After all, he'd been with me in Mexico City when I briefly refused to fight for the gold medal. As the one person who wouldn't gain financially from the fight, Barney could be trusted. He cared about what was best for George Foreman, not for Barney Oldfield; and he wouldn't have wanted me to get hurt, no matter how great the reward. If *he* believed I could knock out Joe Frazier, I could. Though he probably didn't know how badly I needed it, I took the confidence he had in me and made it my own.

"You really think I can win?" Was I asking about the fight or the lawsuit?

"Absolutely," he said.

That conversation was why I fought Joe Frazier.

Chapter Five

I 'LL NEVER TRUST Dick Sadler again." That's what I told Charley Shipes. "I don't want him to be my trainer anymore. What do you think?"

"Well," Charley said. He was thinking.

"I don't want to work with him," I repeated.

"Why don't you bring in someone else? Sadler can stay off to the side. Be more like a manager."

"Who would you bring in?"

"I know a good guy," Charley said. "Archie."

Archie Moore—no relation to James Brown's Mr. Moore—was a former world light-heavyweight champion who'd fought well into his fifties. What I didn't know then is that Sadler had once trained Archie and that Archie had also trained Cassius Clay before he turned pro.

Charley contacted Archie and arranged a meeting so I could explain the problem in person. "Can you help me?" I asked.

"I'll help you," he said.

"How much?" That was my first baby step as a businessman, taking over my own affairs from Sadler. Before he answered, I made an offer. He declined. I offered another sum with a hefty bonus if I won. We shook hands. "I can be with you six days a week, but not on Saturday," Archie said. "I'm a Seventh Day Adventist and have to go to church."

He took superb care of me, rubbing me down every day before and after workouts as I lay on a training table set with a clean sheet. Touches like that made me feel like a champ even before the fight.

"You're fightin' for the heavyweight title, man," Archie said. "This is something unique. Beyond your imagination. It's been around longer than you and me together."

My father's words from when I was a boy came back to me: "Stronger than Jack Johnson. Hits like Jack Dempsey." I started to feel the awe of what I was soon to do. But I still had doubts. *Who are you to fight for the title? These other guys are magical—Joe Frazier, Muhammad Ali. You're not magical. You don't fit in with them.*

Such doubts made the mental training Archie provided even more important than the physical training. This man had been there himself, wearing trunks and canvas shoes. What he had to say came from experience, and his instructions became my Scripture. He spewed mean, vicious talk about what I would do to that blankety-blank Joe Frazier, and forced me to believe it. For a while, I lived on Archie's courage.

"When you see Frazier, you look him in the eye," Archie said. He spoke in a growl, through clenched teeth. "Don't you move your face until you see his face—your face in his eyes. You hear me?"

"I hear you."

"DO YOU HEAR ME?"

"I HEAR YOU."

My instinct had always been to stare at opponents with menace in my eyes, but I'd never channeled so much hate. Hate, that's what Archie thought you needed to be champ. If you had hate, no matter how ignorant you were, or how little self-confidence you felt, you had something powerful carrying you. All I needed was to think about the court case I faced when I returned, and the hate flowed like adrenaline.

By the time I got to Kingston, Jamaica, being mean seemed as natural as breathing. At the weigh-in before the fight, I stared at Frazier with cold, hard eyes, trying to establish dominance the way Archie had instructed. I didn't even dislike Joe Frazier. In fact, he'd always been respectful of me. Now, after a few minutes of my glaring at him, Frazier evidently came unglued. "Man, I'm tired of your stuff," he screamed across the stage. "I'm tired of you. I'm gonna kick your blankety-blank blank back home." He began striding toward me, as though intending to have it out now.

All this time Archie stood behind me, rubbing my neck. Frazier got right up in my face, or as close as his four-inch height disadvantage allowed. "I should kill you right now," he said.

This was déjà vu: Hilton Murdoch and Ickyboo and that night in Houston when I'd backed down. Frazier had stepped on a landmine packed with hate. I exploded instantly. "Shut up," I yelled. "Don't you say another word."

If Joe had taunted me again, or stared in silence, or even turned around and walked back to his seat, I'd have thought he was playing the same game. But he said, "You can't tell me to shut up." He shouldn't have done something that polite. Chink in his armor.

That afternoon some Rastafarians came to my camp bearing news that the stars were properly aligned for George Foreman to become world champ. Then I heard that Joe had begun reading his Bible at night instead of playing craps and cards. Confidence surged in me, until I made the mistake of reading a newspaper story predicting that at such-and-such a time on the evening of January 22, 1973, "that thud you hear will be George Foreman hitting the mat. He has no business fighting Joe Frazier." Just like that, the confidence made a U-turn and went right out the front door.

Man, I shouldn't have read that. This is one of the greatest fighters of all time. Smokin' Joe. He didn't get that name for nothing. I've seen guys, famous guys, tough guys, beat on him until he looked dead. Then he rose up like he'd been getting strength from it. Buster Mathis mopped up the ring with him for nine rounds, and Joe knocked him out in the tenth. Smokin' Joe. This man is invincible. Twenty-nine bouts, twenty-five knockouts.

The heavyweight championship of the world; every seat filled;

celebrities everywhere; Howard Cosell at ringside. Walking down the aisle and up the stairs to the ring, my knees quaked with fear. I started dancing around, because if I'd stood still, everyone would have noticed the Jell-O in my legs. And maybe they'd have canceled the fight, figuring nobody that terrified should be fighting.

Frazier, the beloved champ, ducked through the ropes into the ring to riotous cheering. For the first time, I truly experienced the scope. Fighting for the championship really was bigger than life—"beyond your imagination," Archie had said. I felt as though I'd been watching a television program called *The Heavyweight Championship of the World* for years, and then suddenly I was in it. There was that Joe Frazier character, looking just like he did on the tube. Same hard, stony face. Same little trace of beard. Same jumping up and down to loosen up. I'd known guys in Fifth Ward who'd finish a fight with the help of a gang or a knife—guys who looked like Muhammad Ali. And then there were guys like Joe, whom you didn't bother with unless you absolutely had to—one-man gangs with hands like artillery.

Archie stood behind me and rubbed my neck. "Look at him," he ordered. "LOOK AT HIM. You stare at him. You look him right in his eyes. You look right there until you find yourself in his eyes."

My quivering knees barely carried me to center ring to hear the referee's instructions. I stomped the floor a few times to try to still them. Joe and I faced off. I found his eyes and held them in mine. Archie had taught me that if you could get your man to turn away first in the staring contest, then you'd won the fight. Here, if Joe broke first and looked down, he'd see my knees shaking. I kept telling myself not to be scared but the knees didn't listen.

This was my moment. And I wondered what I was doing there. I'd talked a lot of trash over the years about being champion of the world. I'd bragged that I could knock out anyone. And now I wanted to take it all back, to apologize: "I didn't mean that. I was supposed to say that stuff, but I don't mean it. I don't want to fight Joe Frazier." This wasn't Muhammad Ali, who'd start doing that famous shuffle to get out of the way. This was a man who searches every corner of the ring for his prey. There's no way out against Frazier but to quit.

And yet, despite this knee-quivering fear, I still believed in the person who at that moment didn't believe in himself. I believed in the person who'd overcome a bad break or two. *You're in the ring with a boxer who's trying to hurt you. You're not going to let anybody hurt you, George. Understand? You're going to fight anybody who fights you.*

In the corner before the bell, Sadler said, "Go out there, throw a punch at him like you're going to get him, then stop."

That's what I did: I threw a phantom punch, then got back into position to box again. I jabbed a little. And then, here came that famous Smokin' Joe left hook that had dropped so many guys. *Whoosh!* Missed. What a bullet. *There it is. Now we're acquainted.* The famous Frazier had fired a shot.

Now everything Archie and Sadler had taught me, everything I'd been practicing, took control of me. Joe threw another hook that I partially deflected. I threw one that he blocked. I jabbed, jabbed, jabbed, and decided to test him with an uppercut. Boom! Joe Frazier hit the mat.

I was surprised—and worried. *When Joe Frazier goes down, that's when he gets mad.* But for the nearly three years of my professional career, Dick Sadler had focused on the tools it takes to finish a man, and I was a finisher. Joe got up and I threw another uppercut, dropping him to his knees.

Not until after the third knockdown did I truly realize Joe Frazier was in trouble. After the fifth knockdown, I looked over at Yank Durham, Joe's manager/trainer. "All right?" I said. He didn't reply. Joe was stumbling badly. "All right, I'm going to kill him." That was the only way to stop this warrior, unless someone else made the decision in his behalf. He went down one more time—six in all—before the fight was stopped in the second round. It was a pity they allowed it to go so long. But the referee may have kept the fight going on the belief of everyone in boxing that, no matter what might happen early, I'd eventually tire and Joe would do me the way he did Buster Mathis.

Several moments passed before I raised my hands in victory. I'd been so consumed by the fighting itself that the journey back down the tunnel into the light took extra time. When I emerged, I was the new star of that television series called *Heavyweight Champion of the World*. People who wouldn't have given me air for my tires if I had lost now pitched to be my best friend. Amid the chants of "Champ, champ, champ," I heard someone refer to me as "King of Men." Instantly I was carried away, as by a magic carpet, to another world. And to a twenty-three-year-old lacking either a true friend or a sense of moral direction, that world eventually became a haunted house. It had been unhealthy to feel that I could beat anyone. It was unreal to know that as truth.

I locked the dressing room and prayed aloud for a moment, thanking by name everyone who'd helped me become champ—even Sadler. In the glow of victory, especially Sadler. He would not be my trainer anymore—for that I had Archie—but he could still be my friend and manager.

By my present standards, that prayer was a pitiful little thing I modeled, ironically, on Sadler's "prayers." For years, before each fight he'd be in a lather, pumping me with how badly I was going to rearrange so-and-so's anatomy. Then, in the middle of this mad man's cursing and swearing and describing terrible human carnage, he'd suddenly grab my hand and declare, "Let's pray." And a split second later, he'd complete the prayer sandwich by adding another slice of obscenities. Now, in the glow of the moment, bygones were bygones. He was no longer my enemy.

At last I allowed myself to take pleasure in the knowledge of my baby daughter Michi, who'd been born sixteen days before. While I'd never wanted a child, and frankly hadn't planned this one, peace and gladness descended over me as I thought again of that face I'd seen for the first time when a reporter had handed me a wire photo taken in Minneapolis two weeks earlier. After the birth, Adrienne and I had talked over the phone, and I'd heard my little Michi cry, but at the time other thoughts had occupied my mind. As I'd once told Adrienne, boxing was my true wife.

Even so, I recognized Michi immediately from a place that hadn't existed until then; we'd known each other since before either of us was born. *This is my baby, my beautiful baby girl.*

When legal formalities kept me in Jamaica for a few days, I attended a celebration in my honor at a Kingston nightclub. Don King was there. "George Foreman, champion," he kept saying. He sent over round after round. Of course, I drank only Coke. Soon the nicest-looking young woman in all Jamaica was seated beside me. I was flattered. It didn't occur to me that she wasn't interested in George Foreman, but in "George Foreman, champion."

First stop after leaving was Houston, then Minneapolis, to see Michi. After learning how to change diapers, the new champion of the world wiped and powdered his baby's bottom, washed and dressed her. I was in love with this little creature. But there was bitter as well as sweet. Loving Michi so much made me realize that my feelings for Adrienne weren't comparable.

Some of that was guilt. I'd cheated on my wife that night in Kingston, and didn't know where to put the shame. I'd shamed myself and my marriage. Mostly, I was sad and disappointed, because I understood that my cheating had necessarily destroyed our family—the family I hadn't even known I wanted until I held Michi. I remember feeling afterward that I had to throw away the clothes I'd worn that night, and that no shower could ever last long enough to get me clean again. And feeling dirty, I didn't want my wife to touch me. Adrienne obviously sensed something wrong. But between the baby and the championship, these were extraordinary times. It was easy to confuse confusion with despair.

I stayed only a week in Minneapolis before returning to the small house I rented in Hayward. In a matter of weeks, I became the stereotypical heavyweight champ—surly and angry. If someone asked for an autograph in a restaurant, I'd say, "What do you think, that I'm going to stop eating and sign my name?" Then my eyes would sweep the room in a mean glare. That was as effective as an electric fence for keeping away the unwanted. *So that's how it's done.* I was taking my cues, or so I thought, from

Jim Brown and Walt Frazier. I remembered that night in detail and Technicolor. Strange to think that if they'd embraced me, I'd have become the friendly champ. Instead, I learned the hard way that you'd better treat people well, because soon enough it's someone else's turn.

No one in history had run a four-minute mile until Roger Bannister. Then the dam broke. That's what cheating on your wife is like. The second time is easier than the first, and the fifth's no problem at all. Women seemed to be coming out of the woodwork, and I became increasingly willing to step over a line that now existed only faintly. After all, this was the man who as a boy clung to others in order to be noticed. Pretty women were everywhere. "Hi, George," they'd say. "Mind if I sit down?" I minded less and less. I'd hear a knock. "Hello. Is this where George Foreman lives?"

The more unfaithful I was, the more ashamed I felt. When we saw each other, I could barely look Adrienne in the eye. If not for wanting to be near Michi, I'd probably never have gone to Minneapolis or sent for Adrienne to visit. Divorce appeared to be the only way out.

One evening when she and Michi were with me in Hayward, I asked the old preacher from a local church to stop by. Everyone called him "Fat Daddy." "This man may have some answers for us," I told Adrienne. He sat between us and I admitted everything to him as I already had to her. "What's killing me," I said, "is that I don't like the feeling that I'm a bad guy. And every time I see Adrienne, that's what I feel like. I also don't like the idea of treating these other women like they're lower than my wife." These were the thoughts of a mixed-up young man, but they showed a lot more common sense and virtue than I heard from that preacher.

Fat Daddy asked Adrienne to fetch him something from the kitchen, and while she was gone he bestowed on me his wisdom. "Listen, George," he said. "Men came first; woman comes from man. Men and women are different. What burdens a man doesn't burden a woman. A man's going to be a man. You know what I mean?" He clapped his hands; here came his answer: "Just don't bring it home."

I was dumbfounded. This wasn't helpful. If that's what religion was, I'd never buy it. He hadn't even asked me to ponder whether I loved my career or my child more, nor had he pointed out that I was destroying a family. Instead, he just claimed that I could eat as many cupcakes as I wanted.

"But it bothers me," I insisted.

"Just don't bring it home, George."

Adrienne returned from the kitchen. Fat Daddy rose to leave. "So," he said, "you all work out your problems. You don't need to get divorced."

After he left, Adrienne wanted to know what he'd counseled. I told her and said, "I can't play by different rules, that it's a different deal because I'm a man. I don't think there's any answer. It's driving me nuts. I have to get out of this." Fueling my decision was a profound ignorance. I believed that I could leave Adrienne and keep Michi. That the baby belonged also to the mother never occurred to me.

Adrienne desperately did not want to divorce. So between Fat Daddy's absolving me and Adrienne's wanting to hang on at any cost, I had no justification for my anguish. Somewhere inside, though, I knew that it was right to feel bad—even if I was heavyweight champ of the world, and even if everyone else believed that the champ didn't have to play by the same rules.

Who could I talk to? Not my mother. First, I was ashamed. Part of the reason I sent money home and paid for my brother Roy to go to college in California was because I wanted Mom to think of me as a mature man. I'd blown that image for myself, but I wanted her to retain it. Anyway, I couldn't confide in her. As heavyweight champ, I occupied a lonely position on a cloud in outer space. Everyone else lived at lower altitudes. I thought of Mom on the porch of the house I'd just bought her, happy to wait all that first day for the electric man to come and turn on the juice. That was her championship. She had everything now—except her son. Poverty had joined us; success divided. To reach me, she left messages with answering services.

Alone and bewildered, I pursued a divorce. That's when things got ugly between Adrienne and me. We fought and carried on and argued and quarreled and bickered and squabbled. Until the divorce was final a year or so later, barely a civil word passed between us. We reminded me of my own mother and father, fighting whenever they saw each other. *A man must never hit a woman*, I would tell myself, thinking both of the fights I overheard between my parents and of my childhood friend Charles, whose father often beat up his mother. I'd heard their fighting myself and seen the police come. "I'm gonna kill that man," Charles used to say.

"When you're strong, you can kill a man," I had told Charles. "But you never hit a woman."

My first title defense came early in September 1973 against Joe Roman in Tokyo, where the purse was best and the tax bite least. Showering him with brutal punches, I made a startling discovery: I was powerful enough to knock out someone without hitting him on the chin. I teed off on this man. *Let's see what happens if I hit him up near the ear.* Wham! He became a human experiment. Shots on the top of the head that normally do little or no damage to boxers were knocking him down. I even tried to hit him as he fell. I did not care about right and wrong. I had become something vicious. The fight ended in the first round, when he fell right between my legs. Glowering down at him, I wouldn't move until the referee pushed me back. I didn't even smile when he raised my arm. All I could think about was my punching power. *I'm the hardest puncher I've ever seen.* No wonder the people began booing—booing the champion of the world. Afterward, I answered reporters' questions with a series of "Yeps" because I was daydreaming of my omnipotence. Superman's evil twin. No wonder the public began thinking of me as a thug. I had the act down real well.

Then I ran into Jim Brown again and stole another lesson. It was in the Astrodome, for the so-called battle of the sexes tennis match, Billie Jean King versus Bobby Riggs. There was Jim, sitting nearby. This time, I'd pretend to ignore him. No way was I going to let myself be trampled on again. In fact, I intended to hate him—until he came over. "Hey, man," he said. "You knock those guys out. Wow." I was amazed. He didn't remember that guy who'd introduced himself at the nightclub. But now he stuck out his hand. Even heroes love a winner.

That same September, I attended the Ken Norton–Muhammad Ali fight in Los Angeles, their second that year. Norton had won the first, six months before, and both were trying to get a title shot against me. For ratings value, ABC invited Frank Sinatra to do the color commentary and me to say a few words on camera. When I came off, I saw James Brown's adviser, Mr. Moore. I hadn't seen him since *The Tonight Show,* almost a year earlier. James Brown must have been there.

"Hey, Mr. Moore," I said. "Remember me? Remember I told you I was going to be heavyweight champ."

"I sure do," he said. "How can I find you?"

"I'm in Hayward, California. But you'll never find the house." It was a small house, but isolated. You either knew how to get there or you didn't get there, so I gave him my phone number too.

"I can find anything in Hayward," he said. "That's my name—Hayward Moore."

Sure enough, some weeks later, Hayward Moore came knocking. Good sense of direction, but bad timing. I was holding little Michi when I opened the door.

"I can't talk to you now," I said. "I'm about to get a divorce."

He saw a big suitcase in the entry hall. "Where you going?" he asked.

"Houston."

"What airport you leaving from?"

"Oakland."

Somehow, Hayward Moore got a seat on that flight next to me and Michi. Pushy guy. He was so big he had to ask the stewardess for a seat belt extension.

From that day on, Mr. Moore was with me until he died. Often we talked all night and into the morning. It felt good to have a friend again. My buddies from Houston long ago, Charles and Roy, had abandoned me, saying that I was no longer the George they'd grown up with. They were right: I no longer smoked and drank.

To everyone else, Mr. Moore seemed abusive and nasty. To me, it was just the way he talked, not his heart. Other people used to ask why I tolerated him. I did so because more than his friendship I needed his counsel.

"What do you do for George?" they asked.

"I don't work for George," he said. "I help him spend his money."

With his help I bought a beautiful five-acre ranch in Livermore, California—still the most beautiful home I've ever owned. If I'd never made another dime, that was still a wise investment. And I would need wise investments, because this heavyweight champ believed that to buy anything at a discount carried the stink of failure. And believe me, I was learning how to spend money fast, with fancy, classic cars my biggest weakness (I also spent on clothing, jewelry, women, and animals—especially dogs; a single German shepherd once cost me $21,000). Mr. Moore was the wisest man I'd ever known. Maybe because he'd seen other celebrities hold the world on a string, he offered advice that seemed apropos of nothing until it suddenly came in handy.

Example: We were at the Comedy Store in Hollywood one night, watching Richard Pryor. No one convulsed me more than Richard. Given a chance to see him, I'd go wherever he played. After the show, Richard sought me out. "I want you to come over to my house," he said. "Nobody ever visits. Please come by." He handed me the address. I didn't tell Mr. Moore because I knew his tactless manner put people off. (A month or so before, a woman at Sammy Davis's house had told me to leave him behind if I wanted to come by.) I drove up to Richard's in my Excalibur convertible, top down. I knocked, expecting him to open the door himself. Then we'd sit and talk, and I'd ease his loneliness.

The peephole widened. A voice that wasn't Richard's asked who was there.

"It's George Foreman. Richard asked me to come over."

The door opened onto a crowded party. Several people stood next to a table on which a shoebox filled with white powder was the center of attention. I nearly panicked, but remembered Mr. Moore's advice. He'd told me that if ever I happened on such a scene, just to be cool for a while. "Sit and chat. Then go. But go easy. That way, if something happens and the police show up, they won't suspect you of blowing the whistle."

Richard grabbed me by the arm. "Thanks for coming, man."

He'd lied to me. "You're welcome."

He introduced me to everyone in the front room, then pointed to the powder. "No, thanks," I said. "Give that to Muhammad Ali, 'cause I'm in training." Everyone laughed.

"Make yourself at home, then," Richard said.

I wandered into the back room. Only movie stars were in greater supply than drugs. Freddie Prinze was playing pool. "George, my main man," he said. "Hit me, man. Go ahead. Hit me. Hit me. I just want to be hit by the champ." Needless to say, I didn't do it. I laughed, certain he was kidding. A few years later, he killed himself with a gun.

I walked around a little more, laughing, joking, being cool— and keeping an alarm clock ticking in my brain. When the alarm sounded, I excused myself and sped home. If that party had been busted, my career and life would have been ruined.

Back at the hotel, I told Mr. Moore what happened. "You big country fool," he screamed. "Didn't I tell you never to go to those people's houses?"

I never did again, even refusing invitations from Marvin Gaye, whom I admired and had met through Mr. Moore. Marvin was hardly a square, but he knew I was. When I told him that I'd heard how much profit a recording studio made and that I was thinking of buying one, he pointed out the catch: "If you're going to have a good studio, and you want those guys to work, they're going to have to be able to do their stuff."

"What do you mean?"

"You know, George—do the dope. Especially those rockers. They pay a lot of money to record there. They deserve to relax. You gotta have security. You know, I'm not trying to condone, but that's just the way it is. You don't want to get mixed up in that stuff."

No, I didn't. I'd seen the ugliness and destruction drugs and alcohol had brought on my friends—and even my own brother Sonny. Visiting my mother in Houston, I'd caught him standing outside, shirttail out, disheveled, chugging whisky from a half-pint bottle. It was pitiful to see this fiercely independent man of great character swilling booze like a bum. When he finally saw me, he clumsily screwed the top back on the bottle and tried to hide it in his back pocket. I said, "Man, what's happened to you?"

"Nothing," he said.

Right, nothing. Now I knew why Mom had been so evasive every time I'd mentioned on the phone how I wanted to return to Houston from the Job Corps and become a hard-working family man like Sonny. "Son," she'd said, "you just be yourself." I'd thought she was just offering encouragement to me—not hiding something from me. But the truth, I learned, was that even back then his drinking had begun to win. By the time I saw him, it had cost him his family.

"I have to take care of you," I said. The next day I sent a limo to pick him up at his job and told him that from then on he was working for me. I took him to my ranch and had him checked out by doctors, and it wasn't long before he was able to work effectively. Tirelessly, Sonny ran my business affairs. Even when drinking, he'd always worked. In 1986, years after I'd left boxing, he borrowed two hundred dollars from me. "I know this isn't right," he said, "but I really need it." A year after that, when I got back into boxing and he hadn't yet repaid the loan, he said, "I'm going to rub you down every day, take care of your clothes." And he did. Then he ran my business affairs again, becoming a responsible, church-going man. He had a stroke in 1991, before my fight for the title against Evander Holyfield. Fortunately, his share of my purse for that fight came to a million dollars, so his family was taken care of when a series of strokes killed him two years later at age fifty-two.

Having demolished Joe Frazier, I didn't expect to hear doubts about my skill. But there they were. "George fought a tomato can," some people said after the Joe Roman fight. "What's he so scared of?"

I realized such comments were motivated by my growing reputation as the champ you loved to hate. But I couldn't ignore them. In too many ways I was still the kid from Fifth Ward, fighting to be king of the jungle. I intended to convince every last doubter. *I'm going to kill one of these fools,* I decided. *Then everyone'll shut up.*

The "fool" I chose was Ken Norton. He'd just lost a close decision to Ali, though as a ringside witness I judged the judges wrong. Earlier that year, in the spring, he'd taken their first fight decisively, breaking Ali's jaw in the process. While Ali's victory in the second fight skipped him to Number 1 contender, he himself was in no hurry to get in the ring with me. That was just as well. In my opinion, Norton at the time was the better fighter: tougher and, certainly, much stronger, and as big as me. He deserved the shot. Besides, killing a man like that would undoubtedly earn me universal respect.

That's what I thought. In reality, I didn't have a clue what I needed. I suffered a terrible emptiness that the next accomplishment—first, becoming champ or, now, killing Norton—was supposed to cure. But in fact, the championship had worsened the emptiness by putting the lie to the belief that winning could make me whole. Meanness flowed into that vacuum; I grew meaner by the day. My sparring partners endured malicious beatings. Being nice to my ex-wife in order to arrange weekends here and there with Michi took all my self-control.

Good news, however, came from my lawyers in San Francisco. They'd gotten my corporate contract invalidated through a legal loophole after discovering that professional fighters must have all such contracts approved by the boxing commission in the state where the boxer resides. And that hadn't been done. With pleasure, I paid back all that the partners had advanced me a year and a half before, and got in return their hefty fifty percent proceeds from both the Frazier and Joe Roman fights. Better than the money was the sense that I was not an indentured servant. Funny, though I still blamed Dick Sadler for steering me wrong, freedom immediately defused much of my fury. Before the Frazier fight I'd relieved Sadler of his status as my manager; with Archie Moore brought in, Sadler was trainer in name only. But now, after the court win, I found myself leaning toward a renewal of our relationship. More and more, I listened to Sadler's advice during training, and less and less to Archie's. That was my usual pattern. Whoever got in my good graces last, got my ear.

The Norton fight was to be held in Venezuela in March 1974. I trained with single-minded devotion, as though he were the champ and I the challenger. That included abstaining from female companionship beginning seventy-five days before the fight, not just fifteen. For a twenty-five-year-old whom beautiful women targeted for their affections, this was immensely difficult. Every time I felt my willpower weakening, I ran to the nearest mirror and checked that little bump on my cheek. By the time we finally got to Caracas for the fight, my meanness was magnified by all that suppression and frustration.

Archie no longer needed to coach me on the art of intimidation. I stared at Norton with the intensity of that laser beam Goldfinger aimed at James Bond. *I'm going to kill you.* Kenny refused to look back at me. If I entered a hotel elevator at the same time, he quietly got out.

Not until I climbed into the ring and gazed across at him did I finally see Kenny's eyes. *My God, they're green.* Realizing that I'd never really noticed them before scared me for a moment. Of course, he'd always refused to exchange stares. But I also noticed, probably for the first time, what a remarkable physical specimen Ken Norton was. With muscles rippling everywhere, he looked more like a weightlifter than a boxer. It was going to be tougher to kill him than I'd planned.

We met with the referee at center ring. Lost in a daydream, I picked out my spots on Kenny's head. I know he knew what I was doing because I saw his fear. The crowd must have sensed it too. Their boos rained down on me.

The bell rang.

Unlike my fight with Joe Frazier, whom I'd gone after immediately, I stalked Kenny Norton—a patient predator, in possession of the ultimate weapon, savoring the anticipation of the conquest.

He saw my head up and threw a hook. Missed. Then another. Missed. I hit him in the side, a shot that felt solid the way a bat feels when you hit a home run. He tried another hook. Missed. I followed with a right to the head. Down he went. As he fell against the ropes I swung and connected again. The referee issued a warning before counting. More boos. Kenny got up in time. Round 1 ended.

In Round 2, I became a vicious thug, swinging wildly, connecting with almost every punch. The next time he fell, the referee stopped the fight. Nearly unconscious, Kenny was helpless. "Why are you stopping the fight?" I asked, upset because I hadn't finished him.

I looked down at Muhammad Ali, who was at ringside working the fight as color commentator with Howard Cosell. "I'm going to kill you," I said. I hadn't killed Norton, so I figured I might as well kill Ali. All week he'd been taping segments claiming that Norton was a better fighter than I; that Norton had once beaten him and would therefore beat me; that George Foreman hadn't fought any top fighters; and that if by chance I won, he'd whip me to regain the title. Having won a tough twelve-round decision over Frazier just two months before, he was full of typical Ali bluster. I repeated myself louder amid the boos, "I'm going to kill you." This time, I saw fear in him.

The next day I took a limo to the airport with my publicist, Bill Caplan. The rest of my team was still breaking down camp and would follow in a few days. We got to the Pan American counter, where our tickets were being held. For some reason the agents began whispering to each other in Spanish. Then two guys in bad suits showed up. Now everyone was whispering. Of course, they could have spoken aloud in Spanish, since neither Bill nor I understand the language. Finally, one of the agents said, "I'm sorry, I can't give you your tickets."

"Why?" Bill asked.

"Well," she said, tilting her head toward the suited men, "be-

cause these two gentlemen are representatives of the Venezuelan government. They say that Mr. Foreman cannot leave the
country until he pays his Venezuelan income tax.''

Bill explained that this violated our written agreement with
the government, which had promoted the fight to draw the eyes
of the world via satellite as a means of attracting recognition and
tourism. In exchange, they'd agreed to waive all income taxes.
Which was of course the reason we held the fight there. ''That
was the deal we made,'' Bill repeated.

''That deal,'' one of the men said, ''was with the old president.
We have a new president now.''

I guess the government had changed and we hadn't noticed.
Now all bets were off. The Venezuelans demanded $255,000 in
taxes before they would let me leave. In today's dollars that
would be about a million bucks.

Bill, who's a clever guy with a booming voice, recognized several prominent American sportswriters on their way home from
the fight. ''What,'' he yelled, ''you mean to tell me that you're
holding the heavyweight champion of the world for ransom?
This is outrageous!''

Sure enough, all the writers began running for telephones.
This caused the Pan Am agents enough embarrassment that they
threw up their hands and gave us the tickets.

We hustled upstairs to the boarding lounge. All that separated
us from the plane was passport control—and there were the
same two guys in bad suits. ''I'm sorry,'' one said, ''I can't let you
through until Mr. Foreman pays his taxes.'' Now Bill, his eyes
bugging out, really started a scene. The suits made no effort to
stop him. Nor did I—until a squad of Venezuelan soldiers in battle gear, bearing weapons, marched up the stairs. Bill was still
carrying on when I leaned over and said, ''You'd better cool it,
man. Haven't you noticed these guys've got guns? That's
enough.''

We walked back out of the airport and into the limousine,
which took us to the American Embassy. For five days, the ambassador tried but was unable to work out a settlement. It became clear that for us to leave the country the money would

George at age eleven.
In a household of seven brothers and sisters,
it wasn't easy holding his own.

Nancy Ree Foreman,
George's mother, in 1963

George and J. D. Foreman,
his father

Leroy Moorehead in the U.S. Army.
As an adult, George discovered
that Moorehead was his biological father.

Leroy and George met
soon after the revelation was made.

"Aunt Leola was my favorite of Mom's sisters."

The Foreman siblings.
(*Back row, left to right*) Robert, Gloria, George;
(*front row, left to right*) Willie Mae, Kenneth, Mary, Roy.

George, the fiercest lineman on the E. O. Smith Junior High School football team,
pictured here with Ronald Taylor (*center*) and Tyrone Chandler (*right*)

George shows off his stuff with a fellow new member of the federal Job Corps program in Oregon.

During his Job Corps training, George was transferred to the San Francisco Bay Area, the kind of place he had "no idea existed beyond the Fifth Ward."

George began seriously training (here with Doc Broadus) only after a sparring loss to a much smaller fighter.

On the right is Clay Hodges— the only man to defeat George twice. Here he is beating anotl amateur, Matthew Blow.

George's quick success as an amateur landed him a place on the national AAU team.

...tober 27, 1968.
...orge TKO's Russian Ionas Chepulis
...win the gold.

George poses in classic style
after winning the Olympics.

...ecame a poster boy for the Job Corps:
...gone from a junior-high dropout to an
...mpic gold medalist." George is shown here
...senting a plaque to fellow Texan
...sident Lyndon Johnson.

The scene that startled America:
George waving an American flag after winning the heavyweight
gold medal at the 1968 Olympics in Mexico City

Proud mother Nancy Ree Foreman hugs her son and his manager Dick Sadler after George signs his first professional contract.

(*From left*) Ex-champ Sonny Liston, Dick Sadler, George, ex-champ and trainer Archie Moore, and Judge Perchio

George with his firstborn, Michi

Michi with her mother, Adrienne, in Barbados, 1974

Charlotte Gross,
the mother of Georgetta

Cynthia Lewis,
George's second wife

Sharon Goodson

Pamela Clay

George and Joan on their wedding day

George with George V ("Red")

Natalie

(George with George III ("Monk")

Leola

(from left) Michi, George II
("Little George"), and Georgetta

Freeda holding baby Monk

George with preacher L. R. Masters

George with members of his parish
at the First Church of the Lord Jesus Christ

Street preaching in Houston

have to be paid. But I wasn't going to pay it. Since an agreement in principle had already been reached for me to fight Muhammad Ali in Kinshasa, Zaire, later that year, I insisted that Don King, who was promoting the fight in Africa, pay the fee. He did. Poor Ken Norton, whose boxing future looked dubious at best, had no such angels. Venezuelan officials forced him to pony up $72,000 before allowing him to leave. Meanwhile, they held ABC's TV truck for fifty grand.

Don King had come to me before the Norton fight. "I can put you together with Muhammad Ali," he said.

"Are you sure?"

He said yes.

I called Ali myself to check. "Do you want to fight me?" I asked.

"Yep."

"You're sure?"

"Yep."

Though he said yes, I thought I perceived some hesitation in his voice.

The next time I talked to Don King he claimed he could get me five million dollars for the fight. That was an extraordinary amount of money, beyond anything I could have imagined. The previous highest purse had been the five million split evenly between Ali and Joe Frazier for their second fight, held in January 1974. "Will you do it?" he asked.

"You sign this piece of paper right here," I said. " 'Five million dollars for George Foreman.' Then you've got me."

He came back in a few days. "Muhammad wants five million also," he said.

"Go ahead, give it to him," I said. "I don't care what he gets, so long as I get my five."

I had a feeling Ali wouldn't have fought for less—not as a matter of honor, but because he was afraid of me. He got more afraid, I'm sure, after the Norton fight. Word later came through Don King that the Muslims, on behalf of Ali, were upset. They requested that I stop saying I would kill him. Everyone could see that I meant what I was saying, and that upset them. They asked me respectfully to cool it, because, "you know, Ali's kind of old for boxing. Please."

"Well," I said, "since it's a religious request, I won't say that I'm going to kill him. I'll just say that I'm going to knock him out—in a hurry."

The next time I saw Ali was at the boxing writers' annual banquet, where I was to receive the "Fighter of the Year" award and my W.B.A. championship belt. They'd invited him to be guest speaker. Before we arrived, I told Mr. Moore that I planned to get on Muhammad somehow the same way he always seemed to be pulling stupid practical jokes on others. "I'm gonna tear his coat off."

I'd once run into Ernie Terrell, the boxer who was most famous for refusing to accept Cassius Clay's name as Muhammad Ali. "You can whip that guy, but you've got to watch out for the Muslims," he'd said, claiming that a few days before their fight, he answered his hotel door. A group of men in bow ties ran in, picked up every item that wasn't nailed down, put everything down again, and ran out. "Those are the games they play. They do strange things."

I sat back on the dais, watching Muhammad clowning around behind the podium, snug and smug in his element. These reporters were his prime audience. They loved and appreciated him. His quickness with words made their jobs easier. Me, I grunted and growled. You could have put all my quotable quotes on the head of a pin and still had room left for my sense of humor.

"And now," Muhammad said, picking up the W.B.A. belt, "I'm going to present this to George." Then he stopped for a moment. "Hmm. On second thought, I'm gonna keep it." They were still laughing as I marched over to pick up the belt. Biding my time, I sat down again. *I'll get him at the next joke.* My chance came a minute later. I sneaked behind him, put one hand on each side of the vent of his expensively elegant jacket, and ripped upward.

Muhammad went berserk. Contorting his face into an angry mask, he grabbed me but didn't swing. I'd grown up with guys who'd knock your head off if you messed with them that way. Of course, that was instinct, this was theater. "You Christian!" he screamed. "You blankety-blank!" *Christian? What does he mean— that I'm an American?*

Trying to get his hands off of me, I was laughing, because evidently no one had seen me rip his coat. "What's wrong here?" everyone kept asking. "What happened?" Finally, three or four guys managed to pull him away. Still enraged, he continued spewing an endless stream of obscenities, then picked up some bottles off the dais and threatened to throw them.

Ali's reaction offered insights. I knew without doubt that he didn't like me, but now I saw through his game. Like Joe Frazier protesting that I shouldn't tell him to shut up, Ali's grabbing me—but not taking a swing—gave me an advantage. Also, I began disbelieving his religious commitment. I figured a man who swore so effortlessly and creatively wasn't exactly God-fearing, at least not in the way I understood or wanted to understand.

Later, still wondering why Ali had spit the word "Christian" at me like a curse, I recalled a meeting I'd had the previous year with representatives of Saudi Arabia about a possible deal to endorse Saudi sports.

"What do you hunt for there?" I'd asked.

The answer came through an interpreter. "Christians," he'd said. "We hunt for Christians." Then laughter.

So maybe that's what Muhammad Ali meant: Christians were animals, and the word "Christian" was a slur.

This was discouraging, because at the time I'd been giving Islam serious thought, sort of trying it on for size. In fact, as far back as 1969, *Muhammad Speaks,* the newspaper published by the Nation of Islam, had influenced me to stop eating pork. If I discovered that someone in my kitchen had cooked bacon or ham or pork ribs, I'd throw out all the pans and utensils and buy new ones.

There was something appealing about what the Nation's polite, clean-cut, self-disciplined young men in suits and bow ties represented. And while I wasn't completely ready to adopt their ways, in this time of great emptiness I'd inched closer toward becoming a Muslim—until Ali's poor manners ended my flirtation. I figured if a religion couldn't make you into a better person, it had no purpose at all, and if his was the true face of Islam, I didn't want to see it in my mirror.

Naturally, this didn't end my search for something, anything, to fill the emptiness. Around the same time I became infatuated with the television show *Kung Fu*, which starred David Carradine as a priest from an ancient order of Buddhist martial artists. Each episode contained nuggets of philosophy, sandwiched between the action sequences, that seemed to stick in my mind. *Now this is something I can relate to.* I wondered whether I might be able to learn that religion and become as wise as David Carradine appeared to be—until I saw him and his wife interviewed by Dick Cavett and she breast-fed their infant on camera. *Never mind.*

Before the Ali fight, scheduled for October 1974, in Kinshasa, Zaire, reporters from every major publication in the country—and outside it—came to interview me at my ranch in Livermore, California. One of them was my old hero Jim Brown, on assignment from ABC, the network that would broadcast the event from Africa. I took him on a complete tour—swimming pools, horses, houses, and guest houses. When the cameras stopped rolling and we were alone he said, "Man, George, you've really got it together. I'm going to get it together like you one day."

Like me? Jim Brown's going to get it together like *me*?

I was awestruck. He didn't know what he was talking about. This was Number 32, who'd starred in the first football game I'd ever watched on television, bulling his way over people and pulling five or six of them into the end zone. I hadn't even known who he was then. But I knew I wanted to walk like him. And I wanted my shoulders to be broad like his. And then when he took off the helmet, I saw the face that I wanted to wear. For me Jim Brown had ranked up there with Roy Rogers and John Wayne and *The Rifleman*, Chuck Connors. As a boy, I would close my eyes and pretend to be them. And now one of them was saying that I had it together and he didn't. The world had turned upside down.

Still looking for answers, I took a Bible to Zaire. It had been given to me some months before, when I'd visited a church that was supposed to have a lot of "nice, pretty girls" in the congregation. Nice was the operative word, since pretty girls were constantly throwing themselves at me; some even offered me money. "Is there anyone new to our church who would like to join?" the preacher had asked. To make the proper impression, I'd raised my hand and mounted the dais. Afterward, the preacher had handed me a new Good Book. "Here, George," he said. "In case you ever run into trouble, this will be your strength." I'd never looked at it, but I took it to Zaire. Embarrassed by it, however—feeling that if I was going to cling on to religion that it ought to be an African religion—I hid my Bible from view. Still, I knew it was there in my room, my good luck charm. I even uttered a prayer now and then: "God, help me to get this knockout." But I guess He had other plans.

I was miserable in Zaire, not least because of the food. Tyree Lyons, my cook who'd worked at the Job Corps site in Pleasanton, scoured Kinshasa for edible chow (he eventually came down with some mysterious ailment that swelled his hands and eyes) and found little. But I hated more than the absence of cheeseburgers. My first quarters were an old army base infested with rats, lizards, and insects. Surrounded by cyclone fencing and barbed wire, it was patrolled and inhabited by rowdy soldiers who drank a lot more beer than I like to see in people toting loaded rifles. Finally I found a suite at the Intercontinental Hotel. Worried about someone coming in and messing with me and my things, I hired guards to keep a twenty-four-hour watch outside the room. This was clearly Muhammad Ali country. Sentiment in his favor colored how everyone looked at me—and they did so incessantly, their eyes following me everywhere. Most people wanted him to win back the title as much as he did. As far as he was concerned, he said, George Foreman held the championship taken from him for refusing to register for the military draft. And who was I? The goof who'd waved the American flag. I realized that no matter what happened in the ring, I couldn't win for losing. If I knocked him out, the most I'd get would be grudging respect for vanquishing a legend. And if I lost, there'd be a big crowd at the station, jeering me back to Palookaville.

Two weeks after my arrival in Zaire, and five days before the fight, I was cut over the eye during a sparring session; I had walked into an elbow my partner raised to protect himself from my savagery. Blood spurted. "Hey, I'm cut," I yelled.

"No, you're not," Sadler said. "You're all right."

"Stop everything," I insisted. "I'm cut."

That raised a flag in me. The trainer's job is to protect his fighter. Many's the time less serious finger cuts have caused lengthy postponements, for the simple reason that a championship contest is intended to be a match between both men at their best. Distrusting local doctors, I had Sadler place a butterfly adhesive over the cut in anticipation of flying to Belgium or France for proper medical treatment and regrouping. But, fearing that I wouldn't return, Zaire president Mobutu Sese Seko, who had cut the deal with Don King to sponsor the fight, refused to let me leave until after the bout, which he intended to be a showcase for his country. The month's postponement we did get wasn't nearly long enough for me to heal properly and begin the training cycle again, since the doctors forbade me from sweating for a minimum of ten days. No sweating, obviously, means no sparring or road work.

Like the lazy fox who couldn't reach the grapes, I convinced myself that I didn't need sparring and road work anyway; knocking out Muhammad Ali was a mere formality. Despite his crowing, I still believed he was afraid. I remembered the fear in his eye when I beat Ken Norton. He'd tried to cover with bravado, but having grown up with that stuff, I could spot it across the street. His not swinging at me when I tore his coat meant there was no reason to psych him out further. Yeah, he was scared. I saw it again when I ran into him and his friends at a Kinshasa nightspot.

I thought we were covered. Dick Sadler came to me for $25,000 to slip the referee under the table. I asked why. "Because," he said, "you've got a habit of hitting people when they're down, man. I want to make sure he doesn't disqualify you." I gave him the money, because that's how the game was played. Whether Zack Clayton ever received it, I don't know.

As usual before fighting, I was thirsty. Years before, Sadler had insisted that I dry out before the weigh-in and fight. Hungry to learn and determined to do what's right, I didn't question the wisdom, even though heavyweights aren't disallowed for tipping the scales. One time after a weigh-in I ate the usual poached eggs and toast breakfast with Charley Shipes, who was also on that evening's card. *Man, he must not want to win*, I thought when he drank glass after glass of water. I figured drying out was some secret Sadler weapon to build strength, the way marathon runners would later load up on carbohydrates before a race. Since Sadler had trained or worked with other heavyweight champs, I also figured he must know something.

"Ready for your glass of water?" he'd always ask in the dressing room just before the fight.

"Yeah, give it to me."

"Okay, take a nice drink."

I'd swallow the contents in two big, refreshing gulps.

"How was that?"

"Great."

"Okay, good. Now here's a couple pieces of ice."

A treat.

The feeling of near dehydration, relieved only partially by the short drink and ice chips, contributed to an overall mood Sadler created. I was thirsty, in more ways than one. He'd wind me up with curse after vicious curse, describing the destruction of that evil blankety-blank waiting in the ring. By the time he turned me loose, I'd become an exploding monster. The result: forty fights and forty victories, thirty-seven of them by knockout, most in the early rounds. Why question success?

At four o'clock in the morning, on October 30, 1974, I awaited my fate in the locker room. Later I would read that Muhammad Ali's arrival in the ring was greeted by tribal drumbeats and a crowd roaring "Al-ee, Al-ee." But I was aware of none of that. My thoughts were elsewhere. I wanted to end the fight, collect my money, and get home. Who'd ever fought at four A.M.? But it wasn't four in the morning where it counted: back home. There it was prime time. And we were live via satellite, the focus of the world's attention.

"Are you ready for your water now?" Sadler asked. We'd kept Muhammad waiting in the ring long enough.

"Yep," I said. Just like always.

I took a big swallow and almost spit it back into the cup. "Man," I said, "this tastes like medicine. This water have medicine in it?"

"SAME WATER AS ALWAYS," he yelled.

"All right," I said. I drank the rest, which tasted just as medicinal.

With the aftertaste on my tongue, I climbed into the ring accompanied by tepid cheers and scattered boos. I looked over at Muhammad in his corner, clowning around. When he wouldn't return my stare, I knew for sure that he was afraid of me.

Muhammad's introduction by the ring announcer brought an ecstatic ovation. He was incredibly popular, maybe even more popular than their president, Mobutu. Muhammad Ali was their man. In fact, Muhammad Ali was everyone's man. Everywhere he fought, his opponents faced the same disadvantage I did, receiving polite applause that seemed even more sparse in contrast.

While referee Zack Clayton gave us the instructions, Muhammad finally looked me in the eye. We glared at each other. My only thought was to knock him out early.

At the opening bell, Muhammad became a rabbit. He'd flick a jab at me and run. Me, I rushed him like a tiger, throwing hard shot after hard shot, going for that early shower. But he was one tough rabbit to catch, even for a tiger. Somehow, we always ended up on the ropes or in the corner, with me whaling away and him covering up. I'd jab, jab, jab, then throw several knockout punches that couldn't find their mark. He'd hold on to me, and the ref would break us apart. Still, though, he'd hold on, pressing his elbows against my back as I bent over.

His only offense was that famous flicking jab. It came so fast, you could barely see it, let alone counter it. Each time he threw one, I'd think, *Man, that's a quick jab.* I soon figured out that he was trying to open the cut over my eye. But I wasn't worried. Any minute, I knew, he was going down, just as every other opponent of mine had.

For the first two rounds I unleashed a torrent of punches, none of which really found its mark. Muhammad was a master at covering up. Not until the third round did I land a solid blow. It was a wicked right hand that struck home just under his heart. Blows like that can drive the wind—and the will—out of a man. Muhammad looked at me as if to say, "Hey, I'm not going to take that off you." That made me happy, because I thought then that he'd finally stand toe to toe with me, his pride getting the better of his intelligence. No way could he win a slugging match with me; we both knew that. But when I charged after him, his intelligence prevailed. He backed into the ropes and began covering up to avoid another barrage of heavy shots. I beat on him mercilessly, trying to connect with one of those home-run punches.

At the sound of the bell ending the round, Muhammad's face looked like he'd just seen a miracle. He had: his own survival—he was still on his feet.

Back in my corner, Sadler and Archie Moore insisted that I keep up the pounding. But I was already nearly exhausted. I couldn't understand why. I'd fought only three rounds, yet felt that I'd gone fifteen.

In the next round, we continued playing predator and prey. He'd hit me with one shot—usually the jab, but sometimes a right—then run. He had to, because when he faced me I placed my left foot between both of his feet. That meant his alternatives were to either stand in front of me and fight or move backward. So of course he moved backward and covered up. He was helped by an apparently loose top rope, which allowed him to lean way out of the ring, his head beyond my reach. No one in my camp had checked the ropes before the fight. Why bother? For years now, my fight plan had been to take off my robe, get a quick knockout, put the robe back on, and return to the dressing room. Who worried about the tautness or slackness of the ropes? Now Muhammad was the beneficiary of that lack of attention to detail.

In that fourth round I was able finally to land a thundering right on the back of his neck. It weakened him, and I knew that if I could land another one like that, he'd go down and out. But when I loaded up the weapon and cocked it, I saw something that made me pull back instead. That sight is, in fact, the image I recall most vividly from the fight. It was the face of a "friend," sitting at ringside, who happened to be directly in my line of vision. (What he did bothered me so much that I've put him out of my mind forever; I can't even remember his name.) Between when I threw the first shot and prepared to throw the second, he began waving his arms wildly and screaming, "Bull! He hit him behind the neck. He's cheating." A man I'd considered family was rooting against me. In a state of shock, I couldn't deliver the punch that probably would have ended the fight right there. For the rest of the night I wondered whether he'd do the same thing every time I threw one.

My hurt and disappointment, and that thinking, lessened whatever power I had left. And there wasn't much of it. I wondered what had happened to my stamina, let alone my strength. No matter what the sportswriters said, stamina was never one of my problems; I'd had plenty of it. But because they'd not seen it—with my fights usually ending in the early rounds—they'd assumed I lacked it. I guess they hadn't noticed that I'd gone the distance three times before, and had even once scored a tenth-round knockout (of Gregorio Peralta).

It seemed that this was turning into a déjà vu nightmare of my amateur fights against Clay Hodges. Man, was I tired. I could barely get off the stool between rounds. Even so, Sadler was instructing me to continue my fearsome attack. This contradicted his usual advice, which was to slowly and carefully build to the knockout. "Get him," he said. "He can't last another round."

Archie Moore wasn't as insistent as Sadler; at least, he didn't say as much. This man of great pride had been disturbed and hurt, I think, by my pushing him to the side in favor of Sadler again. If either guy had told me to change tactics, I would have. They could have said to back off a round or two, catch my breath, and let him come to me; he'd have to, if he wanted to win, because by then he was far behind on points. But because these guys counseled me to attack, attack, attack, I did. Their job was to give advice. Mine was to take it.

Every time I went to hit Muhammad, he'd cover up, strike me with that one quick jab or right, then run. The sad part was that my blows, which numbered at least five to one over his, were met by the crowd with either silence or, worse, the reaction of my "friend." Meanwhile, each one of Muhammad's little jabs brought tumultuous cries. I was winning these rounds, but Muhammad Ali owned their hearts and minds more completely with every punch he absorbed. For them, this had become a morality play: Muhammad was good and I was evil. And yet, it was because of me, as champion, that this fight had been staged in Zaire. George Foreman, not Muhammad Ali, had tried to do something grand for Africa, had brought the television cameras to show off Africa to the world, had made the Africans proud of themselves. I'd wanted them to love me, too—and for some reason they didn't. I vowed never to go back.

In the seventh round, Muhammad noticed that I was getting tired, that my shots weren't hurting as much. He said, "Come on, George, show me something. Is that all you got?"

Knowing that he was whistling in the graveyard, I figured, *Okay, I'm just going to play around now, catch him talking, and let him try to hit me. When he tries, I'll knock him out.* As tired and weak as I felt, I always believed that I still had enough for that one shot to end it all. All I needed was the chance, the opening. If Muhammad made the mistake of coming to me, it would be his last mistake that night.

Angelo Dundee, Muhammad's trainer, must have divined my plan. He yelled out, "Don't play with the sucker, don't play." A few years before, he'd been present at a fight of mine in Lake Geneva, Wisconsin, and had seen the ferocious beating I'd given a tough Jamaican boxer. So he understood the damage I could do.

Angelo's warning seemed to sober Muhammad a little. He stopped playing around and talking.

In the eighth, I tried to entice Muhammad to come to me. Dropping my hands, I followed him around the ring, as if daring him to step into my web; there was no way he could hurt me. When we neared the ropes, I began pummeling him again. He was knocked backward near the corner, then bounced to the side. Off balance, I turned to follow him and was leaning his way when he threw a left-right combination whose power was multiplied by both my leaning toward him as I tried to re-balance myself, and his momentum off the corner.

As the combination struck ground zero on my chin, I remember thinking, *Boy, I'm going down.* Muhammad, I'm sure, was as surprised as I was.

My fall to the mat felt that much harder because my legs had been twisted while I was off balance. On my back, I lifted my head and not only was I alert and uninjured, I was actually excited and hopeful: *This guy hasn't mixed it up with me all night. Now, when he thinks he can come in and finish the job, I'll be able to get him. It doesn't matter how tired I am—I've still got enough to put him down when I get the chance. And now I will.*

Though I could have, I didn't get up immediately. Because in the days when there were no standing eight-counts that would allow a boxer to clear his senses before reentering the fray, the custom developed to stay down until eight. Instead of watching the referee's count, you were supposed to look for your cornermen's signal. Even as I did, I could hear Zack Clayton's count. He said "eight" and Sadler motioned me up. I stood at once, but Clayton waved me off with a quick count—nine and ten became one word to me.

It was over.

Clayton guided me to my corner as Ali and the crowd began celebrating. My God, it was over. It was really over. I felt disappointed, less for losing than for not getting a chance to mix it up. Then the magnitude of the loss began to hit me. I would be sorting it out for a long time.

"All right?" Sadler asked.

"Yeah."

Back in the dressing room, the mood was funereal. While dejection had set in, I was still more tired than anything else. Lying there on the training table, letting the thoughts just come and go, I heard questions—impertinent questions—from sportswriters they wouldn't have dared to ask even twenty-four hours before. Now these guys believed they could get away with anything. *So that's how it is? You're either on top, or you're nowhere.*

In short order, I would become depressed beyond recognition, and this fight would go down in boxing history; no less than Norman Mailer wrote an entire book about it.

Muhammad began bragging about his great strategy—letting me punch myself out before delivering the crowning blows. But I know, and he knows, he had no such strategy before the fight. To say he did is to shoot an arrow into a barn and then paint a bull's-eye around it. Muhammad's only strategy had been survival. When I cut off the ring from him, he had nowhere to go but the ropes, and nothing to do but cover up. What's more true than his concoction of some brilliant strategy is that I fought a foolish fight by not letting him come to me more, especially when I was tired and far ahead on points. I hadn't done that because I couldn't let anyone think that George Foreman was afraid of Muhammad Ali, and because my trainers told me to give it my all.

''Rope-a-dope'' the fight got nicknamed when I mentioned to a writer that I believed my water may have been mickeyed. What else, I asked, could account for that medicinal taste and my terrible tiredness? What else could account for how sick and sore I felt for a month afterward?

So was there ''medicine'' in my drink? I can't say for certain. Later, I heard that Sugar Ray Robinson, watching the fight at home in the States, had commented to a friend that I seemed drugged. Maybe sportswriter Jim Murray, aiming for a laugh, was closer to the mark than he realized when he wrote that I looked like ''a drunk trying to find a keyhole.''

If I had been slipped a mickey, why? I can't answer with certainty there, either. Only afterward, when I thought about Sadler and my relationship with him, did it seem somewhat plausible. I remembered some stories he used to tell about boxers who belonged to gangsters—how the fix would be in for this guy or that to lose in order to set up a bigger payday or better betting odds down the line.

Such stories poured out of him when we were on the road and

bored. We laughed about them. I was young and considered Sadler a father figure. Was he joking? I don't know. But surely his message between the lines was that he'd protect me from such nastiness.

There was the tale Sadler told of an aging heavyweight who threw a fight to an up-and-coming champ. After the third round, the trainer put the stool out for his aging heavyweight, who angrily kicked it over backward. That told the trainer that his fighter was going down. A man who's soon to hit the canvas doesn't need the rest.

"I felt so bad," the trainer said. I thought he felt bad because he believed his man had thrown the fight. Then he clarified: "He could've at least given *me* a chance to make some money on it too."

The years since the fight have not answered the question for me of whether I was indeed doped. One verifiable fact is that Muhammad had been the heavy underdog until a late flurry brought down the odds. Was that money bet with the heart? I know only that this fight featured more unexplained happenings than any event of my life, and that in the grand scheme of things the loss ultimately helped to make me a man. Back then, however, I believed that the sky had fallen. I wasn't champion anymore. I didn't know what I was.

As for that Bible I'd taken to Zaire, the one given me by the preacher: I put it away where I wouldn't see it anymore. What good was a Bible if it didn't bring you luck?

Chapter Six

LIFE IS LIKE BOXING. You've only got so many punches to throw, and you can only take so many.

For a twenty-five-year-old who had the world kneeling at his feet, losing stinks. I felt empty, totally empty. I hadn't just lost the title, I'd lost what defined me as a man. I felt as if my core had evaporated.

The day after the fight I slouched on the sofa in my suite, dark glasses hiding my swollen eyes. Mr. Moore came in and saw me moping. He walked over, snatched the glasses off my face, and threw them away.

"Man," he said, "you be proud of that. You let the photographers take your picture like that. And you smile. You're not putting on any dark glasses. YOU HEAR ME, BIG COUNTRY BOY?" He always called me names to get my attention. I wouldn't let anyone else talk to me that way; only Mr. Moore. "What are you? I thought you were a man. You're no man. I'm no fool, and I don't bother with fools."

I picked up the dark glasses—then put them down. Mr. Moore was still the boss.

He took me to Paris and hired a masseur to work on me every day. I called an old girlfriend who lived in Wales and asked her to come over to France. She did. But the more she tried to console me, the worse I talked to her. If she tried to get playful, I'd throw something at her, like an egg off the breakfast tray.

"You're being horrible," she said. "I flew here to help you out."

"Well, don't," I yelled. "What're you trying to help me for? I don't need you, you need me."

She was an emotional wreck when she left Paris. After five days, Mr. Moore and I left, too. But not for home.

"We're not going back there yet," he said.

I was an obedient puppy. We went to Los Angeles and picked up another girlfriend, a student at U.C.L.A., and took her with us to Hawaii. I'd lie on the hotel bed, staring into nothingness, reliving the fight. This girl, who'd always been kind to me, would stroke my head; I'd slap her hand away. Finally falling asleep, I'd awaken with a start in a cold sweat: If only I hadn't dropped my hands; if only I hadn't walked into those punches; if only I'd left Zaire and been treated by a doctor; if only I'd called off the fight; if only the ropes . . . If only. If only. If only. The sweat popped off me as though I'd just gotten out of the ring. She'd try to cool the fire and soothe me back to sleep.

"Who're you petting?" I said. "Pet yourself. There's nothing wrong with me."

She knew I was in pain, and tried to be patient with me. But my insults soon wore her down. "I've gotta get back to school," she said. "I gotta go, George."

"I don't care if I ever see you again," I snarled. "You're not doing me any favors. Who told you to come in the first place?"

After she left, Mr. Moore stuck close by my side. I don't know if he thought I was depressed enough to do something stupid to myself, but I'm sure I looked depressed and stupid enough to do it. I emptied my rage on him, too, ordering him here and there as though he were my servant. But he'd laugh hard enough to make that jelly belly shake. "You didn't talk that way when Muhammad was whipping your blankety-blank," he said.

"I'm telling you, I'm through with you," I said. "Get out. I don't want anything to do with you. Understand?"

Mr. Moore was trying to expose that raw nerve to the air; get it toughened up, callused, so that it wouldn't hurt anymore. "You're talking weak-talk," he'd answer. "Weak-talk."

Much as I hated hearing that, I needed to hear it. And I needed to hear it from him. My quarters were a large, elegant suite, but I preferred to spend my time in his modest room, with his clothes strewn everywhere.

Before we left Hawaii, he said, "Hey, George, you're always talkin' about wanting another Rolls-Royce."

"So?"

"So let's buy you one."

He called the dealer in Chicago and arranged to have a new Corniche waiting for me in Houston. I went along with the plan, because I thought that if I drove up in a big, expensive car, the people in Fifth Ward wouldn't point at me and say, "Uh-huh, Ali beat him."

That first day back in town when I cruised slowly through the streets, hoping to be noticed, I saw my old buddies Charles and Roy. I rolled down the window to say hi.

"Hey, George," Charles said. "What's that? A Toyota?"

I also feared seeing my favorite uncle, Leola's husband, Edmund. A year earlier, after Ali had beaten Joe Frazier, he'd said, "That's a God-sent man."

No, I'd thought, *I'm the God-sent man.* I wished he'd used those words to describe me.

But I wasn't God-sent. And I didn't want to find out that Uncle Edmund had pulled for Ali against me. I'd already suffered the discovery that even in your own family, you're only admired as much as your last win: My cousin Willie Carpenter, who'd been my equipment manager since before the Frazier fight, accused me of taking a dive against Ali. How could he have said that, after what I'd done for him? Until I'd hired him two years before, Willie had been down and out in Los Angeles. As a young boy, I'd promised his mother, my Aunt Mary Lee, to take care of him when I became "somebody." Now, just like that, he quit me.

And then there was my friend Bob Hope. We'd first met by telephone, when he called me during my hotel-lobby press conference after the Frazier fight. He'd offered me ten thousand dollars to appear on his television show. For an hour of work, I was going to make more than I had for most of my previous fights— and wouldn't have to get hit. Imagine, Bob Hope calling me.

I'd done the show and was asked back for the next one, and had then gone to his home in Beverly Hills. Meeting his friends, most of whom I recognized from movies and television, I'd found myself staring at them. The surprise was that these living legends were flesh-and-blood people who treated me as a peer.

I ended up appearing on yet another of Bob's shows, an "all comedian" special with Jack Benny, Don Rickles, and Henny Youngman. Bob had invited me as well, because, he said, he intended to make me an actor after my fighting days. He would spend hours coaching me on how to get the most out of my scripted lines. He acted like my friend. I'd kept reminding myself that my days of attaching myself to others had long passed. Bob Hope liked George Foreman because he was George Foreman.

Wrong. Bob Hope evidently liked only George Foreman the champion. It devastated me that after the loss my "friend" never called or sent a telegram to express condolences or sympathy. A few months later, when I saw him on Johnny Carson's show, he shook my hand mechanically, chatted for a few seconds, and then dismissed me as if we'd met for the first time. Maybe he allowed only winners in his life, or maybe that was just the way Hollywood plays the game. But I interpreted his cold shoulder as a rejection, which added another garbage heap of hurt onto the ache I already felt.

Not every famous person abandoned me. Win, lose, or draw, I was always welcome on Johnny Carson's show; I appreciated that. Then there was Pearl Bailey, who also appeared on the show with Bob Hope. Pearl had even been at ringside in Jamaica. Listening to me complain about how I'd been robbed and that I would someday regain the championship because I hated Muhammad Ali and because I couldn't stand losing, she took me aside when the taping finished.

"Child," she said, "don't say you want to be champion of the world for those reasons. Say you'll be champion of the world again because you *can*. Do you believe you can?"

"Yeah."

"And so you will."

Then she asked if I'd brought home any dashikis from Africa. Yes, a truckload. I gave her one a few weeks later when we were both guest "squares" on *Hollywood Squares.* She seemed thrilled with the gift, and wore it for the next taping. I felt great that she wanted something from an old loser like me.

And then there was my father . . .

"Monk," my sister Gloria said to me one day, "you ever notice you don't look like the rest of us?"

"What are you talkin' about?" I was in no mood for teasing. My torment already felt familiar, something like the anger that had gripped me as a child. I didn't need any more echoes from the past.

"You know Daddy's not really your daddy."

"Stop lying," I said.

"Do you remember when we used to call you 'Mo'head'?" Did I remember? I'd never forget. "Well, we weren't saying 'Mo'-head' but 'Moorehead.' Leroy Moorehead was his name. He wrote Mama a letter saying he'd like to meet you."

"You're lying."

"I'm not lying."

I felt uncomfortable confronting Mom, so I went to her sister. "Aunt Leola," I said, "I was in Madison Square Garden before a fight a few years ago. A man walked up to me and said, 'Hey, son, I just want to tell you that I'm your daddy. My name's Moore-head. Leroy Moorehead.'" I looked at her closely. "And then he said, 'You ask Leola. She'll tell you.'"

Aunt Leola stared back at me. "Don't tell your mother," she said.

She didn't have to say more.

I called Mom anyway and told her the Madison Square Garden story. I asked, "Is it true?"

She cried.

I said, "Please, tell me what happened."

"Well," she said, "your daddy and I were getting into it. We had a breakup, and—" She cried so hard I couldn't get any more details until a few days later, when I called again and asked her to arrange a meeting.

Leroy Moorehead lived in Texarkana, Arkansas, which isn't too far from Marshall, Texas, where our family lived before moving to Houston. The arrangements made, I drove out a few days early, to the ranch I'd bought in Marshall in 1976. That two-hundred-mile drive from Houston is where I did (and do) a lot of important thinking. No radio, no music; just me and my thoughts, usually in a new car I'd bought just for the drive. I needed the three or four hours, and then some, to prepare for my encounter. Or was it a confrontation? How about interview? Maybe an appointment. What do you call it when you're going to meet a man who can explain a thousand and one mysteries about you?

Mom had told me that before I was born, she and Dad used to break up and get back together like the seasons. Well, it was during an off-season when she met Leroy Moorehead. After me, there was a lot more off than on. To get away from the taunts and teasing about how that last baby of hers didn't look anything like the others, she had fled Marshall. When J.D. tagged along, it was mostly to have a place to run away from. The good side of their relationship was a rare love, but the bad side was a slow-acting poison. They fought when they saw each other, and each time he saw me he saw ghosts. Mama worked and spent her money to raise us. J.D. worked, too; he worked hard. But he spent his money on drink and fun. When he and Mama fought, he didn't use me as a weapon against her, but he couldn't pretend nothing had happened. Even so, he loved me like his own.

My sister Gloria wasn't always as kind. "You did this," she'd sometimes accuse me when Mom and Dad separated. My brother Sonny had a similar attitude. He was ten years older than I—old enough to blame me, and old enough to flee the house when I was three or four. Partly because he worked and lived on his own, I looked up to him, wanted to be like him. But not until my teens did Sonny allow me to get close.

I hadn't understood. I'd thought I was *doing* something wrong when, in fact, it was my *being* that was wrong. Now their anger made sense. Moorehead, not Mo'head.

Leroy and I arranged to meet at a church in Marshall. The instant I saw him I knew. He was tall and handsome. He smiled with the smile I smile. We embraced—something I'd never done with a stranger. Then we talked. One thing he mentioned was that he liked to brawl. He said he'd bragged to his buddies about being the father of the world's champ. I silently wondered if he'd seen me on television after winning the gold medal, saying, "Hello to J. D. Foreman in Houston, Texas."

Before leaving for Houston, I gave him my phone number. He called me every other Sunday, but he also made it clear that he didn't want and didn't expect anything from me. Yes, I felt close to him, though not as a son. My heart was thinking clearly: A father is not your seed; a father is the man who raises you. Leroy Moorehead became a friend, but J. D. Foreman was, and would remain, my only father. Leroy was a decorated World War Two veteran, a staff sergeant wounded in North Africa. J. D. Foreman was a railroad worker who spent most of his life loving my mother and not being able to show it. But I wouldn't have traded one for the other. No matter how well I got to know Leroy, he never took J.D.'s place.

At Leroy's funeral in 1978, I stared down at the open casket. *Man, that is my father*—or could have been. That realization made a powerful impression. Headstrong and iron-willed, he'd lived lonely and died lonely. His service pistol and American flag were presented to a son he'd met only four years before. I felt sorry for him in the way you feel sorry for the less fortunate—there but for the grace of God, and all that. I'm pretty sure that Leroy's coming into my life saved me from meeting his fate. We had much in common, from the way we looked to the way we acted. What his death taught me is that, in the end, it's not about how tough you are, but about how much you can give—at least, if you want a family around you. Looking at him, I realized I didn't want to die singing, "I did it my way."

But even before his death, Leroy influenced me. I'd already wanted my children to know who their father was before the old man hit the ground. I'd already decided that they would always be aware of their heritage, and have a sure sense of their identity.

That's why I was determined to name all my boys George Edward Foreman.

Oh, yes, I'd had a son born while I was in Africa, just weeks before the fight. George Edward Foreman, Jr.—Little George.

His mother was Pamela Clay. We'd met through her father, Moses Clay, the athletic director at the Pleasanton Job Corps center. Pamela was living in Beverly Hills when I was down there doing my Hollywood thing and testing my credentials as a playboy. Pamela must have gotten pregnant the first time we slept together. Our breakup after six months had nothing to do with her pregnancy. If anything, I wanted the child as much or more than she. But she demanded a commitment I couldn't give. I was still married to boxing.

When Pam and I split up, people around me began calling her a gold digger, devious and cunning. "That's not your baby, George," one friend said.

I was still heavily under the sway of Dick Sadler's antiwoman paranoia. One reason I wouldn't commit was that I couldn't trust any woman. No matter how refined or elegant or civilized she was, part of me believed she only wanted to get her hands into my pockets. And the more miserable my suspicion made me, the more reasons there were to distrust: How could a woman of honest intentions be attracted to a man as angry as I was unless she wanted my cash and celebrity glitter?

"Come on, man," my friends said. "That girl's pullin' a number. That's not yours. She's not having *your* baby."

I counted the months backward. *January, December, November . . . She'd have to have gotten pregnant that first night.* "No, that's not my baby. Who does this woman think I am? A fool? She's tryin' to trick me." By then I'd decided that it was better to be suspicious than disappointed.

Still, something deep in me hoped that baby was mine. I already loved my Michi so much. She was the joy in my life. God knows, everything else was a mess. When she clapped her hands and said "Bye-bye," I'd melt inside. And even when I didn't see my little girl, I'd call to hear her voice.

"Aaaah," she'd cry.

"Did you hear that?" I'd say. "Tape that for me. Send me the tape." I carried a tape of her murmuring "da-da" for the first time, and played it constantly.

When I returned from Hawaii, I didn't go to see the boy who'd been born two weeks before the fight. I called a cousin in Los Angeles and asked if she'd seen the baby. She had.

"George," she said, "that ain't your son."

Someone else who'd seen him told me, "That's not the Foreman head."

My buddy Leroy Jackson expressed the suspicions of the times best when he smiled at the boy's photo. He said, "Most babies look like you, George."

Too bad. Having been stripped of my manhood in Africa, I would have loved coming home to a baby boy; it would have eased the pain. Twice I went to see him. Funny how Leroy was right—the kid looked like me. I held him because I loved babies, but couldn't give my heart to him.

Pamela filed a paternity suit. So my friends and my suspicions were right. Or were they? It nagged at me that she'd come from such an upright and decent family. I'd known her father for nearly ten years, and gotten to know her grandmother Esther well during the six months Pamela and I were together. Even after the breakup, Esther and I remained friends. We talked almost daily about Pamela and the baby. Together, we worked out a kind of money-laundering scheme to take care of Pamela and the child. I sent the cash to my mother, who sent it to Pamela's grandmother, who passed it to Pamela as her own. That way, Pamela wouldn't think I was admitting guilt. I refused to pay blackmail, but as long as I wasn't being blackmailed, I didn't mind paying—just in case. I swore Esther to secrecy, and she protected me. She was a good friend to both of us.

The lawyer I hired ordered blood tests. The results wouldn't be one hundred percent accurate, but near enough to establish truth.

When the tests came back, I had a son.

I'd written Pamela off as a fraud, while at the same time fighting disappointment that the little boy wasn't mine. Now she wasn't and he was.

George Edward Foreman, Jr. Little George.

Pamela said to me, "I don't want anything from you; not a dime. I just wanted you to know that he was your child."

Because he was, I intended to get him from her as often as possible. In those days, my only moments of happiness were when I was with Michi and Little George. As the boy grew, I recognized his way of sitting and frowning as my own. That was my boy. What I started looking for in girlfriends was not a dazzling figure or great conversation, but an affection for children. Traveling as much as possible with my kids, I decided to date girls who couldn't have been humbler or more plain.

"Can you take care of babies?" was all I wanted to know.

"Uh-huh."

"Good. Come with me."

Trouble always followed when these young ladies realized that I had little interest in them except as baby-sitters. But I inflicted and endured that trouble in order to have my children with me as often as possible. Without them, life looked pretty hopeless. I split most of my time between the ranch in Livermore and a house I bought on a wooded hillside in the Bel Air section of Los Angeles. Because no one could stand me and my anger for long, I was usually alone. And terrified. Both houses were isolated, surrounded by darkness at night, with views that saw only blackness. At the time I was afraid of invisible things—ghosts and the like. Every nighttime sound seemed magnified. Shivering all night, I'd finally drop off to sleep—only to awaken with a start and in a sweat. In my dreams I was still reliving that fight. *All I would have had to do was back away; breathe a little; jab, jab. Why did Sadler tell me to stay down? I could've jumped up, maybe caught him with a lucky shot.* Sometimes I counted seconds until the housekeeper showed up in the morning. Her familiar footsteps and noisy vacuum became my lullaby.

Losing had knocked me off my axis. The heavyweight title meant much more to me after I lost it than when I held it. Without it, I was nothing. As champ, I'd imagined that people considered me the ultimate man. Now I imagined that I could hear them laughing at the loser. I had a dozen cars, three houses, a ranch, and all the money I could spend. But the way I felt, none of that meant a thing. One day while racing up a hill in my Excalibur, I wondered how it would be to continue over the edge. *If I die, then people will see the pain I'm in; then they'll understand.* I wasn't suicidal, but that thought came with increasing frequency for several weeks. Fool that I was, I never considered that if I really did die, I wouldn't be there to say, "See?"

Desperate to climb back to the top, I stepped on people. I drained them of their goodwill. I remember a sweet girl I met in Los Angeles, a Cal State College student from a good family who had the misfortune to think highly of me. While we were courting, she told me that her childhood boyfriend was playing basketball for a college in Washington state. As it happened, U.C.L.A. soon invited me to attend their basketball team's game against the Washington team. When the announcer introduced me, I forced her to walk with me across Pauley Pavilion's floor, both of us the center of attention. Such was my cruelty. That young man was humiliated, and so was she. At halftime, she went out and cried.

I said, "What're you crying about? You don't want to be with me?"

Even then I knew I was confused and angry enough to need help from someone who could offer perspective. But who? Only crazy people went to shrinks.

My mother, my siblings, my aunts and uncles? I considered these people poor and ignorant. They'd never owned anything. How could they give *me* advice?

Mr. Moore? What did he know about losing? He'd never had anything to lose.

With nowhere to go and no one to trust, I decided to rebuild from the inside, to become again the man who hadn't yet hit the canvas in Zaire three months before. The only way to do that was to win back the championship.

The idea consumed me. I resolved that if I ever got into a title fight again, I'd die before losing. The only way to count me out now would be on a stretcher.

But getting that title shot wouldn't be easy. No matter how much money might be in it, Muhammad Ali didn't want to risk fate again. So it was strange when Herbert Muhammad approached me to say that if I signed with Dick Sadler again, I'd get my rematch. Impossible. Not only would I die before being counted out again, I'd die before signing with Sadler again. (We'd been working without a contract since after the Frazier fight.)

"I don't want to deal with him," I said.

"That's your problem," he said. "You don't want to deal with anyone. If you don't, you won't."

"I won't." To this day I don't know why Herbert Muhammad took an interest in Sadler.

No, I was going to have to bring in the fans, make them clamor loud enough that Muhammad Ali couldn't refuse me. I needed to show them the new George Foreman, the people's champ. That meant plenty of publicity.

Bill Caplan told me about a new magazine called *People*, which had just been spun off from *Time* magazine. He said that if we cooked up a juicy angle for them, the editors would probably be willing to send out a photographer. Okay. Here's the angle: I'd "prove" that I was the world's strongest man.

On my ranch in Marshall, I stationed five burly guys at the head and five at the tail of a seven-hundred-pound cow—all ten of them just outside the camera frame's outer edges. With me in the middle, smiling casually, it would appear that I alone was holding him up.

All of us lifted on the photographer's cue. Then somebody at the tail slipped, starting a chain reaction. Within moments, sure enough, that cow lay on my shoulders like a shawl.

No one rushed to help me, probably because it had happened so fast and the result paralyzed them. They all watched, awestruck, as though they'd just seen the Red Sea part. "I got him, I got him," I kept saying.

After the photo appeared in *People*, the promoter Henry Winston came to me with a bright idea cooked up by Marvin Gaye. He proposed that I fight five guys in one night, each minibout to go a maximum of three rounds. It sounded hokey, but Henry convinced me that I could use these exhibitions to prove my toughness. "Toughness" was the magic word. Just fighting an ordinary fight wouldn't prove what I wanted to prove, that something had to have happened to me in Africa. Beating one guy wouldn't do it; beating five guys would. Henry promised to sell the network broadcast rights so that the rest of the country and the world could see that the loss to Ali had been a fluke.

Preparations began well. Henry immediately found some good, credible fighters like Boone Kirkman and Terry Daniels. But when he had trouble getting either a locale or an interested network, Don King stepped in, and the project became a three-ring circus—because Don, whatever else can be said about him, is the quintessential ringmaster. He guaranteed to deliver both ABC and an arena. I agreed on the condition that he not push Henry aside. (As it turned out, Henry disappeared anyway.) Now I had Don King, a site in Toronto, and the Howard Cosell–Muhammad Ali sideshow providing commentary.

Throughout the televised exhibition on April 26, 1975, Howard kept repeating in that nasal twang what a "travesty," a "disgrace" and a "discredit" to boxing this was; that the event mocked the legitimate sport of boxing. Ali naturally agreed with him, and heckled me from his ringside seat. Why did neither man mention that Ali himself, beginning his comeback trail in 1970, had performed in this type of exhibition? Or that the great Jack Dempsey fought ninety-eight exhibition matches in 1931? Besides, if what I was doing was so heinous, wasn't their presence giving me undeserved legitimacy?

All five fighters hoped to gain instant fame by beating the former champ. They took their bouts seriously and fought hard. I knocked out three of them—Alonzo Johnson, Jerry Judge, and Daniels—then battered Charley Polite and Kirkman over three rounds each. A sparring partner for Joe Frazier and Chuck Wepner, Charley kissed me on the chin when I was glaring down at him during the referee's instructions. While one had nothing to do with the other, he was the only boxer of the five I didn't knock down at least once.

Despite Cosell and Ali, I felt proud of having gone twelve rounds. A cracked rib proved I'd taken some wicked punches.

My only real mistake was getting into a jawing match with Muhammad. When he began jiving, I jived back. That put the fans in his corner against me, and gave the exhibition the smelly aura of professional wrestling. The crowd booed me, then chanted "Al-ee, Al-ee." Trying to show that they didn't bother me, I flexed my muscles and postured like a muscleman. I meant it in good fun, but this was strictly Ali's domain. I couldn't avoid looking like my usual sour self.

Still, by establishing that I had twelve-round stamina, I believed I'd furthered my comeback cause. I began to feel hopeful—until the following week, when I decided to drop in on a woman I'd known so well that her four daughters considered me their Uncle George. (One of her daughters was named Michi, which she told me means beautiful and smart in Japanese. That's why I named my own daughter Michi.) The moment I walked into her house, she reacted as though I'd committed a crime.

"You're a mad man, a bad man," she said, informing me that I was no longer welcome in her home. "What's happened to you, George?" she added. "You've changed."

My goodness, if a real friend had watched my exhibition matches and bought the bad-guy image, then the rest of the world must have seen Jack the Ripper. I guess the camera doesn't lie. It had captured me perfectly: George Foreman, the man you loved to hate. I was shattered.

But not deterred. Never deterred.

To get what I wanted, I focused on who already had it. Muhammad. What stuck out in my mind was his religion. So when a business manager–agent named Tom Collins suggested that I start speaking at certain church groups about how important God was in my life, I didn't automatically call him crazy. (This was before Collins was accused of losing millions of dollars for Kareem and other athletes in bad investments.) Coming from a somewhat religious background himself, Tom contended that there was no better place to begin rehabilitating an image than in church.

Well, the thought of talking about religion to religious people took as much getting used to as there is. For one thing, I had Mr.

Moore butting in the way he did. "You gotta watch this religious stuff, man," he said. "It'll get you down. You'll lose your career and your money, and then they're through with you. No one wants anything to do with you."

I didn't need Mr. Moore's doomsday warnings. I had my own objections for other reasons. I remembered being in Canada with a woman who'd brought a friend along. This friend happened to know a lot of athletes—had slept with a lot of them, I think.

"Guess what," she said to my girlfriend. "Guess who I met?" She named a star Los Angeles Dodger. "He's born again."

"Get out of my face," I overheard my girlfriend say. "Found God? He's lost his mind."

I sat listening to their conversation, their ridicule of a man they'd once admired, and thought to myself, *I hope that never happens to me. He was a fool to tell a good-looking woman something like that.*

A while later, my sister complained about going to see Al Green in concert. "Next thing I know," she said, "he's singing church songs. Well I didn't go there for any sermons. I know where to get *my* religion. He must've flipped out to do that."

Absolutely, I believed, you never wanted to talk religion in public. Never. That's why I sort of crawled into a hole before and after appearing at Reverend Robert Schuller's church in Garden Grove, California. (His Crystal Cathedral wasn't built yet.)

"I've never done this before," I said.

"Don't worry," Reverend Schuller said. "It's just a little gathering after church."

"What am I supposed to say?"

"Well, Ali's always talking about Allah. Why don't you say something about Jesus?"

Piece of cake. I stood up and mentioned Jesus by name. They applauded. I did it again, and they applauded. A few more times. Then I sat down.

When nothing happened to help my career immediately after doing the same thing at another church, I said forget it. It was true. Religion was for losers. I wasn't going to be a loser anymore.

For a while I tried getting involved in Hollywood again. I met some people who were as famous as I was, but seemed normal. I saw they could be role models. That was important at the time. Best of all I got to meet Roy Rogers. We were paired on celebrity *Bowling for Dollars.* At first I just stared at the legend in person. Then I took pictures with him that I still have. He couldn't have known what he'd meant to me when I was a kid. What impressed me most was that the mythic Roy Rogers still acted human.

I was invited back to *Hollywood Squares.* There, too, I met celebrities who seemed as though they changed their own clothes. I laughed, I made jokes, I let people see that George Foreman could be decent, that they could allow themselves to be on my side. Little by little, I tried to chip away at my monster image.

But my smile was always just a word away from anger. When I appeared on *The Joey Bishop Show,* Joey and I joked and joshed until he mentioned Muhammad Ali. I suddenly turned serious.

"Hey," I warned. "Don't bring up that name."

"Okay," he said, not understanding that this was not a joke. "We'll just say 'M.A.' "

"You're getting close," I scolded. "Too close."

That ended my time with Joey.

The Ali fight had created a line I couldn't cross over, or go around, or get past in any way. I needed an exorcism to get rid of that devil in me. Until I did, I could have smiled all day long on national television, but nobody was going to buy it. If I was fooling anyone, it was only myself.

I soon teamed with Jerry Perenchio, the man who'd promoted the first Ali-Frazier fight and whom Don King had outmaneuvered to promote my Ali fight. Jerry signed me for one of the first outdoor bouts, at Caesars Palace in Las Vegas. This was in the days before Vegas became America's boxing Mecca. Perenchio promised that the fight would attract widespread attention, and that if I beat a top-ranked contender, Muhammad would move me to the top of the list. What choice did I have? I agreed to fight Ron Lyle, a guy my size who they said punched like a mule's kick, on January 24, 1976.

To train me, I hired Gil Clancy, who'd trained Emile Griffith and Jerry Quarry. Gil insisted that I needed a tune-up before meeting Lyle in order to regain my breathing and timing. He and Perenchio arranged an exhibition match against Jody Ballard at the Concord resort in the Catskills to benefit the U.S. Olympic boxing team. With a 22–3 record, Ballard was a good young fighter. If I lost, the Lyle fight would be history. And so would I.

I enjoyed wearing my red, white, and blue trunks again. I enjoyed standing in the ring again for my first real bout since the infamous "rope-a-dope."

This young man Ballard came from Houston, and I was told he admired me. I didn't care. I'd ignored him during the several days we were at the hotel. Now I stared at him as though he were Muhammad Ali.

Feeling more like the bad old George with every punch, I beat that boy badly, hitting him with my best shots instead of tactical ones. When the referee stopped the bout early in the second round, Ballard had already been punished unnecessarily. Punished for my losing to Muhammad. Punished for my "friend" at ringside rooting against me. Punished for my cousin who thought I threw the fight. Punished for every teacher who hadn't taken me seriously and every older kid who'd called me a bad name. It was inexcusable viciousness, the kind I was to put away when I returned to boxing years later. That night, it was on display.

Three weeks after Jody Ballard, I took four rounds to finish a tough kid named Eddie Brooks in San Francisco.

Now it was time to prepare for Lyle, five weeks away. I trained the way I should have trained for Ali. The difference this time was confidence: I didn't have as much of it as I'd had the year before. And maybe cruelty. Which I had in excess. I treated my sparring partners as I'd treated Ballard—and planned to treat Ron Lyle. I hoped to knock him out before he broke a sweat. Going toe to toe for several rounds with a guy who could hit as hard as Lyle was not in my best interests.

The fight was staged in a tent in the Caesars Palace parking lot. The only difference I could see between a tent and inside arenas was that my dressing room was a trailer.

I began the fight with knockout in mind. Then Lyle stood up to me. This man was neither frightened nor intimidated. I don't know why that surprised me. He and I got into it, using each other as punching bags. And suddenly I was on the canvas.

He'd hit me so hard it didn't even hurt. I still don't remember either the punch or falling from it. But as I was lying there, the crowd cheering—hoping, I think, that I'd stay down—I thought about what the world would have to say about George Foreman now. This time I wasn't going to think about the crowd. There were no more excuses to give; no loose ropes to lie back on; nobody poisoning my water. Nothing. Nothing to blame but his fierce right hand.

Staring in my rearview mirror at Africa, I jumped up without waiting to clear my head, without waiting for Clancy or my other trainer, Kid Rapidez, to give the signal. And *boom!*, I got knocked down again. The crowd was in a feeding frenzy. I tasted blood. So did they, I guess.

As I sat on the canvas, I thought, *I'm going to die.* That's what I hadn't done in Africa—hadn't pushed myself to the breaking point. That's why I could barely stand myself now. I'd wake at night wondering, *Why didn't you die? If you did everything you could, why didn't Muhammad have to kill you to beat you?* That I hadn't given my all was what tormented me. I wouldn't repeat that mistake now. *Didn't you vow that you'd die before you get counted out again?*

As I jumped to my feet, my arms felt strong. I knocked Lyle down. He got up. I knocked him down again. He got up again.

The slugfest went on for four rounds. Both of us looked like we'd been in a knife fight. At the bells between rounds, it took both of us half the time just to stagger to our corners.

Eventually, Lyle just sank to the canvas, his will more than his senses knocked out of him. He realized that nothing short of a bullet between the eyes would stop me. If the fight continued, someone was going to have to die.

When the referee raised my hand in victory, I felt that I'd been redeemed. I was wrong about needing to win the championship again. Having proved I could get off the mat, the core that made me a whole man reappeared. Just the possibility that I really might have beaten the ten-count in Africa restored my dignity.

The win established me again as Big Bad George, at least with the sportswriters. After all, this was the type of brawl no one had seen since, well, maybe never. It wasn't about winning; it was about surviving. Just when you thought Lyle was going to win, George got up on wobbly knees. And just when you thought George had it, Lyle would get up, his knees also wobbling. What a sensational slugfest it turned out to be. Maybe it was my imagination, but I thought that my victory had also won me some hearts as well.

Next stop: Muhammad Ali. But Jerry Perenchio had other ideas. "The road to Ali," he said, "goes through Joe Frazier."

I wanted to get to the destination, all right. I just didn't consider Joe Frazier a scenic rest stop. No matter that I'd beaten him already. Fighting Joe again seemed a needless risk. Though he'd reached the advanced age of thirty-three, six years older than I, he was still Smokin' Joe, as he'd just proved a few months before to Ali in their third bout. Losing on a T.K.O. in the fourteenth round, he'd still showed his same pit-bull tenacity and cement fists.

"I'll fight other guys, because I know I have to," I told Jerry. "But not Frazier. And besides, what happened to that promise about getting me Ali if I beat Lyle?"

Jerry offered me $600,000 to fight Frazier. When I turned him down, he added a hundred grand.

"This isn't about money," I said. "I just don't want to be in the ring with that guy."

He upped the purse to $800,000. Still, "No."

Jerry had Joe Louis call me. "Joe," I said, "I know what you're going to say. And I respect you as much as anyone in the world. Maybe I need another tune-up or two before Ali—but not Joe Frazier."

"That's what Joe is for you, George," Joe Louis said in that foghorn voice, "a tune-up."

I was so complimented that Joe Louis thought Joe Frazier would be an easy fight for me, I decided to think over my decision a second time. While I was thinking, Jerry Perenchio called again. Before I could tell him that I'd changed my mind, he said,

"All right, this is my last offer—a million bucks, plus a percent-age of the closed circuit, to fight Joe Frazier."

"I know this is hard to believe," I said. "I'm gonna fight Frazier, but not for the money."

At the pre-fight press conference, Joe was in a playful mood. But I couldn't bring myself to play along. I became old doleful George, not cracking a joke or even a smile. A reporter asked about my attitude.

"I'm gonna teach that man a lesson," I said gruffly, without looking in Joe's direction.

I trained well and hard. I knew that Ali had said he planned to retire in three months, after fighting Ken Norton. But Gil Clancy and I both believed that if I beat Joe convincingly, he'd postpone retirement because of demand. Muhammad Ali wouldn't risk speculation that he was afraid to meet a renewed George Foreman.

No surprise, the majority of fans in New York's Nassau Coli-seum cheered for Joe, who showed up with his head shaved. And no surprise, they booed me. At the bell, Joe came out danc-ing. Eddie Futch, his manager, had prepared him well. The fight plan, evidently, was to take me into late rounds. They still thought George Foreman lacked stamina. Joe backed up and jabbed a lot; no sign of the Smokin' Joe left. He must have thought he was Muhammad Ali, because at the end of the first round he dared me to hit him. The crowd laughed. For them and for Joe, his lasting a round unscathed was a victory.

He made it through the second and the third rounds, too, though in the third I gave him a taste of things to come with a combination to the head, followed by an uppercut. At the end of the fourth, I missed badly on a hook and left myself open. Joe connected with a left that stung.

In the fifth, I caught him on the ropes with a shot that opened a cut over his eye and sent his mouthpiece flying. Then I threw another, and followed with a flurry of punches. Joe crumpled to the canvas. He was up at four but took the mandatory eight. Seconds later, I dropped him with a combination. Seconds after that, he dropped again, this time staying down till eight. He rose and stood on shaky legs. His eyes looked glassy and blood poured from the gash on his forehead. I'd really put it on him.

Leaning on the mat, Eddie Futch tried to attract the referee's attention. Before I could deliver what I knew would be the final blow, the ref saw Futch and signaled the end. As I stood over him, glaring, the crowd booed. I stared out defiantly at them, trying to enjoy their boos.

This was Joe Frazier's final night as a fighter. "I think it's time to put the gloves on the wall," he said afterward. Of his thirty-two career victories, twenty-seven had been by knockout. His four losses had been divided equally between Muhammad Ali and me.

My record now stood at one loss and forty-two wins—almost all of them by knockout. I'd showed the world that I was ready for Ali.

But Ali wasn't ready for me.

He beat Ken Norton, all right, but in a lackluster way. I knew, he knew, and everyone knew that he would have gotten whipped if it had been George Foreman in the ring with him that night.

"Foreman *is* the heavyweight division," *Sports Illustrated* declared soon after my fourth-round knockout of Dino Dennis, who'd won all of his twenty-nine previous bouts.

That fight had been promoted by Don King, whom I'd approached after Jerry Perenchio abruptly quit the boxing game—in part, I suspected, because he couldn't deliver Ali. But Don couldn't deliver him either. Even though I'd become top contender, and the guaranteed purse would have put him on Easy Street forever in an overstuffed leather chair, Ali saw that this George Foreman wouldn't be the dope he'd roped in Africa. I had to keep fighting and winning, hoping that eventually either the fans or the boxing federations would force him into a rematch.

Don King's plan was to showcase me on television, the Dennis bout being the first of three scheduled ABC telecasts. But ending the fight so early, I'd hardly given the network any time to sell beer or razors. The second fight, against Pedro Agosta in Pensacola, took the same amount of time. The third fight was to be in San Juan, Puerto Rico, against Jimmy Young. Young had recently fought Muhammad Ali. And in my opinion and the opinion of many, he'd won, even if the judges hadn't given him the decision. That's why our fight was set up, as an unofficial elimination bout, with the winner to get a rematch against Ali. Young was known best not for his knockout punch, but for putting together some wicked combinations. Beating him was a certainty; it just wouldn't be easy.

My new girlfriend's name was Andrea Skeete, though I thought of her more as an executive assistant and cook than as a lover. Her role was to do everything for me while I was in training. She even removed my shoes when I came in from running. After I beat Lyle and felt like a man again, I repaid her kindnesses with contempt. I figured I was on top and wouldn't need her so much. Then she told me she was pregnant.

Pregnant? Well, I was certainly leading the strangest of lives.

"Are you sure?"

"How sure do I have to be?"

We went to a doctor I knew. As we sat across from him, he asked me, "Do you want the baby?"

After we left his office Andrea told me, "That man didn't even think to ask me—didn't even look at me—and I'm the one who's having the baby," she said. "That isn't right."

Andrea, who was originally from the island of St. Lucia in the Caribbean, disappeared somewhere into San Francisco. I lost track of her until a paternity suit was filed on the unborn baby's behalf. I brought her to Houston for proper medical care. She gave birth to Freeda George in late 1976. (Freeda was the name of the girl who'd first stolen my heart as a young teenager. I never even kissed her. Though she wrote me a "Dear John" letter when I was in the Job Corps, I invited her to visit me after I won the Olympic gold medal. "We'll just talk," I said. "Oh, no," she said, "my fiancé is coming in town." That hurt like a knife to the heart. I told her, "You'll never have anyone love you like I loved you. But I'll never bother you again." That pain kick-started my season as a playboy.) Still willfully ignorant, I assumed that I would raise baby Freeda myself.

"I'm not giving you my child," Andrea declared. *"I'm* taking her."

To be with Freeda, I tried to make a go of it with Andrea again, but we couldn't find a single brick on which to build a relationship.

Other women looked after me. One of them was Charlotte Gross, a country girl from a good family in Jefferson, Texas. She did her job well and best of all had a boyfriend.

"You'd better stop trying to get so close with these girls," Mr. Moore had said. "Maybe if you find one who has a boyfriend, she won't go crazy and think that you've got to marry her. And you won't get sued."

Charlotte took good care of me, and when Michi and Little George came to be with me, she cared well and lovingly for them, too. Sometimes I sent her to check on Andrea.

"Maybe," I said, "Andrea will give me Freeda if you show her that you'll help me look after her." It wasn't a well-conceived idea, and didn't work. Still, things were beginning to go better. Until, of course, Charlotte called to say she was pregnant.

"What do you expect me to do about it?" I asked. "Why are you telling *me*?"

"Because it's your baby."

We'd slept together here and there.

"Who says it's mine?"

"Look, I know whose baby I'm having."

I'd never seen Charlotte so upset.

"I don't know why you're telling me," I said. "Where's your boyfriend?" Now I wondered whether there really was one.

"I don't know," she said. "What am I going to do?"

"Well, I guess you're having a baby." I slammed down the receiver. Tough guy.

Then it struck me what the doctor I'd taken Andrea to was really talking about—abortion.

I phoned Charlotte back in a hurry and changed my tone. "Oh, I didn't mean what I was saying. I'll do anything for you.

Whatever you want. What do you want to do? What do you need, money?"

"No," she said, "I just wanted you to know I was pregnant."

"Well I'll take care of everything. I'll do everything for you."

"No, you're not doing anything. I just wanted you to know that it's your child."

Obviously, I'd stepped in it again. *Man, what is happening to your life?* It was one thing to be foolish, and another for all that foolishness to bring forth babies.

Knowing I was soon to have another child, I went to Marshall to train for the Agosta fight. Mom came to care for my household needs. Mr. Moore had taken sick with brain cancer, and for understandable reasons, Mom was the only person left I really trusted. I slept in the back bedroom and let her use mine. Everyone who had my phone number knew not to call after dark, because during training I went to bed early and rose early. If someone did happen to call, Mom tried to snatch the receiver immediately.

One night I heard half a ring, then went back to sleep; I never heard who called.

After the fight, I returned to Houston and inquired about my Aunt Clara, Mom's sister who'd been ill. "She's all right now," Mom said. Then she changed the subject.

When I went to visit Mom's sister L.C., I said, "I've got to see Clara."

She said, "Clara's dead."

"Why didn't anybody tell me?"

"Nancy said she didn't want you bothered."

Mom had laid down the law to everybody, brothers and sisters, aunts and uncles, not to tell me about Clara's passing away until after the fight. "If you go down there," she'd said, "let him go about his business. He's preparing to box. He doesn't need anything on him."

So I'd missed the funeral and memorial service; the chance to say good-bye to my beloved aunt. Disgusted, I tried to walk it off outside. I hadn't intended to be protected from something like that. *No one's that important.*

When I went back to Marshall to train for Jimmy Young, Mom again accompanied me. At two A.M. one night, the phone rang. Mom picked it up on the first ring. This time I listened in; I had to know who had the nerve to call at that hour. My sister Mary Alice.

She was calling from a hospital in Houston, crying. "But the doctors said that he's in a coma." This was her five-year-old son, whom she'd named George—George Edward Dumas—two years before I had my first child. I thought of this boy, my nephew, as one of my own. Mary Alice had rushed him to the hospital after he suffered a seizure. "He can't move," I heard her tell Mom. "And they said that even if he does come out of the coma, he'll never be able to walk or speak."

I replaced the phone gently in the cradle so they wouldn't know I'd heard, and got back in bed. *I didn't hear that. I didn't hear that.* Then I jumped out of bed and ran into Mom's room.

"You tell them that I'm George Foreman, former heavyweight champ of the world," I yelled. "You tell them to fly in the best doctors in the world. I'll pay for it."

"Son," she said, "they've got the best doctors. They're doing all they can do now."

I grabbed the phone from her hand. "You tell them who I am," I told my sister. "I don't want them playing with this kid. You help him."

I went back to my room thinking how unfair it was that this boy's life was becoming a tragedy, and that all my money wouldn't buy a different outcome. Before getting into bed, I instinctively got down on my knees and prayed aloud.

"If there's really a God," I said, "why mess with this boy's life? Please don't. He hasn't traveled. He hasn't gotten to do anything yet. Leave him. Please."

I jumped into bed. *Uh-uh, this doesn't feel right.* Then back on my knees.

"Okay," I said. "If you really are God, and if you really are up there like they say, I'll make you a deal. You save this boy's life, I'll give up all my money. Just give it all away to charity."

Back into bed. And back out.

"Okay. If you really are the really true, real God, the one people say helps people who need help, if you're really up there, I'll give up boxing. I'm through with it. You can have my money and my boxing. Just save this little boy. If you're God, you can do that."

Under the covers, eyes closed. *Uh-uh*. On the floor. Crying.

"Okay," I said, "take *my* life instead. Let that boy live. I'll die instead of him."

This time I fell asleep immediately.

Next morning I called my sister. She said she saw George's feet move. "Are you kidding?" I said. "Great."

"Yeah," she said, "but they say he'll never speak."

She called the following day. She said she'd told George, "If you can hear this, blink your eyes." He did.

And a day later, he spoke.

When he came home from the hospital, he kept saying, "I gotta go see my daddy."

"What do you mean your daddy?" she asked.

"George Foreman's my daddy."

Today, George Dumas is bigger than I am. And he can talk the ears off a chocolate bunny.

In the middle of March 1977, a few nights before my fight against Jimmy Young, I stood on the balcony of my San Juan hotel, staring out at the lights of Puerto Rico and reflecting on the journey I'd taken since leaving Fifth Ward. I thought of my fourth child, soon to be born to a fourth woman; yet I still didn't have my own family. A rung or two from returning to the top of the ladder I'd been climbing all my life, I wondered why I felt so little pleasure. When would I stop to admire the view? The Lyle win had restored my sense of manhood, but that same old emptiness had survived all my victories and accomplishments. Now I knew it would survive my win against Jimmy Young, and the one against Ali as well. For whatever reason, I began a prayer to a being I wasn't even sure existed. "God," I said, "maybe you can take my life and use it. Maybe you can use me as something more than a boxer."

Next day, Don King took me aside. "Listen to me, George. The networks love you, baby, but hey, you're knocking these guys out too quick. They can't make any money. You gotta let them go a few rounds, sell a few more commercials."

I was flattered that Don King believed I could determine how long each fight lasted. Maybe he was blinded by dollar signs. He knew the World Boxing Association planned to strip Ali of his title if he refused to meet me after I beat Young. And since this was to be the final fight in my ABC contract, all three networks would be bidding to broadcast Ali-Foreman II on a delayed basis. So, between the network licensing and the pay-per-view revenues, my purse for that fight, he said, might reach ten million dollars—"If you play it smart." Meaning, I shouldn't knock out Young so early.

Jimmy Young and I fought in Robert Clemente Stadium, an arena named for the great Pittsburgh Pirates star who was a hero on the field and off. It saddened me to be booed. But for the first time, I think I understood why they were doing it. I wasn't the humanitarian Clemente had been; I wasn't acting like a hero.

The thick, stifling air of a Puerto Rican jungle permeated the stadium, dressing rooms included. Sweat poured from me as if I'd already finished the bout. Where all that moisture came from, I don't know. I'd gone two days without water.

One dry day had been proper in the world according to Sadler. But this was the new world according to George; two dry days would be a hundred percent better.

In my corner awaiting the opening bell, I looked at the sellout crowd and remembered Don King's last-minute words: "You've got a full house, George, and the ratings are going to be great. Don't try to knock him out too early."

I didn't. I toyed with him, jabbing casually. I eased him in and out of the ropes. And when I finally hurt him in the third round, I heard Charley Shipes yell, "Now, champ, now. Do it now." As much as I wanted to, I wouldn't; it was still too early. (Years later, Charley told me that he thought I was throwing the fight.) Letting him off the hook that way increased Young's confidence. He believed he was still standing because of his skill. He began bobbing and weaving with increased confidence. But he had none of Ali's style. He ran, he stuck his head out of the ropes, he held me the way wrestlers do.

Midway through the fight, I glanced around the ringside seats, as I always did, hoping to find Mr. Moore. When I remembered that he was gone now, dead of cancer, grief suddenly filled me again. I had to put the pain aside to continue the fight.

Like every boxer who'd seen my fight in Zaire, Jimmy Young intended to test my staying power by taking me into late rounds. And the longer the fight went on, the more it looked like it was going to be a long night. The stadium heat was getting to me. Still, I'd trained well and felt confident that time was on my side.

In the seventh, I landed a shot high on his head. His knees buckled. I thought he was going down. But instead of delivering the crowning blow, I wondered whether Don King would be satisfied with a seven-round bout. In those seconds of indecision, Young's wits returned, and he ran for his life. (Years later, Young told *Sports Illustrated* that the punch had put him out cold for a moment. "I was asking God to help my soul," he said. "All he had to do was push me with his little finger.") I pursued him without success during the two remaining minutes of the round. At the bell, feeling that he'd outlasted my worst punishment, he threw up his hands in victory. That incited the crowd to stand and chant: "Jee-me Young, Jee-me Young . . ."

The consummate finisher, I'd missed another chance to finish the job. And, unlike the first missed chance, this one didn't come again. I felt drained and weak. My trying to knock him out became an exercise in futility. Sensing that, he fought more aggressively.

By the eleventh round, I couldn't be sure anymore that I was ahead on points. In the twelfth, I swung a desperate right uppercut. He countered with a wild shot. Because I was chasing him, it caught me with a kind of power he didn't otherwise have. It turned me around and dropped me to one knee. He was more surprised than I was. Up at the count of one, I immediately resumed my chase of him, then spent the last ninety seconds hoping that one of my punches would take the decision out of the judges' hands. At the final bell, I believed in my heart of hearts that I'd won the fight, yet knew with as much certainty that they'd already decided against me.

I stayed to hear confirmation of the judges' decision, then hurried to my dressing room as Gil Clancy told me I'd been robbed. Though defeated, I felt none of the shame or hurt of the fight in Zaire. I'd given my best and, for the first time, gone the distance.

The dressing room was the usual postfight scene, with managers, trainers, assistants, and stadium officials milling around. Thinking of how racehorses are walked around the track to cool them down after racing, I paced back and forth. Never in my life had I been so hot.

"Man," I said, "where's the window around here?" Somebody cracked the transom, but to no good effect. Not even the hint of a breeze blew in. Out of panic, I started to pace faster.

Maybe it was the heat that made my thoughts come in such a rush. *All right, George. You don't have to worry about this fight anymore. You can retire if you want. You can do television and movies. You just signed a contract with ABC to comment on fights. You're still the world-famous George Foreman. You can always find something to do. And if you don't want to do anything, you don't have to. You've got that fine ranch to live in, and your other houses. You've got money to travel. You've got everything you want. You can retire and die.*

Die?!

How did that get in there? You're not dying. You're not going anywhere. You've got everything to live for—cars, money, houses, safety-deposit boxes; things hidden away nobody knows about. You don't have to worry about boxing anymore. If you want to, you can go home and retire and . . . die.

That word again. I didn't understand where it came from or why. In no way was I considering suicide. In fact, I felt more excited about living than ever. But no matter how hard I focused on positives, my thinking was dominated by death. My pacing back and forth was no longer about cooling down; it was about staying alive. Walking soon escalated into calisthenics, and while the deep knee bends and jumping jacks didn't change my perspective, they did raise eyebrows. Mine would have been raised, too, if I'd seen a fighter do this after twelve brutal rounds. I didn't dare share my reasons with them, nor my thoughts.

My internal struggle went on for—well, I'm not sure whether it was seconds or hours. I considered confiding in someone until I realized that he'd have mistaken my admission for depression. I was fighting for my life, and at that moment understood for the first time how precious life really is.

You've heard of athletes dying after fights. Yeah, but not me, I'm not going to die.

Then a voice interrupted my thoughts. Though it came from inside my head, it definitely wasn't my own: *You believe in God. So why are you scared to die?*

Who was that? I, George Foreman, didn't really, honestly, truly believe in God. No one had thought less of religious people than I had. My own voice would have known that about me. Unless of course it was referring to my prayers on the San Juan balcony and at my Marshall bedside. Oh, and there was also that time in Reverend Schuller's church, when I was trying to be liked. But none of those counted as proof of devotion. None of my prayers had ever counted. They had been pretend prayers, for effect only.

Still, the voice insisted: *If you believe in God, then why are you afraid to die?*

I blotted out the words with another recitation of what I had to live for. *I'm still George Foreman. I can still box. I can still give money to charity. And for cancer.* (I'd recently given ten thousand dollars to the American Cancer Society in the name of Dr. Anderson, the man who'd delivered me, who was suffering with the disease.)

As if offended, the voice grew urgent: *I don't want your money, I want* you!

Now I believed I really was dying. The invincibility I'd always felt had been an illusion. Life can end as quickly as a smile.

From somewhere came my own voice, "God, I believe in you—but not enough to die." To this day I don't know whether I said the words aloud or just heard them in my head.

As I fell to the floor of my dressing room, my leg crumpling beneath me, my nostrils filled with the stink of infection. I recognized it instantly as the smell of absolute despair and hopeless-ness.

Then I felt myself transported to a far-off place, to an enor-mous void, to the bottom of the bottom of the bottom. This was the literal idea of nowhere—not someplace you talked about as nowhere, not even a place you could imagine unless you'd been there; but the real nowhere, the place where hope doesn't exist. All I could see was nothing. Nothing but nothing. Over my head and under my feet—just nothing.

A sledgehammer of crushing sadness—the most desperate sad-ness squared—stopped my breathing at the realization that all the cars, houses, and money for which I'd worked counted for nothing in this nowhere place. They were like ashes that crum-ble from burned paper when you touch it. When I looked back, I saw it all crumbling behind me. What counted was that I was going to die, and I hadn't told the people I loved how much they'd meant to me. Did I even know? I'd taken them for granted—Mom, my children. I'd not said good-bye. I'd not held them. I'd exchanged harsh words. I'd ignored them. I'd ex-pressed my love mostly through gifts.

One after another, at light speed, my regrets whizzed passed. As they did, the sadness continued to squeeze the life from me. *I'm dead. This is death. This is what it's like to die.*

I said, "I don't care if this *is* death. I still believe there's a God." I had nothing else to lose; this was my last punch. It was as if I'd already died. And I didn't care anymore.

At that, a giant hand lifted and carried me out of that nothing-ness. Suddenly, feeling blood flowing through my veins again, I was back in the dressing room, lying on the training table. They must have carried me over after my leg crumpled. I looked up at the circle of faces surrounding me—my brothers Roy and Sonny, Gil Clancy, Charley Shipes, my bodyguard Lamar, and my mas-seur, Perry Fuller, who was crying.

"Hey, I'm dying," I said cheerfully. "But tell everybody I'm dying for God." That great hand had rescued me from a horrible place. I was going to trust it now. I wasn't scared.

They all humored me: "That's all right, George." "You're

going to be fine, George." "Don't worry, George." And then: "You're a man, champ. You can get another fight."

As I lay on that dressing room table, I suddenly felt something sucking me from one place to another. In each place, I became a different person, speaking his language, feeling what he felt, worshiping his religion—living his life. And just as soon as I became comfortable somewhere, I'd get sucked somewhere else. The journey seemed to last a long time, but it probably all happened in a single moment.

For some reason, I yelled, "I don't care where you take me. I'm George Foreman. I just lost a boxing match. I'm in this dressing room. I don't want to be anybody else. I'm who I want to be. I'm George Foreman. I lost the fight. I don't care where you take me. That's all I'm ever going to be. And I'm never going to forget that."

That's when I stopped moving here to there.

Keith West, the doctor who traveled with me, grabbed my head. "Hey, Dr. West," I said, "move your hands, because the thorns on his head are making him bleed." What I saw was blood pouring out of my forehead. And it wasn't from the boxing match.

He didn't say a word. He just smiled wearily.

"Hey, Mr. Fuller," I said, "move your hands. He's bleeding where they crucified him." I saw blood on my hands.

"You're all right, George," he said, tears streaming down his face. Everyone had such pity for me.

"Hey, Jesus Christ is coming alive in me," I yelled.

They humored me some more: "It's okay, George. You'll win another fight. Don't worry."

"I'm not talking about boxing," I said. "Jesus Christ is coming alive in me."

Then Roy came over. I think he was playing around. "Yeah, George," he said, "but you're not clean enough."

"I have to get myself clean," I said.

Pushing them away, I aimed for the shower. Someone called out not to let me in because there was no hot water and the cold water might send me into shock. Everyone grabbed a limb and held on. Before someone got hurt, Dr. West ordered them to let go.

Standing in the water I shouted, "Hallelujah, I'm clean. Hallelujah, I've been born again." Afterward, I didn't towel off. That's when something took possession of me. I felt it below my stomach; I couldn't even control my breathing. I began reciting passages of the Bible I didn't know I knew, and running my mouth. Then I told everyone how much I loved them.

I grabbed Gil Clancy. "Come here," I said. "You're an Irishman, and I love you. You're my brother." I kissed him on the mouth.

"Come here, Mr. Fuller," I said, kissing him on the mouth, too. "I love you."

One by one I did the same to every man in the room. When I got to Sonny, he refused. But I wouldn't accept that. We struggled until Mr. Fuller ordered, "Just do it, Sonny. The man's losing his mind."

They must have figured that my next move was outside, where there were a few thousand people to kiss. That, they couldn't permit, if for no other reason than that I was still naked. I must have understood; I let them lead me to the training table. I lay down.

Then came the voice again: *I come to my brothers, and they don't believe me. I come to my friends, they don't understand me. So now I go to my father in heaven.*

I started to yell again: "Don't let Jesus go. Don't let Jesus go." A loving farewell from the other side. At that moment I was utterly at peace. I'd achieved all the greatness I'd aspired to. I was everything I'd ever wanted to be. The feeling that rocked me was the one I'd never experienced as the world champ. I finally had it all: fulfillment, peace, contentment. And the voice said, *Now, I go.*

And just like that, it went. I reached out to grab my experience, but it was like trying to recall a spectacular dream that recedes with every waking second.

Looking up at all those faces I'd just kissed, I was the most embarrassed man on Earth. Now, suddenly, I was an old boxer, naked and wet, who couldn't explain what had just happened.

All I could do was pray and hope that all these witnesses would soon forget what they'd witnessed.

My next memory is of lying in an intensive-care hospital bed, watching the bottle dripping liquid into my veins and a machine monitoring my heartbeat. *As long as that machine keeps beeping, then I'm alive.*

The doctors couldn't find anything wrong with me. One of them said I *might* have been slightly dehydrated. Another gave a highly technical explanation: "Well," he said, "you got your bell rung."

Gil Clancy came to visit the next day. "The media's outside," he said. He tried to pretend that he wasn't embarrassed for me. "I told them you had heat prostration. That's what you tell them, too, when they come in."

Heat prostration? "I've never used those words in my life," I said. "I can't even say them. Tell me again."

"Heat prostration."

"Heat prostration, heat prostration, heat prostration, heat prostration," I said. "All right, send them in while I can still remember."

"Heat prostration!" I yelled, the moment the first reporter entered.

"What's that?" he asked.

"It's—"

Gil filled in the blank.

Lying on my back for two days, I didn't relive the fight. Nor did I retrace the steps that had brought me, at age twenty-eight, to this Puerto Rican hospital. Instead, I concentrated on my desire to go home and see my mother and children. I'd been given the gift of a second chance. Closing my eyes, in my mind I held each of them tight. I had to make them know that I loved them, in case they didn't see me tomorrow.

Chapter Seven

I WENT BACK to Houston and hugged my mother as if it were my last chance to hold her. "What is this?" Mom asked. "George is in *my* house?"

After the Ali fight, Mom had briefly lived in my huge new home in Houston. When she finished furnishing it, I'd told her to hit the road. I wanted to bring in women without her looking funny at me, or them at her. Now, without family or love, my house felt empty. I preferred Mom's. I needed her presence. At her home, even when she wasn't in the room her presence was, so I stayed there.

I sent for my three children and couldn't stop hugging them. The words sprang from my heart to my mouth: "I love you, I love you, I love you, I love you." I was trying to compensate for the twenty-eight years of silence and anger. My eldest, Michi, wondered aloud why Daddy was all of a sudden so cuddly. I laughed, remembering that at any moment I might be whisked away once more to that awful place of nothingness. Never again, I thought, would I imagine that I had a firm grip on life; never would I forget life's fragility. *Death could happen at any minute.* I didn't want to regret missed opportunities. No longer could I pretend that presents and toys were a substitute for loving my family in a way they could feel.

During the three weeks at Mom's house, I tried to explain to a stream of visitors bits and pieces of what had happened in Puerto Rico. Still sorting it out myself, I had more questions than answers. My ignorance of church and religion was total. I'd never heard the term "born again," so I couldn't relate my experience to anyone else. Education was to come slowly. Mom neither asked nor was told. All she knew was whatever she overheard while coming and going. She saw that I'd left home a confident brute and returned contrite—and that now I needed her love. Plus, I was wolfing down her cooking.

"Maybe God is trying to tell you something," my sister Gloria said. Handing me her Bible, she suggested I read the Book of Revelations. I did, and when she said to read more, I read more. Unsure what the verses meant, I phoned the only preacher I knew well: Fat Daddy, in Oakland. His advice on marriage and lovers had been awful, but whether or not I wanted religion, religion wanted me. And I needed advice. I didn't know then that there are good preachers and bad preachers the same way there are good doctors and bad doctors. "Why're you calling me, George?" he asked. I told him my story and he said only, "Mmm-mmm-mmm. Isn't that something. Man, it's like you're really coming home." End of conversation.

Bewildered, I called the Reverend Schuller, at whose church in Garden Grove I'd spoken two years before. "I believe you," he said. "And listen, I want you to come to my congregation next Sunday. Just say what happened." I resisted until he said, "Be encouraged. This won't hurt you. Everyone needs to know this."

I flew to Los Angeles and told three thousand worshipers at the Garden Grove Community Church what had happened to me in Puerto Rico. That they were all believers helped me overcome my embarrassment. "I was dead," I said. "And all of a sudden I came alive again. I couldn't control what I was saying. I shouted, 'Jesus Christ is coming alive in me.' " They applauded every time I mentioned Jesus.

After church, Reverend Schuller's son listed some Scripture verses he thought would be appropriate for me to read. But I didn't yet own my own Bible. As soon as I got back to my hotel room in Los Angeles, I asked my cousin Dorothy's husband, John Fowlkes, to buy me one. When he wanted to know what kind, I said, "Call your mother in Alabama. Find out what she's got and get me the same." It was the King James version.

Two weeks later, while reading the newspaper, I spotted an ad for Dr. Schuller's *Hour of Power* television show. "Listen to George Foreman's testimony how he found Jesus Christ," it said. What flashed in my mind was the memory of those two girls, laughing about that baseball player who'd been born again. *Now people will be saying that stuff and laughing about me.* I was hurt and angry. I hadn't known that cameras were taping me. "Everyone needs to know this," Dr. Schuller had told me. Well, I didn't think so. Embarrassed, I decided to go home and stay home; not to leave my house. I dropped completely out of circulation. Nobody could reach me. Through another friend I announced that I'd quit boxing. Then I wrote a letter to ABC, resigning my new contract as color commentator alongside Howard Cosell. Some of that was my discomfort at being seen in public after my exposure on the television show, which was reported in the news. Mostly I believed that boxing no longer held a place in my life. Boxing had been a funnel for my hatred. To knock a guy out, I needed to psych myself into a state of viciousness. But that George Foreman didn't exist anymore.

I proved that after Sonny went to pick up some of my animals at the ranch in Livermore and drive them to the ranch in Marshall. Upon arriving in Livermore, he discovered something startling: every possession in both the main house and the guest house was missing, from wallpaper to carpeting, including irreplaceable trophies and a lifetime of memorabilia. As it turned out, the property's caretaker, an elderly retired police officer, had placed an ad in a newspaper: "George Foreman Estate Auction." People had come from hundreds of miles.

Worse, I discovered that Leroy Jackson had somehow managed to sell the property without my knowledge. The proceeds were actually in escrow, and the closing was to be in a few weeks. This was the same Leroy Jackson whom I'd lifted out of the Job Corps to work for me; the same Leroy Jackson who, six months before, had conspired with a banker in Oakland and stolen half a million dollars from my bank account. I'd had to hire an attorney to get that money back.

I didn't stop the ranch sale, because I knew I'd probably be leaving that house soon anyway. I just accepted the proceeds. As for the caretaker, I refused to pursue him.

It was when I went to San Francisco to give a deposition on the house sale that I knew anger had left my life. Standing in the hallway waiting my turn, I saw Leroy. Seeing me, he froze in terror. The George Foreman he'd worked with for seven or eight years would have pulverized him. He didn't know that that George Foreman had died in Puerto Rico. The fear on his face made me ashamed of myself. I reached for him and gave him a bear hug. "Hey, Leroy," I said. "I'm so glad to see you, man."

He didn't utter a word until he called me at my hotel that afternoon. "I thought you were going to kill me," he said.

"I'm sorry you felt that way," I replied. "I don't do that anymore."

The emotion of anger was no longer in my computer programming. This was nothing like being hungry and forcing yourself not to eat. The anger just wasn't there.

I went to Marshall and walked through my home gym, where the punching bag had always assumed the face of my next opponent. I used to beat that bag until the man died. Now the bag looked only like a bag, not a faceless opponent.

One night when I was back at Mom's house, Gloria invited a young couple over. At her urging, I retold my story. This was the first time Mom had heard it from beginning to end. She listened and said nothing.

When I finished, the couple took turns relating the Bible story about Paul's vision on the road to Damascus, and about Cornelius, who saw an angel.

"That's it," I said. "That's it. That's what happened to me. Is that really in the Bible?" They showed me where. "Wow." *I've had a Biblical experience.*

"Brother George," they said, "the Lord's giving you a calling. He's wanting you to work with Him."

They explained about God this and God that. And the longer they went on, the more they sounded like fanatics, the kind I'd always made fun of and hoped never to become. The difference this time was that the words went straight to my own experience. "This is real," I exclaimed.

"It's real," they said.

They sang some hymns and invited me to stop by their church. But I was still timid, still getting acquainted with the new George Foreman. Still self-conscious.

I left Mom's and moved back home. It was like a perpetual open house. People were always dropping by unannounced. One night, Shawn came over. She was a beautiful young woman I'd chased madly before going to Puerto Rico, but she'd never consented. After we visited a while, I excused myself to shower. As I was soaping up, in stepped Shawn—naked. In the past, that come-hither look she had would have made me happy; here was that chance I'd wanted. And now, nothing. She stared at me, and I at her. An awkward moment. I threw her a towel, then wrapped one around me and dried off.

Puzzled and embarrassed, Shawn asked what was wrong. This wasn't the George Foreman she'd known, the man who'd wanted her so voraciously just a few months before. In clumsy language, I explained that I'd discovered a measure of peace and intended to hold it. My instinct warned that such casual relationships disturbed the peace.

I told Shawn that I was getting dressed to go to a church I'd read about where the preacher was going to be discussing blood sacrifices. Thinking that his words would relate somehow to my experience in Puerto Rico, I'd asked my Aunt Leola if she knew where the church was. She'd said she'd prayed there before.

"Do you want to come with me?" I asked Shawn.

She stared at me for the longest moment. I don't know whether she was more incredulous at my question or her answer. "Okay," she said.

I put on my best suit and we climbed into my fancy Stutz Blackhawk—wire tire mounted on the rear, real gold inside, hand made. We must have passed the church a dozen times searching for the address. I'd had my eye open for a building that looked like a cathedral, not a 7-Eleven without neon. This was the Church of the Lord Jesus Christ. I stood at the door, afraid to enter. Inside all the pews were filled. I didn't want anyone to spot me. When we took seats at the rear, I turned my head to the far side of the room and saw the couple who had told me Bible stories in Mom's living room. The man returned the gaze and nodded knowingly. This was their church. I didn't know what to think. Had I been brought here by God?

During the service the preacher made me uncomfortable by directing his comments to me. He was looking into my eyes when he said, "If anyone would like to pray, come down to the altar." One by one, until a large crowd had assembled, people stood up, walked to the altar in front, and knelt in prayer. Praying aloud, their voices created a deafening racket. I figured no one could hear me anyway, and they were too lost in prayer to notice another body. Still, I was too afraid, too self-conscious, until I saw the preacher turn around and go down on his knees. When I decided he couldn't see me either is when I joined them. "God," I said, "I've got enough. I've really got enough. Maybe you should worry about someone else." Then, concerned that He wouldn't hear my voice above the din, I spoke louder. Others must have gotten the same idea, because soon everyone was shouting and no one's voice could be distinguished. I confessed to God my secret fears and doubts. Mostly, I asked for answers to my thousand questions. The most prominent was: "When are you going to snatch me out of this life again?" The next time, I believed, would be for eternity.

The more I prayed, the more passionate I became, the closer I got to the spirit that had filled me in the Puerto Rican dressing room. It bordered on ecstasy, and I prayed for it to last. I felt brave.

But that bravery vanished like a blown-out match when I returned to my seat. I began wondering if anyone had heard me. Convinced that they had, I left with no intention of coming back.

Lying awake that night and for several nights after, I decided that that feeling wanted to come into me. Question was, would I embrace it?

I visited church again the following week and joined the prayer at the altar. This time, nothing happened. Nor did it the following night or the one after that. I didn't mind hanging around, though, listening to the sermons and the group prayer and the Bible passages. I felt safe.

After three months, someone suggested that I attend Sunday services. I'd thought this was only a night church.

I convinced my cousin Linda Gayle to come with me. She'd been there before with her mother, my Aunt Leola, who also accompanied me from time to time.

Days, I sat home alone or visited Mom. And I began reading the Bible. I bought several more Bibles and studied them all. I made notes in the margins and after church discussed my thoughts with the preacher, L. R. Masters. When I told him about Puerto Rico, he said, "I believe you, Brother George." He pointed to passages in the Bible as scriptural confirmation of my experience.

Now I was Brother George and he was Brother Masters. The words came out of me with all the enthusiasm of a child who's first learning to read. "This Jesus Christ really lived," I said. "Jesus is really the Son of God. He really lives. God's son walked on this planet. I'm telling you."

He laughed; this was no big deal to him.

We'd stay up talking about God and the Bible until the early hours—when he'd fall asleep and I'd let myself out. Because he was so polite and accommodating, it never occurred to me that he worked a real job during the day. I could go home to kick back and sleep all day if I chose, as Mr. Moore and I used to do after talking all night. I missed Mr. Moore badly, and wondered often what he would think about my new passion. His warnings about religion still echoed in my ears. But those fears didn't matter anyway. How could religion damage a career that no longer existed?

One night Brother Masters and I got onto the subject of sex. I told him about my new practice of avoiding relationships with women outside of a sacred covenant. "That's just the feeling in me," I said defensively, thinking that he would offer the same line Fat Daddy had about not bringing "it" home. "I can't explain why."

"Well, I *can* explain it," he said. "What you're talking about is in the Bible." He pointed out the passages. *God's law.*

That scriptural verses affirmed what I'd begun to believe on my own drew me more deeply into the Bible. When I read, I kept a dictionary nearby so that I could be certain of nuances.

Soon I began having dreams and visions. The first vision came to me when I was at my mother's house, resting on her bed with my eyes closed. I saw myself carrying my favorite black and gold briefcase from Gucci. Then my brother-in-law Paul Dumas, Mary Alice's husband, appeared, wearing a suit and tie. People were heckling him, yelling, "Hey, Rev." A pained expression on his face, he said, "Brother George, when I got married, nobody understood why. But I got married because it came from within me." Then he and everyone else disappeared. I opened my eyes and was back in my mother's room.

The next day I described my vision for Brother Masters to interpret. He laughed gently, a laugh of recognition. "You're going to be a preacher," he said.

My brother-in-law Paul represented the apostle Paul, who was knocked down on the road to Damascus before becoming a preacher. My carrying the briefcase referred to my carrying the word of God. The marriage represented my marrying Jesus Christ. "People will laugh at you, too," he said, "but you should listen to your inner voice."

As time went by, my vision became fact. People did laugh at me; others avoided me. And some did both.

I'll never forget walking through Houston's Northland Mall shopping center. Across the way I saw my brother Sonny with his new fiancée and her mother. Sonny turned away, as though he hadn't seen me, even though our eyes had locked onto each other. This man who'd always been so proud of me, especially after I'd rescued him from alcoholism, was now embarrassed by me. Truly, I was the man with the briefcase, enduring the laughter.

. . .

Three months after my return from Puerto Rico, Charlotte gave birth in Houston to my darling baby Georgetta. I'd never seen a child with such a full head of hair. Cradling her in my arms, I felt whole and complete, blessed by God. On her left arm was a birthmark identical to the one on my left leg, a cream-colored blotch that looks something like Texas. Though she obviously couldn't understand, I repeated over and over how much I loved her.

Whatever her mother, Charlotte, needed or said she needed, I gave her or bought for her. After leaving the hospital, she stayed in my home for a few days to regain her strength, though I made it clear that I didn't want a girlfriend *or* a wife.

Charlotte was now my responsibility, but I had other responsibilities, too. Attending church and trying to live in God's way, I wanted to avoid the appearance of impropriety. People were bound to get the wrong idea, so I sent her and Georgetta to my house in Marshall.

After several weeks, when she seemed strong again, I said, "Well, now that you're up on your feet, I think it's time for you to seek out your own life." I offered to help her land a job, find a home, buy a car, even go back to school if she wanted.

My words grabbed her by surprise. She became upset and angry. Apparently, she had misinterpreted my being nice to her and my taking care of Georgetta as a kind of courtship.

"I'm not going to marry you," I said. "I'm not going to marry anyone."

With that, she stopped speaking to me, which only made visiting Georgetta more difficult. I didn't try to soothe Charlotte. I didn't try to change her. She had her own crosses to bear.

My life centered on my children and church. Michi, who was nearly five, flew down often from Minnesota. The more time she spent with me, the sadder she acted when she had to return home.

As often as possible, I gathered all my children together. These were my happiest days—buying clothes, doing their hair, cleaning up after them. When we went shopping, Michi would want to walk with the purse and decide what Little George, Freeda George, and Georgetta got to buy. Having stared at the head of

Leroy Moorehead in his coffin, I dreaded it every time when they returned to their mothers. Our days together were never enough, and I would almost fall apart when the door closed behind the last one out.

One day I got the idea that if I were married, I'd be entitled to have my children with me more often—maybe even permanently. Then, too, my new religious life begged for the stability and respect you get with a wife.

I'd met Cynthia Lewis some years before, when she'd just finished high school and her mother, whom I'd dated a little, called to ask for help getting her enrolled at U.S.C. Always trying to help out my friends, I ended up paying for her tuition there and buying her a car. One of her boyfriends was the football All-American Ricky Bell. Over the years she would come by to visit me whenever I was in Los Angeles, but she was just a little girl then.

Now, at twenty-one and about to graduate, she wasn't. When we became reacquainted, I told her about my religious conversion. To my surprise, she expressed curiosity, and declared that she too had been praying and reading the Bible. She seemed serious and sincere, an educated young woman on a right path. When she mentioned during a visit that she and her latest boyfriend had broken up, I made an executive decision.

"You know," I said, "I've really helped you in your life, maybe you can help me in mine."

"How?"

"Well, if we got married, maybe I could get my kids."

"Oh, George, I'll help you," she said. "I know what you're trying to do. I can be a mother to the children. And a wife to you." Then she sighed, and smiled with wet eyes. "That's what I always wanted, to marry you. There's never been anybody I loved but you."

Seek and ye shall find.

I'm sorry that this wasn't as romantic a moment for me as it was for Cynthia. But I'm sorrier that her feelings weren't closer to mine, because with her great expectations came great heartaches.

Cynthia and I were married at the courthouse in a ceremony that lasted almost as long as our marital peace.

My ex-wife, some cousins, the mothers of my children, and my own mother reacted poorly to the marriage. For years I'd been a wealthy single man, caretaker of his family, generous to everyone. My taking another wife looked to them like an end to that long run. And so the declaration: "She's a gold digger."

Our marriage was a live lobster in a big steam pot. Cynthia had believed that we were the stars of a movie: guy finds religion, is lost in the clouds, finds girl, and drifts back to earth better than ever. She expected me to be, once again, the great George Foreman she'd always known, the one she'd proudly brought her friends to meet as I taped television shows in Hollywood.

If Cynthia got less than she bargained for, so did I. My children seldom came to visit now, because they felt unwelcome in my wife's home. I sat alone for hours just reading the Bible, and rarely went anywhere. She wanted more.

I resisted the obvious emptiness of our marriage until the day she took Michi's picture out of our bedroom. "That's the past," she said. "Let's worry about our future." I insisted that she put the picture back. She refused.

"Look," I said, "we're not making it. This isn't going to work out. I'll get you back into school so you can pursue what you were doing and move on with your life."

We fought until she understood that my change was permanent and that I'd never again be the man she wished me to be. Staying in Marshall at the time, we talked for a week or two about how she would return to Houston, find a place to stay, and re-register for college. I promised to help her get back on her feet. When everything seemed finalized, I suggested taking her to the airport in Shreveport, Louisiana, which isn't too far from the ranch.

"Well," she said. "We don't really have to break up right now." She'd already once told me that she didn't believe in divorce.

"No," I said. "It's best this way. I don't want any more trouble—arguing and stuff." Shuddering at the memory of my own parents' bickering, I remembered that I'd said the same to Adrienne when she'd insisted on staying together.

In the car, Cynthia was quiet. "Are you sure?" she asked once. "I'm sure."

Suddenly she grabbed on to the steering wheel with both hands and fell to the floor. We were going about seventy-five miles an hour at the time. If I'd slammed on the brakes, the car would have gone out of control and we'd have run into a tree or turned over on a hill. While fighting her for the wheel I slowed the car gradually. "Please don't do this," I cried. "Please don't." When I finally regained control and she'd slumped in her seat, I said, "See? Do you see what's going to happen between us?"

"I see," she said. "I see." She began crying.

I saw her onto a plane and then drove home, planning to begin divorce proceedings as soon as possible.

While I remained in Marshall, I soon began hearing from the people I went to church with that Cynthia had a big belly and was claiming that I'd impregnated and abandoned her. Then, evidently, one of the little kids pulled up her shirt and discovered that she'd stuffed a pillow under there.

When it was time to go to court for the hearing on our dissolution of marriage, she showed up with her big belly and told the judge she was pregnant. I could only conclude that her hurt and disappointment were more powerful than her shame.

"She's not pregnant, Judge," I said. Not wanting to embarrass her, though, I didn't mention the pillow.

The judge must have known anyway; it didn't look very realistic. He ordered her to take a blood test, the results to determine his course of action.

When we returned in two weeks, the judge had the results in front of him. "Young lady," he said, "you're not pregnant." His voice didn't hint at any surprise, pity, or anger.

I said, "Judge, this woman's lying."

Then I stared at Cynthia. "How could you do that?" I asked.

She contorted her face into a look that said, "Who do you think *you* are?"

The judge dismissed the case, I gave her some money, and we went our separate ways. Eventually, we were granted a divorce.

. . .

When my brother Sonny pretended out of embarrassment not to recognize me that day at the mall, I realized that I was without company on a path I had to follow regardless of where it led. Even my family had grown tired of hearing me talk about heaven and Jesus Christ and salvation and Scripture. Their tolerance for my playing the same note over and over again frayed to the point that several of them asked me not to come around anymore.

In early 1978, I decided to shave my sideburns, mustache, and beard. I had a good reason. Naked and unadorned, my face became my own again, not Jim Brown's, nor any other hero's. To cut my hair, I bought a clipper from Sears that adjusts to any length. I didn't want to hang out anymore at barbershops, where there'd been a lot of uninformed gossip about why I'd stopped boxing and found religion. Anyway, the clippers were pretty foolproof technology. You inserted separators that allowed you to choose the length of hair you wanted; it wouldn't cut shorter than that. For months, that's how I kept myself groomed.

Later, I was in Marshall and giving myself a haircut, partly in preparation for seeing a girl who worked in an ice cream parlor I sometimes visited for a scoop or two. Being just me now, no longer playing a role, I was shy and uncertain how to respond to young women. So I at least wanted to look my best. But while cutting, the separator slipped and the clippers mowed an *S* around the top of my head. The only way to even it out was to cut all my hair off and let it grow back the same length. I began wearing ski caps when I went off the ranch and into town, especially to the ice cream parlor.

One day when I was ordering my cone, I saw the girl snickering. When she walked away, I wondered why. Then I climbed into my truck and knew why. *Good gracious! So that's why she was laughing.* There was my hat, lying on the seat.

All the way home, I felt the heat of humiliation in my cheeks. I knew I'd never go back to that shop again.

But while studying my head in the bathroom mirror, I suddenly asked myself why I was embarrassed. *Just because you don't have any hair? Man, you've worked all your life for wealth and fame.*

You can run for miles, lift weights with the strongest of men. You've found God. How can you run from something so stupid as embarrassment? Ashamed, I decided to confront my vanity. From now on, my head would be clean-shaven, a shining pate.

Another vision came to me one day in Houston, while I was visiting my Aunt L.C., Mom's youngest sister. I saw the apparition of an enormous, open book stretched out in her living room. On both facing pages was written "evangelistic 21." Never having seen that word, I didn't understand its meaning. When I told Aunt L.C., she said, "Isn't that something? Sometimes, son, the Bible's just kind of telling you something."

I thought about the vision for a long time before asking Reverend Masters about it during one of our nighttime conversations.

Pausing for a moment, he glanced up toward the ceiling. I could tell by his eyes darting back and forth that he was thinking. "That's a prophet's fast," he declared.

"A prophet's fast? What do you mean?"

"It means a twenty-one-day fast. It's a way to purify and concentrate the soul."

"I don't know what you're saying."

"Well, you go twenty-one days and twenty-one nights without food."

"That's impossible."

"Well, I once went forty days myself. Like Jesus and Moses."

Twenty-one days without food? Even a few hours without eating could bring me misery.

"If I were you," he said, "I'd drink water."

I told Masters's assistant pastor, W. R. Lumbart, what I was planning. "Brother George," he said, "I've been on fasts before. After about seven days your skin starts to dry up on you, and you get really jumpy, kind of nervous." He recommended a few practice fasts to get the hang of it before attempting such a long one first time out of the cannon.

"I'm gonna do it," I said. "Twenty-one days."

I began at home in Houston weighing about two hundred thirty pounds. After three days I gave myself permission to quit the following day; I wasn't sure I would make it even that far.

But after the fourth day I couldn't bring myself to pass food or liquid over my lips. On the fifth night I attended services and visited Reverend Masters. He handed me a glass of water and ordered me to drink. The water tasted cool and sweet on my tongue. But only when I was with him would I drink—just to let him know I was okay.

On the eleventh day, when I was down to about two hundred pounds and my jacket and shirt hung as if my shoulders were a clothesline, my mother said I was crazy. "How can you do this?" she yelled. "You're going to die." This was what the vision with the briefcase and people laughing had foretold.

After two weeks, my extraordinary dreams included Bible readings. I'd see a page obscured by shadows. Suddenly, a particular passage would be highlighted the way the light fell on Ingrid Bergman's eyes in *Casablanca*. Illuminated by this hidden spotlight would be a verse from, say, Corinthians about man not thinking better of himself than of God. It was at these moments that I began to fasten my life to the Bible. This experience was no fluke. This was now my reality.

By the seventeenth day I began to notice that all the world was composed of signs advertising food—milk, cheese, eggs, meat, fruits, fast food, fine food, turf and surf, daily specials, weekly specials, seasonal fruits, frozen desserts. A Big Mac and fries. The only way to stay on my fast was to hoard some food in anticipation of its end. At the supermarket I bought a cart full of groceries for that day to come.

I don't know how much I weighed on the twenty-first day. My best guess is one-ninety, though it may have been less. I woke up the twenty-second morning and rushed to disregard all previous advice for treating the fasting stomach with restraint. No bowl of oatmeal for me. I ate a regular egg breakfast, except twice as much. And I chased it with a drink that, since childhood, had made me gag me unless poured over cereal. I chugged a gallon of milk—and got hiccups that lasted a week.

For the next six months, no meal was complete without a cow's worth of milk. Then, just as suddenly as I'd loved it, I reverted to revulsion at its sight. What did remain, though, was an appreciation of food's beauty and importance. I've said grace, silently or aloud, before every meal since.

The fast erased my embarrassment over Dr. Schuller's television show and my brother's snub. I also understood that others knew now that I was the real thing, not some guy with religion temporarily under his fingernails. Masters came to me after the fast. "Brother George," he said, "why don't you tell the whole church your story about Puerto Rico?"

"I'm no preacher," I said.

"You don't have to preach, brother," he said. "Just tell them what happened, the way you told me."

When I said okay, he announced that the following week I would be giving my testimony. The church was full on that day. I started in a sputter, but the words came more easily as I went along, and as I went along the old feeling began to flow.

I testified again the week after, then the week after that, and on and on. And every time I told my story, the feeling returned. I couldn't have gone on otherwise. Without the feeling, I'd have been too ashamed to repeat myself. With it, mine was a story worth repeating. My performance didn't matter at all to me. I wasn't looking for greatness as a preacher. I'd already tasted greatness as a boxer. That's what I'd told God my first time praying in that church: "I've got enough."

About the middle of 1978, two fourteen-year-old boys befriended me at church. Nice kids—and poor. I'd take them out for cheeseburgers. We'd talk about God and the Bible. They loved it when I drove them home in my fancy cars. One time I brought them to the ranch in Marshall for a visit.

One of the boys, Dexter, said he wanted to go out in the street and preach. He pushed and taunted and dared me, but other than to tell my testimony, I was inhibited. By now I had a pretty good grasp of Scripture, so if I could get past the stage fright, I'd have something to say.

"All right," I declared, "We're going preaching." We bought a portable amplifier that connects to a hand-held microphone, and drove to Shreveport, stopping at several large apartment buildings in close proximity to each other, where there'd be plenty of ears within range. Dexter grabbed the microphone first and began pacing back and forth, stepping immediately into the role: "Well, praise the Lord, brothers and sisters. I'm not here to lift up me. I'm here tonight to lift up Jesus . . ."

He went on beautifully for fifteen minutes, but I couldn't concentrate on him all that well. I was next, and my hands dripped more sweat than before my first fight. *What am I going to say?*

"Well, praise the Lord, brothers and sisters," I said when my time came. "I'm not here to lift up me. I'm here tonight to lift up Jesus." Same as Dexter. Word for word, as best I could remember.

I was wearing a flannel shirt under some old overalls, and by then had gained back all the weight I'd lost on the fast and then some. There was just stubble atop my head and my face was clean-shaven—a big, happy face now, not a scowl. If you didn't know who I was, you wouldn't have known who I was—and you'd certainly never have guessed mean old George Foreman. Dexter wanted me to identify myself. I resisted. Boxing didn't impress me anymore. But when I ran out of words, I said, "Yeah, folks, that's right. You're looking at George Foreman here, former heavyweight champion of the world. Yes, I fought the great Muhammad Ali." Now people stopped. Someone ran and told some others, and the crowd got bigger. It was my gift, having that ammunition. How can you save souls if you don't have bodies?

"Is that George Foreman for real?" I heard someone say.

"Yeah," I said, "this is George Foreman in the flesh. God saved me. I was lost in sin, and now I'm saved."

One after another, people came down from the apartment buildings. Soon it became an almost biblical flow. "I can't believe it," they muttered. "I can't believe it."

For the twenty minutes that I talked about how God could help everyone find peace, I didn't care that the crowd was probably listening for curiosity's sake. At least they listened. And I was getting the feeling.

Next night, the boys and I drove to Tyler, Texas, and did the same. This time I began, "Yeah, this is George Foreman . . ."

We hit most towns in a reasonable radius, setting up shop near rows of apartments. Different places, same story: "Wow, I can't believe that's George Foreman." They gathered and listened, and I got the feeling. A force took over and guided the testimony from my heart. I heard the words as they came out, same as my listeners did.

News of the rookie evangelist spread quickly. Requests for my presence came from churches around America and Canada. I was invited to appear on Jim and Tammy Bakker's *PTL* and *The 700 Club*. Wherever I went, they'd have to turn people away. I was asked to join an evangelical mission to Africa, and I testified before sixty thousand people in Kinshasa, Zaire. This time, they cheered.

In late 1978, I was ordained as a minister by Brothers Masters and Lumbart at the Church of the Lord Jesus Christ. It was a lavish, laying-on-of-hands ceremony. I wouldn't have thought to do it if not for my visit a few months before to a hospital where I'd been invited to come and pray for a boy who'd been shot four times. In the past, despite being a lay clergyman, I'd had free run of Methodist Hospital in Houston, where heart surgeon Michael De Bakey had operated on Joe Louis and encouraged me to pray for his recovery. But at the hospital where the shot-up young man was fighting for his life, only ordained ministers with proof of their ordination were allowed. So I prayed for him at home, in church, and in the waiting room. (He pulled through.)

That refusal turned out to be a disguised blessing for me. Because once I became ordained, I was able to preach at other hospitals, too, and even prisons. The most memorable engagement was at San Quentin. Dozens of the hardest criminals formed a line that snaked out the door, waiting to be baptized in a small tub. I watched vicious men become as little children.

My own life had changed completely. Where once I'd had suits made to emphasize my athletic physique, I now bought clothes that hung straight, with comfort as the only criterion. I was embarrassed by anything that reminded me of my athletic past—or called attention to me. In the gas lines of the early 1970s, people had recognized my Rolls-Royce and sent me to the front for an immediate fill-up. Now I drove a Chevette, and in the gas crunch of 1979 had to wait my turn like everyone else. Before, when I shopped for anything, the clerks fell over themselves to assist me. Now they often ignored me. I was happy not being a celebrity, and began hating anything associated with fame and privilege. Though I could afford to, flying first class seemed wrong. I wanted to be an ordinary man. I was. And yet, people still went out of their way to treat me well. I remember a stewardess whispering to me as I was scrunched in my coach seat, "Hey, big guy. Let's put you up front. I won't be able to get you a meal, but I want you to be comfortable." It was an offer that was hard to refuse. Another time I left my headlights on in the car and the battery died. A cowboy drove up, pulled out his booster cables, and got me started. "How much do I owe you?" I asked. "Get out of here, big 'un," he said. Wherever I went, people wanted to take care of me, as though I were an infant. They called me "big boy," "big man," "big fella." Since leaving Puerto Rico, I'd become a block of fresh clay. The experiences of each day molded me into a man who saw the best side of humanity.

At the church in Houston, I always volunteered to help any-one, whether the need was replacement of a faulty water heater or repair of a creaky porch. And soon, my popularity at the pulpit rivaled that of Reverend Masters. "Brother George, are you going to speak tonight?" people would ask. This didn't sit well with him. I'd see him roll his eyes and comment out the side of his mouth. One night I brought some bongo drums to beat on. I wailed on them as the feeling flowed in me. "You know, Brother George," he said in front of the congregation. "The Bible speaks of all instruments." He named those he could think of and gave the citation. "But did you know there's one instrument that the Bible never speaks about? Drums." He paused a moment, in case I missed his meaning. "And did you ever notice in all those witchcraft dances, the people are beating drums? And when the Indians go on the warpath, they paint themselves and do what? Beat drums. So we're gonna stop beating those drums in here."

Brother Masters knew that I respected and admired him. Be-sides seeking his advice and counsel, I'd shared with him some of my visions in which he was dressed in white shirts, white signifying purity. But in the one vision I hadn't shared, I'd seen a trace of some old dingy longjohns under his shirt when he shook hands. My interpretation was that he had something up his sleeve. Of course, to my family, such a realization hardly required a gift of vision. "That man is a crook," they declared.

"I don't believe you," I said. "In all the world there is one righteous man. And this is a righteous man." I loved him anyway.

"Brother George," Brother Masters told me one day, "we're planning to build a bigger church." He described a larger version of the small church and explained that if I loaned them a hundred thousand dollars, they would pay me back a certain amount each month. He also asked me to donate fifteen grand for the air-conditioning system. I happily complied with both requests, and the church was remade.

One day I happened onto a confrontation between Masters and a young couple. He ordered the woman and her husband never to return to the church. "You've got to go," he said as the wife sobbed.

"Masters, you're wrong," the husband yelled. "You're wrong, you're wrong. I'm gonna tell the truth on you. You know you're wrong."

"Get out," Masters said. "Just get out of here."

I didn't need to ask what was going on. I figured these people must have been terribly wicked for Masters to excommunicate them.

Some weeks later, as I preached on a street corner, several members of the congregation gathered to wait for me. What was unusual was not their presence but their grim mood. It bothered me that they acted sad while I was trying to generate a little happiness.

When I finished, one of them explained their heavy hearts. "There's a rumor," he said, "that Brother Masters kissed one of the sisters. She says he drove her home one night, and when he thought no one was looking, he cut the lights off and kissed her, then drove away."

Impossible. A married man in his early fifties with two beautiful children, the Masters I knew would never violate the sanctity of either his marriage or family or that of a young woman. Surely he'd never subscribe to Fat Daddy's philosophy.

I confronted him about the rumor. "It's no rumor," he admitted. He seemed kind of pleased.

"Well," I said, "you were just saying good-bye. It was just a friendly good-bye." I wanted to give him an out. But he didn't want to take it.

"No," he said. "She needed kissing, and I kissed her."

Masters explained that the young woman in question reminded him somehow of his first wife. "She had the same spirit," he said.

He explained that she was single when he'd kissed her, and afterward she had gotten married in another church.

I was shattered. I'd invited people from everywhere to meet this "righteous" man, and had been personally responsible for reconstructing his church and bringing in more members.

Then it got worse. Fourteen-year-old Dexter, who had his ear to the church rails, said that the woman I'd seen Masters excommunicate with her husband was the one he'd kissed—which was why he'd sent them packing. Devoutly religious, they'd come that day to plead for acceptance because she'd gotten pregnant (by her husband) and felt she needed her church. "Masters told her that this was the devil's baby," Dexter said. "He told her if she wanted to come back, she'd have to have an abortion."

"You're lying, Dexter," I said.

"I told her she'd better not do that," Dexter said.

"You're lying."

"He's making her go get an abortion tomorrow."

I hurried to Masters.

"Brother George," he said, "if I don't know what's right, then nobody knows what's right."

Crying, I dropped to my knees before him. "Man, don't do that," I begged. "Please, please, don't do that. You mustn't." He ignored me as though he were deaf and blind.

I fled Houston for Los Angeles, where I stayed with my cousin Dorothy, Aunt Mary Lee's daughter. I bought half an hour a week on a local radio station and broadcast an evangelical show. I spoke at Christian schools and colleges all over California. I intended to stay for a long time, establishing my ministry. But after a month I had a dream about getting back to Houston. I woke up, jumped in my car, and drove all the way home. I went back to see Brother Masters.

"Brother George," Masters said, "I loved this woman. I always loved her." He began crying. The pressure on him had worsened.

How foolish I felt. How deceived. This man whom people like me would have followed into battle turned out to be ordinary. Out of jealousy, he'd forced a naive young woman into an abortion and run off her husband. And now he planned to leave his wife and make a play for her. Most amazing to me was that everyone in the congregation knew the truth about him—and didn't seem to care.

But Masters cared. Having been found out so nakedly, he now seemed close to a nervous breakdown. He could barely talk without crying.

"Man," I said, "you've got to get it together."

The next day I visited his wife. "You've got these two kids," I said. "It's your duty to patch things up for their sake. You can't just break up and leave."

"He doesn't want me anymore, Brother George," she said. "He doesn't want me."

"Oh, yes he does," I said. I didn't know for a fact that he did. But I believed that there was still goodness in him, and that he wouldn't want to throw away his marriage if it could be saved.

I went back to Masters and argued that he and his wife needed only a vacation to heal. "As long as I've known you," I said, "you've been talking about wanting to see those redwoods on the West Coast. Well, now's the time. You and your wife. You just go."

It took a little more work to get them into that car aimed northwest. Next day, the assistant pastor, Lumbart, led services for a full house. Everyone sensed that the pall had been lifted; there was a renewed spirit. I jumped up during a prayer and asked to speak.

"You probably read," I said, "about this fellow named Jim

Jones, how all these people followed this man to death. They came to his church to walk closer to God and Jesus Christ." Pause for effect. "The message is that, when someone's wrong, he's wrong. Leave people like that alone. Have nothing to do with them." Again I paused. "Masters is a bad man."

I continued on about his betrayal of God, and when I got through speaking every voice was dead quiet. I thought I'd reached them when a woman's voice rang out.

"Well, it's like this, Brother George," she began. "The church is hurting enough. We don't think you should be bringing that kind of stuff up anymore. We should just let that heal in peace."

"So you all just want to follow something like that?" I said. "Is that what you're telling me?"

"No, we're not saying that. But you are just plain wrong to even bring that up."

"That's a preacher's job, to tell people right and wrong."

Another woman joined in to take up the cause against me. Then another, and another and another. Soon there was a unanimous clamor: Forgive Masters—and forget me. They didn't want to hear the truth. And the truth was that I felt more hurt and more betrayed than they. So they just ran me off.

There was a moral to this experience. I learned that my biggest barrier as a preacher would be overcoming people's fear of changing the status quo. The parishioners may have felt miserable and cheated, but they didn't want anyone tampering with what they'd become accustomed to. I knew as I left that church that I was going to have a job ahead of me, telling the truth. But I'd resolved to tell it anyway; that's what God wanted from me. Having begun, I wouldn't turn back. It was like a massive tree that needed chopping down on my ranch. When that first woodchip flew from the first lick of my ax, that tree was as good as down. I didn't care how long it took; I never got discouraged, I never panicked, I never grew impatient. I choppd all day, went to bed at night, and returned every day until the job was done. So when I walked out of that church, I decided that I was going to keep whacking away at people's resistance to the truth, and eventually that, too, would fall.

I went to a Houston radio station and bought thirty minutes a week for my preaching. Except for family, that was to be my only contact with Houston. The other six days I lived in Marshall. Then some of the people I'd invited to join Masters's church asked me to pray with them.

First there were two of us; then three; five; nine. Eventually they asked, "Can we have church services in your home?"

Yes, absolutely.

As the groups got bigger, I had to keep borrowing larger homes. Eventually I sold a tractor for twenty-five thousand dollars and used the proceeds to buy a small lot on which an old, dilapidated building barely stood. We renovated it, wooden floors to roof—a communal effort, which made praying in it all the more meaningful. Alongside the building, I erected my revival tent that I'd bought with the intention of traveling around the country like the old-timers.

I loved to preach, and the more I did it, the more I loved it. There's nothing greater than to stand up there and tell the truth. Five people or five hundred—I gave them everything I had. The good feeling swelled my chest; the words spoke themselves. I talked a lot about boxing, how it meant nothing to me now compared to the Lord. I figured that was something they could see in me and know was true.

"I'll die before I get in the ring again," I said. "You take all of Kennedy's money, and all of Rockefeller's money, and you put that together—it wouldn't come to a down payment on my getting back in the ring. I'll die before I pick it up again." (I was speaking from experience. Several months after my retirement, Muhammad Ali had begun calling me, begging me to come back and fight Ken Norton. "They want me to fight him, but I can't beat him," he'd said. "You can, George." He'd offered me full use of his training facilities and another shot at him and the title if I agreed. "I'm not a boxer anymore," I'd told him. "I've given my life to God.") Everything I shared with my congregation had to do with the ecstasy I felt in God.

Chapter Eight

IT WAS MAGIC SEEING my own congregation grow larger every week. Life now, aside from my children and family, was about maintaining and expanding the church, and becoming the kind of preacher who deserved such wonderful company. Being the main man is different from being the pinch-hitter or special guest preacher. Leading the prayers day in and day out means sharing your profound insights into the Bible, which means, first of all, having profound insights to share.

I prayed to have them, and in a vision the Good Lord asked what I wanted. "Wisdom," I said. "And a wife." The wisdom to pass on to my congregants; a wife, because I thought a proper preacher was supposed to have one.

When my hours of memorization and thinking produced sermons with the same messages Masters had preached, I figured the wisdom God promised me was the same wisdom He'd given Masters. Then one day I realized that it was the voice of Masters I'd been hearing in my mind's ear as I read the Bible. It was his rhythm—and so his interpretation. Now I rediscovered the words I'd repeated a hundred times each. They jumped off the page at me. I read them with new eyes and understood them as I believed they were intended. What I did differently was to follow the punctuation precisely. Where Masters and other preachers selected phrases out of context, I read them as written—that is, with all the periods, commas, semicolons, and colons in place. And they made all the difference in meaning.

I also found that Masters had occasionally changed the text to suit his purposes, such as when he turned the phrase from First Corinthians, "It is good for a man not to touch a woman", into "It is *better* for a man not to touch a woman." I saw that the word "better" corrupted the message, which is that it's *not bad*. By inserting an antonym for "good" and other words in other passages, I was able to comprehend what had been obscured. In that way, synonyms proved useful, too. For instance, people often interpret the word "let" (as in "Let every man") to signify a commandment. But substituting "allow" clarifies the intent. By the same token, the word "thou" is usually interpreted as referring to us all. That is sometimes so, but not always. What I discovered was that way back there in the text is an antecedent for "thou," and that the message may pertain only to that person being addressed and not everyone.

Many of the women in my congregation had husbands who were still jitterbugs. These women loved coming to church, but their other preachers had emphasized the biblical verse, "Be not unequally yoked together with unbelievers." Rather than leave their husbands behind, they stopped coming themselves. To me, that seemed silly. There was no reason why a God-fearing woman shouldn't tend to her spiritual needs and "allow" her man to find his own way. Better one soul saved, it seemed to me, than none. Besides, I saw a number of women leave otherwise healthy marriages when their husbands wouldn't join their church. And some of the single men hoped for that. All the way around, such dogma caused a lot of misery with little good in return. So I began preaching from First Corinthians: "If any brother has a wife who is an unbeliever and she consents to live with him, let him not send her away, and a woman who has an unbelieving husband, and he consents to live with her, let her not send her husband away, for the unbelieving husband is sanctified through his wife, and the unbelieving wife is sanctified through her unbelieving husband."

So what happened? A lot of single women sent themselves

away from my church, figuring that I'd given single men license to seek wives outside the faith. Others left when my prayer for a wife was answered, I think because they'd been quietly plotting my betrothal to themselves.

Sharon Goodson and I had known each other since she'd posed for an advertising poster for my fight against Ali four years before. When we met then, only a few days remained before training began in earnest and I wouldn't be able to touch a woman. I'd planned to spend those days with her, but dinner and talk was as far as I got. For years, all I'd had to do was smile at a woman to get what I wanted. Not Sharon. She was a good girl—only about seventeen at the time, a teen beauty contest winner soon to begin studying at U.C.L.A.—while I was a bad boy. She was smart and sure of herself, and uninterested in what I wanted. "I'm not ready for this," she'd yelled. "I hope I never see you again."

She was the one I'd emotionally abused in Hawaii after my loss to Ali; and who, in Puerto Rico before the fight, had read me to sleep; and who'd visited me in a dozen places, coming to my room after the other girls had gone to help me pack my belongings, give me a quick kiss, and send me off. She was my special girl. I always admired her for holding out on me.

Having heard that I'd turned my life around, Sharon stopped to see for herself while she was visiting other friends in Houston. By then, 1980, she'd earned more than one college degree and a professional pilot's license. I drove her around and we talked about old times. Being with her, I remembered what a nice girl she'd always been. Being with me, she saw how much I'd changed for the better. When she left, I wrote her a letter telling her how much she had meant to me. We talked on the phone a lot. In my next letter I wrote, "Why don't you come down here and help me win some souls for God. Marry me."

She called with a yes. Then she said, "Well, I've always wanted to take some classes at the University of Houston."

I'd always loved Sharon. She was what I'd hoped for in a wife. Surely now that I had her, the mothers of my children would share custody with me.

Too bad neither of us thought through our marriage. Here was an educated and sophisticated woman, whose thrill was to shop, becoming the wife of an austere preacher who demanded that she wear only dresses, not trousers, and no makeup. Sharon was now expected to conform to the strict practices I'd taken on unquestioningly from Masters.

She struggled to accommodate herself to my way of life, but this was to be another ill-fated marriage. Soon after we wed, Adrienne sent Michi to live with us. "I'm happy for you, George," Adrienne said. "Michi loves you and needs you." I finally had my baby, at least the first of them.

But all of sudden, Sharon seemed to me to become unstable. When a mood struck, she would fly home to Los Angeles, parking her car at the airport until she returned. Now that I was on a fixed income—my earnings were limited to interest on investments from the principal I earned during my fighting years—and had learned to admire a dollar, it bothered me almost as much as her leaving that she allowed those parking fees to accumulate.

Over the few months we were together as husband and wife, Sharon began disliking so many things about me. For example, I'd say a little prayer—as I still do—before each meal: "God, I thank you for this food." It didn't take long before that offended her. She'd get up and walk away. Once she said, "You did that last night. You going to do that after every course?"

One time she said to me, "You just going to let your body go?" The George Foreman she remembered had walked around with a tape measure around his thirty-three-inch waist, making sure that another quarter-inch hadn't snuck on there after dinner. Now I was a hefty man of about three hundred pounds, and in her opinion looked less like an athlete than the "before" picture in a Weight Watchers ad.

When a television camera team came out to do a feature on me in church, she said, "I hope they didn't get a picture of me in there."

The only photo Sharon kept of me and her together had been taken in my pre-conversion days. It was clear that she wanted her old George back. But old George was gone and wasn't coming back.

Worst of all, Sharon didn't care for Michi, and because of that, Michi began reacting badly. To my eternal sadness, I had to send Michi back to Minneapolis. Sharon's obvious happiness as she packed for the child to leave told me that our marriage was over. I knew suffering was around the corner.

At church one Sunday, talking with friends, I saw her waiting outside—waiting to tell me something I already understood and didn't want to hear. After eating dinner as usual following services, I went home and found the house empty and all of her clothes gone.

I cried all that night, and all the next day, and for days and days afterward. I cried out of the brutal realization that keeping her meant I couldn't be the type of man I aimed to be; and that my becoming the man she wanted meant my giving up the calling. The two choices were incompatible. To get her back would mean a lot of compromising my values. There was nothing to do but cry. I nearly drowned in my tears. I knelt in prayer: "Well, God, I don't want to get over this. I don't want help." Then I remembered that men in white coats with butterfly nets put straitjackets on people who cry uncontrollably as long as I had. So I cried in the closet, where I thought the neighbors couldn't hear my wails. I covered my head to blot out all the light; it hurt to see anything. My bed was too soft, and there was no one to hold on to. And no one even to tell. I was a preacher now, someone who'd been telling other people that everything was going to work out, no matter how shattered they were. That's what I preached at funerals, comforting wives who'd been married forty years and parents who'd suffered the pain of pains with the loss of a child. Hardest of all was to get up for Sunday services and sing "Yes, Jesus loves me" with a smile. I'd cry all the way home, where I held back the tears, parked the car, and waved to the neighbors as if I were the happy preacher I longed to be.

Now I prayed again: "God, if you just let me get over this, since I feel like dying anyway, I'll tell this story and help somebody else. Just allow me to live through this."

For a long time—months—I stood close to madness. With the divorce soon to be final, I was nowhere near healing. I'd begun to question whether I even wanted to live with the relentless pain. While driving one day to pick up Freeda—the road hard for me to see through the blur of tears—I asked God, "Why are you letting things happen to me?" A moment later, a verse from the Book of Job appeared as an apparition to me: "Though he slayed me, yet will I trust him."

Instantly, I felt relief. Comfort came from the realization that Job's faith had survived miseries and tragedies that I could only imagine. Though he'd had every right to abandon his beliefs, he'd maintained his devotion to God. And in the end his faith was rewarded. I was just going to have to trust in Him and believe that what He had in store for me was peace.

When I got to Andrea's, I picked up Freeda in my arms and swung her around with reborn happiness. *My beautiful, beautiful baby girl.* She was five then. I hadn't seen her for more than a year, since Andrea had taken her to stay in St. Lucia, her home island in the Caribbean. Taking her back with me was like eating again after a fast.

Andrea called a few days later. She said she'd heard I'd broken up with my wife.

"Yeah," I said, "I'm through." No pain.

"You know," she said, "nobody will ever love you as I did. I was the only one who would ever take care of you. You'll never meet anybody else like me."

"Okay," I said, "then marry me." Just like that. Having thrown off the chains of Sharon, I overreacted to freedom. Besides, I was looking at Freeda at the moment. I wanted my child with me.

"Are you kidding?"

"No, I'm not kidding."

"Well, then, yes."

Days after my divorce became final, Andrea and I were married at my mother's house. My mother groaned as she had at my marriage to Adrienne. My decision didn't jibe with the George she'd begun to admire and respect after I left Masters, whom she hadn't trusted. Seeing me disown a man I'd loved and respected, she'd said, "Hey, this guy tells everybody, even his friends, if they're wrong. I'm going to church with this boy." She'd become a member of my congregation, because she was able to see me not only as her son, but as a preacher worthy of his flock.

For our wedding night, Andrea bought a new nightgown. She changed in the bathroom while I waited in the bedroom. Proud and loving, she came out and put both arms around me. At her touch, I became ill and ran into the bathroom, locking myself in, the way they do on television sitcoms. *This isn't Sharon. This isn't Sharon.* I couldn't get into bed with that woman. I couldn't touch her and wanted nothing to do with her. Why had I been so stupid again? Guilt and shame threatened to suffocate me. I prayed: "God, you just can't let me do this."

There was some quick reckoning to do. The thought of Andrea's wearing that new nightgown, a symbol of her expectation for everlasting happiness on her wedding night, tore at me. I would just have to muster the will to be a good man, to make my feelings less important than my doing the right thing. *You're going to love this woman. She wanted to marry you. She's not running, and you're going to love her back.* That's what I did—at least, pretended to do. And she pretended not to notice—until she got pregnant and left me.

We were on St. Lucia at the time, visiting her family. We'd come because Andrea had accused me of treating her like the employee she'd once been. "I want you to see," she'd said, "that I've got a decent family. You'll respect me more." I admit to dominating her, to acting the paternal preacher as I had with Sharon. I regret that she mistook the booming voice that came out of my three-hundred-pound body for something to be afraid of; and I regret that she believed I didn't respect her. I did. I just wasn't in love with her. But I wanted us to be a family anyway. That's why I'd brought Michi and Little George to be with Freeda.

Andrea announced suddenly one day that she was leaving and taking Freeda. No words could dissuade her, nor would she tell me where she was going. After a few days of hoping and waiting, I flew home to Houston with Michi and Little George, and returned them to their mothers. When I didn't hear from Andrea after several more days, I called everywhere to find her and Freeda. Nothing. No trace.

A month later, she called me. "I'm in Houston," she said. "This isn't working between us. I'm pregnant and I'm not ready to have your child again."

"What are you saying?"

"I'm standing across the street from an abortion clinic. I've made an appointment. I'm getting rid of this baby."

I began screaming, not in anger, but in anguish. "I'm sorry for everything I've done to you," I said. "I promise I'll never speak meanly or rudely to you anymore. Just, please, don't do that."

"Why shouldn't I? Go ahead, tell me why. I don't need to go through this again in my life. I don't need to have another baby to look after."

"Andrea, please. This baby didn't do anything wrong. No matter what I've done, this baby is innocent. Please don't make the child pay for my sins."

"That doesn't mean anything to me."

"Where are you?"

"I'm not telling."

I continued to beg and plead through my tears, and at one point dropped to my knees and prayed aloud for her to hear: "God, what have I done that you're going to take my child?" That being growing in her womb was already my son or daughter, as entitled to life as the others.

She hung up.

I broke down. This time, I went to Mom's. Thanks to my playing Cupid, she and Dad were living together again. I wouldn't cry in their presence, nor complain. As a preacher now, I felt I had to act as if everything were fine. While Mom and Dad never said anything directly either, they knew that Andrea and the kids had left; they knew I was deeply troubled. It was comforting just to sit with them. The days passed with excruciating slowness. It hurt my mother to see me dying inside.

"George," she said. "There's a church song we used to sing when I was in school. It goes something like this: 'How well do I remember, when Jesus brought me through. I walked, I prayed a night or two. I said, God why don't you take and use me? That's all that I can do. I give my life to Jesus. What about you?' " Then she started singing, "What about you? What about you?"

I wrote the words down and read them a few times, then put them in my wallet. Every day I asked God, "Why don't you take me and use me?" I felt some strength in that.

Two weeks passed before Andrea finally called from St. Lucia. "I've made up my mind," she said. "I'll have the baby."

Thank you, Jesus.

She said that when she decided not to abort, she also decided not to come back to me; but she'd changed her mind on that as well.

My second son, George—we called him "Monk," like me—was born in January of 1983, the happiest child imaginable. He slept in a crib next to our bed. Where other babies would wake crying, Monk woke laughing and cooing, watching the mobile above him turn in all directions. I loved to see that big head of brown hair every morning, moving every which way.

It seemed to me that Andrea and I were doing all right. Sure, we had our problems like other married couples, but none I considered major. A devoted family man, Andrea's husband didn't drink or swear or run around. I was living the preacher's moral life—living by example. I preached, went to church, came home, read the Bible, spent time with family. The house didn't even have a television. But as it turned out, Andrea was still waiting for that guy's opposite number to reappear—like Sharon and Cynthia before her.

Monk was nearly six months old when I accepted an invitation from a German television company to give an evangelical speech. Before leaving, I kissed Monk, Freeda, and Michi, who was living with us for a time. Then I kissed Andrea. She smiled and wished me well.

In Atlanta, I changed planes for the flight to Frankfurt. On a hunch, I called home. No answer. I called again eight and a half hours later, after landing. Still no answer.

Mustering my courage, I spoke to the German congregation about the power of Christ, all the while praying silently that my family was all right. When I finished, I called home again. No answer. Now I called my sister Mary Alice and asked if she'd heard from Andrea. She hadn't. "Look," she said, "why don't I go out there and check?" An hour later she phoned me back. "Andrea's gone, George. The children are gone too."

"What about Michi?"

"Michi's at Linda Gayle's."

My silence meant that I was dumbstruck.

"And George," she said, "the crib's gone, the rug's off the floor, the dishes aren't in the cabinet. It's gone, George. Everything is gone." I stopped listening well when she said the crib was gone.

Before flying home, I called St. Lucia looking for Andrea. As before, she was a hard woman to find. Frantic and panicked, I spent virtually every minute contacting someone who knew someone who referred me to someone else who heard about someone who maybe knew someone who knew where I could find Andrea and the kids. When I slept, it was only out of sheer exhaustion, and only for an hour or two. Mary Alice had been wrong, though. The crib was indeed there—stripped of its bedding and the mobile—an awful reminder of who was missing. All of my babies had used that tiny bed.

A month passed before Andrea called to say that she planned to raise Freeda and Monk by herself in St. Lucia. "You can see them when they're in college," she said.

"Please bring the kids back," I said.

"I'm never coming back, George."

"I'm sorry, Andrea, I'm sorry. Whatever I've done, I'm sorry for it and I'll make it up to you."

"No, George. I'm not coming back. You know, I don't love you."

After hanging up, I shook with rage. I called her back. She hung up on me. I called her brother and her cousins. They hung up. I phoned night and day, pleading. One time, Andrea let me talk to Freeda. "Listen, darling," I said. "It looks like your mother and I are never going to be together again in that way. She's going to divorce me. But I want you to know how much I love you."

Freeda broke down. This young girl's voice became a hollow rasp, like an old man's death rattle. The agony in that sound shredded me inside. Just when she and I had grown close, her father had been taken from her. Later, in tears, I called Andrea and pleaded again.

"Leave me alone," she said. "You make me sick."

You make me sick. I believed her, and there was nothing else to say; no line of reasoning to invoke, no conscience to appeal to. "Okay," I said. "I'm sorry." And I hung up.

Through all the pain, I suddenly became clear-headed. I realized that I would have to put aside the hurt and embarrassment I felt at being a preacher whose personal life failed to lead by example. *George, those are your kids.* Did Andrea honestly think they were unimportant to me, that I would allow her to keep them, that I would not do everything in my power to be their father? She must not have been paying attention. Either that or she decided that religion was now my wife, to the exclusion of all, the way boxing had been years before.

I thought of Leroy Moorehead, how there'd been no authentic bond between my biological father and me. I thought of Freeda and Monk growing up to speak another language, or with a different accent than mine; of their not appreciating football and basketball, "The Star-Spangled Banner" and the Fourth of July. I couldn't let any of that happen.

The question wasn't if I would retrieve my kids. The question was how. And the answer lay with a woman I'd met nearly ten years earlier.

Irma Cumpton was from the island of St. Lucia. We had dated in early 1974. She liked me enough to want to make me her husband, but that was more than I liked her. Soon we became just buddies and liked each other the same. It was she who had introduced me to Andrea, and she got a kick out of that.

Before I fought Jody Ballard in the Catskills in 1975, she showed up to say hello. When she knocked I was sleeping and didn't hear her. Then she rang through on the telephone. "How are you doing?" she said.

"Fine." In those days, especially near a fight, I wasn't particularly talkative when awakened from a deep sleep.

"Well, I made it in."

"Good."

"Okay, well, I'll be in my room," she said.

I called Andrea, who stayed elsewhere in my suite, and asked her to check on Irma.

Half an hour later, Andrea came back looking awful. Her clothes were in tatters. "Irma beat me," she said.

"What?!"

Irma had dragged her into the room and begun swinging at her. Andrea had managed to free herself and stagger back to me some minutes later. I stomped over to Irma's room.

"You don't come in here and do that to my friend," I said.

I must have been blind with rage, because I evidently pushed her a few times and scared her to death. I don't remember doing it, but I did it. This was my season of wrath, as proved by the cruel and merciless way I went on to beat the Ballard boy.

After I left her room, I called Leroy Jackson to check on Irma. He reported back with horror on his face, and the horror became fear in my presence. He stared at me as though I was Dracula with an eye on his neck. I'd known Leroy since the Job Corps. He'd witnessed my brutality before. But never had he seemed so shaken. He was afraid that I'd do to him what he thought I'd done to Irma.

Soon Mr. Moore came in. "My Lord, George," he said. "What is wrong with you? Didn't I warn you about this kind of goings-on?" Yes, he had.

There was nothing to say. I couldn't explain why I'd done what I had. I'd lost it. Me, the young boy who'd cried with his friend Charles when his father or mine beat our mothers. We had vowed to kill men who hit women.

Mr. Moore took Irma to my home in Bel Air. He cared for her, soothed her, made certain she healed properly. One day she announced she was leaving and said to me, "I'm going to sue you."

I diagnosed her as still being in love with me, and saw the threat as either blackmail or revenge. My guess was that she wanted me to pay her in exchange for silence. At the time, ABC was negotiating to sign me to a three-year contract as a boxing commentator. Such bad publicity would be the death knell for that contract. "You're not going to get anything out of me," I told her.

My friend Bill Caplan offered advice. "You know what you should do?" he said. "The old guy you used to admire has had a lot of trouble like this. He may be able to give you some insight in getting out of it."

Jim Brown had certainly been involved in more than one physical encounter with a woman. I called. "I don't know how to stop her," I said. "Can you help me?"

He agreed to help, but when he phoned Irma, she hung up. "Who is this man calling me?" she asked.

I said, "That was Jim Brown. He's a prince of a fellow."

At my request, he called her again. This time, she took the call and agreed to a meeting. At that meeting, she fell in love with him.

I don't know whether they ever graduated to a reciprocal relationship, but Irma stopped talking about suing.

"Let me have ten thousand dollars," Jim said one day. "No questions; just give me the money."

I wrote a check and mailed it off, and was soon at my attorney's office, where Irma signed an agreement not to sue. Jim told me that she was planning to promote a Bob Marley concert on St. Lucia. He'd been introducing her to people who could possibly help with financing.

Many months later, while in New York City for a press conference to announce the ABC contract, I heard from a friend that Irma was down in the dumps, living in the worst part of the city. "Not Irma," I said. I couldn't imagine her impoverished, this woman who spoke with a proper English boarding-school accent and corrected my language. I remembered her acquainting me with gold collar stiffeners (which I still wear). This was a woman of pride.

After checking into my hotel, I withdrew five thousand dollars from a bank and, ignoring Mr. Moore's advice, called Irma.

"George," he'd said, "curiosity killed the cat. Don't be curious how people are doing. Just leave them alone." I couldn't listen. She needed a friend now, and I was determined to be one. Besides, a guilty voice in my ear whispered that I was somehow responsible for her downfall.

Irma came to my room. We laughed and joked. She said nothing about her circumstances, didn't ask for help. Then she decided to spend the night with me. Where was that little voice when I needed it, to keep me from sprinting down that road paved with good intentions?

Next morning, before the press conference, I handed her an envelope and said, "Look, I have some money for you. I want you to make sure you take care of yourself. I'm getting ready to leave now, so you'll have to go."

Irma raced from zero to one hundred in less than a second: "What am I? A whore that you sleep with and then offer money to? I am not a whore. I'm not. How dare you? I don't care about your money. I'M NO WHORE." She took the money from the envelope and ran to the bathroom.

"Oh, no," I yelled. "You don't flush money down the toilet. Don't do that."

A step behind her, I reached over her shoulder to grab the bills from her hand. When she turned around, her nose was bleeding. I did *not* hit that woman.

"You hit me," she said, crying.

I ran cold water over a towel and pressed it to her nose, then ran down the hall to fetch some ice. When the bleeding stopped and she'd calmed down, I said, "Please, just hold the money."

"I don't want your money."

"Well, just sit here, please. I'll be back in a couple of hours." I was about to be late for my own press conference. As I left, I thought the matter had been resolved because she'd ended up clutching the money.

When I returned, Irma wasn't there, but Mr. Moore and Don King were—along with half a dozen N.Y.P.D. detectives and uniformed officers. "Mr. Foreman," they said, "you're under arrest. We're going to have to take you in."

"Oh, man, I did not hit her," I said. "She's just trying to get money out of me."

"Well, sir," one of them said, "she says you hit her. If she presses charges, we've got to take you to jail."

"Where is she?" I asked. "Where'd she go?"

"She's on the phone."

I held the receiver. "WHY ARE YOU LYING?" I yelled. "You know I didn't touch you. You're not getting a cent from me by lying."

Mr. Moore snatched the phone away from me. "Lighten up, George," he said.

"But she's lying. If I'd hit her, I wouldn't be arguing. When I'm wrong, I'm wrong. But I didn't do it. I'm not going to be tricked." It was important to me that at least Mr. Moore believe me innocent. Given what had happened last time, he had good reason to disbelieve me.

He spoke to Irma in a calm, assuring voice: "Irma, please tell all these people not to put this man in jail."

I grabbed the phone back and screamed: "You're a liar."

Now Don King took over. "You know, Irma," he said. "George is kind of hard-headed. You're just gonna have to tell these people not to take him to jail." He listened for a while, then: "You want to ruin him? Is that what you're saying?" He listened some more before handing the phone to the ranking detective.

"Forget it," she told the detective. "It's just a little personal problem."

But while Irma had dropped the criminal charges, she soon filed a civil suit against me. I didn't care how much the attorneys cost. I wouldn't pay for what I hadn't done.

About a year later, when it appeared the suit would die of inertia, I gave an interview to a reporter from *Ebony* about my new relationship to God. Intending to admit past sins, I said something to the effect that "I was a mean guy. I didn't care. I'd hit man, woman, or child." It was just common lingo, meant casually, not literally. But Irma saw the article, published in late 1977, as a grenade to lob back at me. She chased damages more ferociously than ever.

In those days, while learning the Bible, I refused to leave Texas. I spent all my time in either Houston or Marshall, and sent relatives to bring my children from out of state. So I was not about to fly to New York to give a deposition, no matter how righteous my case. I was told the suit could be settled, with no admission of guilt, in return for a modest five-figure sum. That figure was evidently the amount of Irma's legal fees. I signed, though not gladly, and thought no more of Irma until I heard that her young son, born before she met me, had been murdered in New York. She took her grief on board a merchant ship, traveling several times around the world. Then she moved home to St. Lucia, where her brother was prime minister, and founded a business.

Six years later, when Andrea and I visited St. Lucia during her second pregnancy, Irma stopped by the hotel. I rose to greet her and shake her hand. By the time she left, she knew I'd changed my ways. So a year after that, when Andrea stole the kids, she was the logical person to call.

"I know where they are," she said.

"I just have to get them back," I said. I explained that I'd hired a lawyer in St. Lucia to serve Andrea with the divorce papers, and told her that I didn't expect any satisfaction from the courts there.

"Well, come and get these children out of here," Irma said. "I know what this woman is doing, and it's not right. I'm glad you want them so much. I'll help you. And bring lots of cash. You're going to have to spread it around."

That wouldn't be easy. Several months before, I had dreamed I was on a talk show, admitting that an accountant had embezzled my money. Upon awakening, I'd called the bank to verify funds. I was supposed to have a total of about half a million dollars—the same money Leroy Jackson had stolen; after recovering it, I'd had it wired to Texas. The rest had been set aside in a trust to generate an annuity in years ahead. But the somber voice of the banker had confirmed the dream's prophecy. My accountant Gordon Eldridge, using the power of attorney I'd granted him, had mismanaged my money. Like so many other athletes,

I'd trusted not too wisely but too well. In response to my lawsuit, Eldridge had visited my house with a friend, whom he probably considered a bodyguard. "George," he'd said, "I'm sorry. I blew all your money. You can sue me all you want. And you've got every right. But you can't get blood from a turnip. I just don't have it. It's all gone." And with that, he'd walked out the door.

I dropped the suit when I overheard one of the attorneys say that Eldridge's marriage had broken up over the stress. "He's so mixed up, he couldn't find his way to his car," the attorney said. Here was this man who'd clipped me out of everything, and I was feeling sorry for him. (A year later, Eldridge came over to my house to tell me that he'd stopped drinking and been born again. He knew in his heart that I'd be happy for him. For him to feel safe with me after what he'd done to me made me believe that there must be something about me I didn't fully understand myself.)

Since I was now a preacher committed to a simple existence, my relative poverty didn't outwardly affect me, and it's unlikely that anyone had suspected my financial downturn. Only now, needing money that wasn't there, did I truly feel the loss.

I borrowed tens of thousands of dollars from the trust, put the cash in a briefcase, flew to Barbados, called Irma from my motel to confirm final arrangements, then shaved my head clean of stubble. The shaving symbolized my commitment; I cared about nothing other than bringing my children back. To pass the days while I waited for Irma's signal, I ran on the beach and exercised. I also prayed.

Each evening Irma caught a small plane from St. Lucia and flew about half an hour to Barbados, bringing me fresh vegetables and fish. After dinner, she would disappear into the darkness, not to be seen until the next night.

At last the arrangements were completed. A private plane and pilot flew me to St. Lucia. Through her connections and my cash, Irma had arranged for a smiling customs officer to take my bags and usher me into a waiting car, which dropped me at a hotel in Castries, the capital city. Irma was waiting in my small bungalow. We went over the plans that she had devised after watching

Andrea's movements from afar. On Monday morning, two days from then, Andrea would drive Freeda to school, where I'd be waiting and hiding. When Andrea drove off, I would take Freeda. Then, while Andrea was doing her chores, we'd go to her home and take Monk from the baby-sitter. By the time she finished, the kids and I would be in the air on the way to Barbados.

Before leaving the hotel, Irma said, "Do not step out of this room until I tell you. No one can see you here."

The next day we reviewed the plans again. "It's all set," she said. "The car will pick you up at eight-fifteen tomorrow morning."

Growing more nervous and impatient by the minute, I began coming up with other plans. Irma told me to be cool and wait. But that night, she made the mistake of calling. "George, you can't believe it," she said.

"What?"

"I just went over there, knocked on the door, and the housekeeper said, 'Hi. May I help you?' There were both kids, just sitting there on the floor. This isn't going to be any problem at all."

"Then I'm getting them now," I said. "Let's go."

"No, no, no, no, no, no," she said. "You'll ruin everything. You've got to wait. Remember the plane."

"I don't care. I want them now."

"But—"

"No. Just get the driver and let's do it this second."

I waited outside for Irma and the driver. We drove into the countryside. It's a lush island, covered with forest and tropical vegetation and fruit trees, though it was too dark and I was too nervous to appreciate the sights. After half an hour, we arrived at the building that had been converted from a hotel; outside staircases connected the bottom-floor apartments with the top-floor ones. I knocked on the door while the engine ran. The housekeeper, dressed in a nightgown, opened the door. She was young, late teens or early twenties, and pretty.

"How do you do?" I said.

"Fine," she said.

"Is the children's mother here?"

"And who are you?" she asked.

"I'm the children's daddy."

"Oh, okay."

"I don't want any trouble, ma'am," I said. "I don't want any trouble with anybody. But these are my kids. And I just want my kids. I'm going to leave with them, and I'm not going to hurt anybody. I don't want any trouble. I just want my kids."

Freeda saw me, ran to the door, and jumped in my arms. She got all the hugs and kisses that daddy's little girl had missed for three months.

Holding her, I walked into the living room where Monk crawled on the floor. He wasn't smiling; didn't seem like the happy boy who'd cooed in the crib next to my bed.

I turned to the baby-sitter. "I don't mean any harm, ma'am," I said. "Where's the mother?"

The baby-sitter whispered, "Upstairs."

Then I, too, whispered, "Okay, be quiet." Something or someone was telling her that the children were better off with their father and to trust me. I nodded in thanks and headed for the door when she said, "Take me with you. The baby's going to cry. I just can't leave him like that."

"All right, fine, but let's go right now."

She grabbed a scarf and wrapped it around her waist. We all climbed into the car and drove to the hotel. I figured that Andrea would sleep until morning; by that time, we'd be in Barbados, preparing to fly home.

Hours later, I spotted some figures creeping around outside my bungalow. I pointed them out to Irma. "Wave at them," she said. We did.

There was a knock on the door. "What do you want?" I yelled out.

A man's voice: "This is the police. We want the children."

"These are my kids," I said. "I'm George Foreman. The baby's George Foreman the third, and the girl is Freeda George Foreman. I have both their birth certificates. They're American citizens, and I'm taking them home. That's their birthright, and you can't stop me."

"No," he said. "You're not taking the kids off the island."

"You're not getting them back," I said.

"We demand that you give them back."

"No."

"Open the door."

"If you want it open, you're going to have to break it down. And if you do that, you're going to have to kill me. These children are going home. They're going to their country. And they're going with me." Challenging them was a bluff that could have backfired. But I felt ready to die for this cause. There was only one way I would leave the island without them—horizontally. "Go ahead, break in."

"Well," he said, "we just may have to do that."

I looked through the curtains out the window and saw a combat vehicle, like the humvees that the National Guard uses, rolling to a stop. A dozen or so soldiers in full battle gear, automatic weapons in their hands, jumped out and aligned in formation. Soon Andrea arrived, and her brother. They too had connections. With St. Lucia's population only 150,000, most people probably had connections.

Watching the soldiers pace back and forth, thinking that they were starved for action on this sleepy island and anxious to prove themselves, I'd never felt more frightened. I closed the bathroom door behind me, dropped to my knees, rested my elbows on the toilet seat cover, clasped my hands, and prayed. "God," I said, "I don't want to die and be known as a violent man. Have mercy on me and my children."

As I walked back into the bedroom, there was another knock. "Go away," I yelled.

"We want the children."

"I told you, you're not getting the kids unless you kill me."

I heard Andrea's voice: "Go ahead, shoot him. Just get my kids. I want my kids. He's not taking them."

Irma called out, "Hey, you can't do anything here. This man's an American."

She picked up the phone. It was dead. "I'll be back," she said. "I'm going to make a call." She cracked the window quietly, climbed onto the ledge, and crawled out like a worm. I saw her hide in the bushes until the soldier patrolling that side of the bungalow turned his back. Then she scampered off. This brave woman became a hero before my eyes.

It occurred to me that my daughter might prefer not to be involved in a *Mission: Impossible* escapade. "Tell me, Child," I said, "what do you want to do? Go home or stay here. Tell Daddy the truth."

"I want to go home," she said. "I want a Big Mac." How good it was to see her smile. I wondered whether my willingness to die for her was something she would keep close to her heart.

"Your wife told me what a horrible husband you were," the baby-sitter said. "But when I saw Freeda run to you, I knew the children loved you."

Another knock on the door and another man's voice: "This is the minister of police. You've kidnapped the baby-sitter. She's a St. Lucian citizen."

"Nobody kidnapped me," she yelled. "I can leave anytime I want. I'm coming out." Before slipping out, she handed me Monk and motioned toward the door, as if telling me to lock it behind her.

"Nobody else leaves this room," the police minister barked after she'd left. "We'll settle this tomorrow in court."

Tomorrow seemed an eternity away. But at least the issue would be settled. I didn't doubt that the judge would honor my children's American citizenship. So why was I so jumpy?

Monk fell in and out of sleep. When awake, he cried. He didn't recognize his father anymore. Freeda wouldn't lie down. She insisted on keeping me company. "I'm going home, Dad," she said every few minutes.

About three in the morning, I saw the soldiers climb back onto their vehicle and drive away. I called outside the front door. There was no one on that side, either. This was the miracle I'd prayed for. Then a knock.

"Irma, that you?"

"Yes."

I unlocked and opened the door. "Where'd they all go?" I asked.

"They're gone," she said.

"How'd you do that?"

"Magic."

"We're going to court tomorrow," I said.

"There's not going to be any court," she said. "They'll listen to everything you have to say. Then they'll say 'Thank you very much,' take the kids, and put you off the island."

"So let's get out of here now."

"No planes are leaving the island, George. But I have another plan. I'll need more cash."

It was a pleasure to give her what I had left. She gave some of it back.

Irma had already arranged to have a man drive us to the other side of the island. The kids and I had to get down on the floor of the truck so we wouldn't be seen. Having to go slow and carefully through the mountainous interior made the trip longer than it looked on the map. I could feel Freeda's heart pounding. Mine, too. Monk wouldn't stop crying. Both Freeda and I petted him. Nothing calmed him. If he was crying because he missed his mother, I was sorry. But what choice did I have?

I lifted my head and saw the ocean as the sun was coming up. Beautiful. Finally the truck stopped by the water. There was an old, leaky-looking trawler, about twenty-five feet long. For a moment, I thought about laughing. For years I'd intended to save up some money for an ocean cruise. And now I'm supposed to escape to freedom with my children in this raggedy boat. This was one of those situations in which right, left, and backward aren't even options.

Irma explained that her "friends" had been instructed to take the kids and me to St. Vincent, a nearby island just south of St. Lucia that belongs to a group of islands named the Grenadines. From there we'd easily find a way to Barbados, the next island to the east. She said good-bye as Freeda, Monk, and I went below and lay on our stomachs. It smelled musty and dank. The baby wouldn't stop crying. Freeda could see my frustration and got brave in a hurry. "Here," she said, "give him to me."

Two Rastafarians jumped on board. "Who are you?" I said.

"We going to take care of you, mon," one of them said. "You just be cool, mon." He showed me the exit visa they'd brought from St. Lucia and the entry visa for St. Vincent. There was a space left for us to fill in our names.

For at least an hour, I suffered. I was frightened, certain we would be captured at sea. After two hours, I raised my head and gazed out at the daylight. The opening above framed a square patch of blue. Freeda and Monk had fallen asleep. I went to stretch my legs on board. When I climbed out, I saw that St. Lucia was a speck in the distance, as was St. Vincent in the other direction. We were all alone. Only a plane could reach us now, and the sky was empty. I breathed deeply and noticed that the deck was covered with marijuana, drying in the sun. I looked over at the two Rastafarians with a mind to lecture but heard a voice in my head: *Man, these guys are trying to help you. So shut up. Go sit back and relax.*

They weren't smoking, so the drug was easier to ignore. I struck up conversation with one of them. He said he'd studied navigation at Harvard. I had no reason to disbelieve, so I didn't. Besides, I saw the way he worked out intricate calculations about where to land based on his charts. While he worked, the other guy began talking to me about religion. It was fascinating stuff about the anti-Christ and other strange things. I just listened. He said they called people who didn't wear their hair in dreadlocks, as they did, "Bald Heads."

"Like me," I said, running my hand over my shiny scalp.

I think they had a feeling for me and the kids, because after we got to St. Vincent, they made sure we got through passport control before leaving. (They'd hidden the marijuana.)

When the guy in the blue cap stamped our passports, we were free—or so I thought. We took a cab to a hotel, where I phoned the American Embassy in Barbados. The ambassador explained that though legally the St. Lucian government had no authority on either St. Vincent or Barbados, a sense of family joined the peoples of these three neighboring islands. He warned me not to trust anyone, not even the lawyer I'd hired in St. Lucia; and not to tell anyone who I was or why I was there. He hinted that someone doing a favor for someone else in St. Lucia might take it upon himself to hold us under a kind of house arrest until the St. Lucian authorities arrived. "We'll make the airline reservations for you guys," he said. "You just get here as soon as you can."

He obviously knew what he was talking about, because as soon as I hung up, the lawyer called. How did he know where I was? Andrea was in his office. "Please, please," she cried. "I want my family back. Please give me one more chance."

"I don't trust anybody who'd run off with my kids," I told him to tell her. "I'm taking them home. You want to see them, that's where you come."

The kids and I cleaned up and caught the next plane to Barbados. Irma flew to the island and met us at the hotel. By now the sum of the stress and fear had reduced me to tears. "Listen," she said, "you pull yourself together. These kids, they don't need to see you crying like this."

She was right, and I appreciated the advice. It came as a bracing slap of reality. There wasn't any place for frailty yet.

When she heard the baby still crying, Irma said, "I'd better help you get home." We all went to the American Embassy, which granted her a visa so she could accompany us to Houston.

"You've got your kids now, George," the ambassador said. "Good luck."

Not until the plane was safely in the air, and my children were next to me, did I breathe easily. Almost as soon as we arrived in Houston, I called my friend in New Jersey Dave Macmillan, whom I'd had the pleasure of marrying to his second wife. Dave knew this terrain well, having traversed it himself. He had been involved in a painful custody suit with his first wife. Dave offered me several suggestions, and referred me to the attorney he had used, who referred me to a family specialist in Houston.

"You know what you should do?" the specialist said. "You should find that girl who took care of your children in St. Lucia. See if she'll come here to help you. When we go to court, she can testify as to what kind of father you are, and who's the better parent, you or Andrea."

It was a great suggestion, not only as legal strategy for earning

Bob Arum (*left*), George, and Don King after a Vegas fight

In an early professional fight,
George defeated Gregorio "Goyo" Peralta in ten rounds.

Livermore, California, 1974.
George poses with Mr. Moore, his mentor and adviser.

George trains for his highly anticipated first fight with Joe Frazier.
Charley Shipes consults on technique.

Kingston, Jamaica, January 22, 1973.
George won the heavyweight championship
after defeating Joe Frazier in the second round.

Tokyo, September 1, 1973.
In a decisive and brutal first round, George knocked out Joe Roman
in the first defense of his heavyweight crown.

Caracas, Venezuela, March 26, 1974.
In his second defense of the heavyweight crown, George won
in the second round against contender Ken Norton.

George, seen here with Don King, was in Zaire longer than he expected
in preparation for the Muhammad Ali fight.

In Zaire: Doc Broadus,
brother Sonny, a local police official,
and George, with a look
that says it all

Muhammad Ali and George during a light moment
promoting their fight in Zaire

Mr. Moore implored George to show his battle wounds
after the stunning Ali defeat.

George fools around with Bob Hope
on the set of one of his comedy specials.

On the set of *Let's Do It Again*
with Bill Cosby and Sidney Poitier

George and Howard Cosell teamed up
for ABC Sports.

James Brown and George flank
the "women of the Ali-Foreman fight."

Joe Louis was an admirer of George.

Uniondale, New York, June 15, 1976.
In a rematch, George defeats Joe Frazier in a fifth-round knockout.

Having unwittingly taken on a "bad-boy" image, George stares into the crowd while Frazier gets the count.

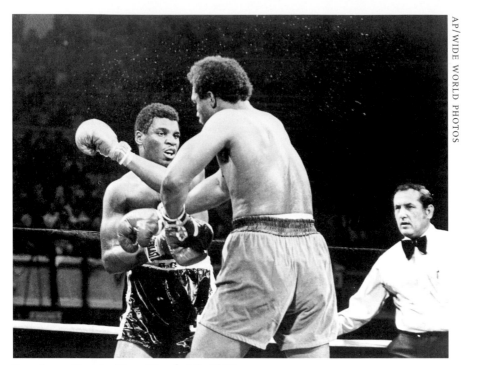

San Juan, Puerto Rico, March 17, 1977.
Jimmy Young surprised George with a unanimous-decision win.
Afterward, George underwent a religious experience.

George didn't fight
from 1978 through 1986.
He turned his attention
to God, family, and his
youth center in Houston.

Sacramento, California, March 9, 1987,
George's first professional fight in ten years. He forged a
comeback trail that began with a fourth-round knockout of Steve Zouski.

Atlantic City, New Jersey, January 15, 1990.
George knocked out Gerry Cooney in the second round,
twenty straight wins into his comeback.

George and defending heavyweight champion Evander Holyfield
promote their title fight at a news conference in Los Angeles.

George and his attorney
Henry Holmes show their joy
at the latest comeback.

George delivers a knockout sermon
on Sundays at the First Church
of the Lord Jesus Christ in Houston.

Las Vegas, Nevada, November 5, 1994.
George on his way to a stunning
tenth-round knockout
of Michael Moorer.

At forty-five, George Foreman became
the oldest man in boxing history
to win the heavyweight championship
of the world.

custody of Freeda and Monk, but because I dearly needed someone to help me with them. Irma volunteered to find the girl and
make her an offer in my behalf. And after my new friends at the
embassy in Barbados got her a U.S. visa, Irma accompanied this
girl back to Houston. Then Irma rode off into the Caribbean
sunset.

Her leavetaking wasn't marked by emotional good-byes. I had
no words for my gratitude, and no tears left to cry. We were now
friends and had said everything there was to say about the people we'd both become.

Chapter Nine

MARY MARTELLY was nineteen when I met her. She had been raised deep in St. Lucia's interior, a world away from the island's capital city of Castries—a world of plantation work and factory labor. One day when she was walking down a lane, a woman named Andrea stopped and asked for directions to a nearby house. Mary led her there. Andrea went to knock on the door and, when it was opened, said a few words. Mary overheard a girl inside exclaim, "I don't want the job. I don't work servant." The door slammed. Before Mary could walk away, Andrea asked her whether she knew of anyone who could watch after her two children, a girl of about seven and a six-month-old boy. When Mary said she couldn't think of anyone, Andrea asked if she would be interested in the job. Mary said she already had a job running a sewing machine at Bell's Fashions, which made brassieres for export to America. Her sewing machine had just broken, she explained, but would be fixed in a week. Andrea asked if she would be willing to watch her children until she went back to her regular job. It would give Mary work and give Andrea a chance to find someone permanent, she said.

"Why not?" Mary said. Agreeing to work for a week, she went off to Castries.

Mary established an immediate rapport with the little girl, and fell in love with the baby boy. When she asked Andrea about the children's father, it inspired a long tirade about the miserable, abusive man she'd left behind in the United States. Mary pictured a cross between Jack the Ripper and Godzilla. A few days later, a bald King Kong showed up at the door. Mary had never stood next to anyone as big, she told me later, in Humble, but she knew as soon as she saw me that the man Andrea had described to her wasn't the man who'd come to claim his children.

Still, though she'd come to Humble (I'd sold my big Houston home and moved to this suburb in 1980), she seemed afraid of me. Every night when she took Monk with her to bed, I'd hear the latch turn in her door. When she came out of the room to get him a bottle she'd carry him on her hip. Then she'd go back in and turn the latch again. Even during the day she preferred to remain with Monk behind the locked door. Whenever I saw her, she was fully dressed. I wondered if she'd even brought that nightgown she'd worn in St. Lucia.

I was an imposing figure, reciting Bible verses while wearing a flowing African robe around the house. "You must be Jim Jones or something," she said. I thought that was funny, and it broke the ice a little.

Monk adored her. He cried if she left him. Most of the time he camped at her side. Neither too strict nor too lenient, she showed an easy rapport with both children. Mary had an integrity that showed in the way she carried herself and in her character. You could just tell that she thought no one was better than she was.

About two weeks into her stay, she told me she wanted to take a shower. "In my country," she said, "we shower with cold water. The water here is so hot. I hate hot water."

"Oh," I said, "here let me show you. You just turn the handle to the left for cooler water—all the way left for cold."

"I knew that," she snapped with a dignified air.

Neither of us laughed, but I know we both thought this was funny. In any event, the exchange was the most intimate moment we'd had together since that incredible night in St. Lucia. It wasn't too long before Mary didn't lock her door every time she went into her room.

After several weeks, when my court date came up, she testified that I was a good father and provided a good home for my children. Almost entirely because of her testimony, my lawyer later said, the judge ruled for joint custody.

"If anyone goes puddle-hopping again," the judge said, looking at Andrea, "I myself will track that person down to the ends of the earth and put him or her *under* the jail. These kids had better not be taken out of town." That was a victory for me. All I wanted was for the children to remain in the United States.

Usually in custody battles, both sides dredge up everything nasty there is to say about the other. My testimony concerned only Andrea's stealing the kids. What stood out for me in Andrea's statement was her complaint that I didn't own a television. No wonder I didn't know what I'd done wrong when, pleading for her to return the kids, I'd apologized to her for "whatever I've done wrong."

With money I gave her, Andrea returned to Houston. With my money, she bought furniture. With my money, she found a place to live. And with my money, she paid her attorneys. Financially, I'd been soaked. But I had my babies near me.

Andrea was bitter because, while the law technically allowed her to live anywhere in the state of Texas, the effect of the ruling was to confine her to the Houston area. I'd gotten Freeda George enrolled at a good school near my house and the judge had stated that he absolutely, positively did not want her to have to change schools again. Under the custody terms, if Andrea wanted to see her children, she'd have to stay close. She'd drop off Freeda at school, where I'd pick her up in the afternoon and bring her to Andrea's after dinner. Meanwhile, I was Monk's day-care provider. And we alternated taking the kids on weekends.

At least, that was the plan. In reality, Andrea sometimes just dropped both of them off for days at a time, without asking whether I had other plans. I didn't mind.

About a year after the court decision, I began looking at Mary a little differently. Up to that time I'd seen her as a wonderful girl to help me with the kids. Now I thought she might be wonderful for *me*, too. Watching the way she acted with the children—including Michi, who was now eleven, Little George, ten, Georgetta, seven—I wondered if it was possible for me to experience an *Ozzie and Harriet* type of family life after all. Mary treated each child with respect and expected the same in return. She wouldn't back down. No matter how tense things got now and then, the next day everyone would be eating out of the same plate. You could see that Mary liked children—the more the better. I never worried for an instant when I traveled.

I'd had four wives, and until I began thinking about Mary so much, I figured that married love would forever be the one empty place in my life. But I've never been anything if not stubborn. Besides, I'd prayed for a wife and had had the vision of one, so I knew that God was going to give me a wife. If He hadn't been planning someone for me, I wouldn't have told Mary that I hated the thought of her ever returning to St. Lucia. I asked her if she'd marry me.

We were in a shopping mall. I walked into a jewelry store and, for less than a hundred dollars, bought a ring with a diamond so small you had to squint your eyes to see it. I got on my knees at her feet, slipped the ring on her finger, and popped the question.

At the time, I'm sure I didn't love her as much as I needed her. I reminded her of how well we all got along. She was like food and water to me. You don't love them as much as you need them to live. I admired Mary more than I could say, and respected her enough to show it. That's what the other four marriages, and my every other relationship with a female, had lacked. While Mary and I didn't begin as Juliet and Romeo, we had a good foundation, a chance to get somewhere without ending in tragedy. The better I came to know her, the happier I was. And for the first time in my life, I felt contentment. I thought then that if I had to die, I'd go out with a smile.

Years later, I don't think like that anymore. Now the thought of dying makes my heart race, because I never want to have to say good-bye to her. I'm like a fish who has swallowed the bait and gotten the hook caught in his gut. She's what keeps me here. Ours is a love from God.

My religious ways weren't originally Mary's. The strict religious rules I lived by, which had driven away two women, allowed less freedom than she was used to. While I'd learned not to impose my rigorous ideas of dress and makeup on her (dresses only and no makeup), she adopted them anyway. They fit her personality. She was born unpretentious.

The year after we married, I took her to a store to try on a two-carat diamond. She looked at me as if I'd cussed in her presence. "I'm not going to wear that," she announced.

"Don't you like it?"

"Don't I *like* it? Don't you *know* how many dresses I can buy with the money this cost?"

That microscopic diamond in her engagement ring was what she cherished.

Day by day, Mary became the preacher's wife I'd hoped and prayed for; out of affection, I began calling her Joan, and the name stuck. She was now Joan.

Now that I had a solid home, Adrienne let me have custody of Michi, Pamela gave me Little George, and Charlotte allowed Georgetta to spend more time with me. And because their mother dated and needed baby-sitters, Freeda and Monk were in my house at least half the time. There was also Natalie, who immediately became my own dear child, as much a Foreman as the others. (All she's missing is a George in her name.) We were a family. With kids crawling all over me, and a good mother in the house, life was perfect.

When the U.S. Olympic Committee invited me to visit and, they hoped, inspire the boxers on the 1984 team, I went to Lake Placid, New York. While there I met Mal Whitfield, who'd been an Olympic track star in the 1950s and was also a Korean War hero. Now he was heading an organization called Athletes in Africa. Its goal was to inspire and motivate African youth through excursions sponsored by the United States Information Agency. Mel pleaded with me to accompany a group on their next trip, which was to Cameroon and Nigeria.

"I heard you're a preacher," he said. "Come on, there are a few churches we can arrange for you to preach at."

That was the hook that got me leaning in his direction; also, this "next trip" was in six months so it was easy to say yes—it seemed so far in the future. As always, though, the future became the present in a few tomorrows—and Mel was calling to finalize plans.

Before leaving I met with a U.S.I.A. representative who'd lived a long time in Africa. Boy, did he cram my brain full of warnings and fear about Nigeria.

"These people are bad," he said. "You've got to watch them all the time. Be careful. They'll steal anything."

He cautioned me about so many things—theft of my luggage, valuables, and shoes; soldiers who'll kill you for fun; food that makes you sick; rudeness; and illness—that I wondered why anyone would live there and regretted agreeing to go.

The first leg of my flight was to London, then to Nigeria. I wasn't staying, however. After a seventeen-hour layover in Lagos, I was to fly east to Cameroon, where I would catch up with the rest of the group. All that brain-washing had made me so wary that I intended to spend all seventeen hours of the layover sitting on a bench in the airport. I left to eat only because a guy who identified himself as a police captain recognized me and offered to take me to a nearby restaurant.

I wasn't scared so much as paranoid to the point of skittishness. Even my dinner companion noticed. He suggested that I take a hotel room until the plane took off. No way would I do that. "They'll steal everything out of your hotel room," the U.S.I.A. guy had said.

I preferred the openness of the airport. I clutched my bag as I sat and wished the hours away. Someone walked right up to me with his eyes on my shoes. "Those are real nice," he noted. "We don't have those over here." Soldiers casually slinging automatic rifles were nearly as plentiful as regular travelers coming and going. Some of these people seemed as though they were being rude on purpose.

It was basically the same situation when I reached Cameroon. No one had said anything bad about Cameroon—there was nothing bad to say—but I couldn't quite relax. For my entire seven days there, I dreaded the eleven I was going to have to spend in Nigeria. I'd already spent more time in Nigeria than I wanted to. Even the Cameroonians warned me about Nigeria. At the end of the seven days I had to return there.

Except for the speaking engagements I'd been booked for, I kept to myself in my locked hotel room. On the fourth night, I dined on the same menu I'd had the previous three nights—sardines I'd brought from home. Sardines. And bottled water.

Only seven more nights to go. So far I'd managed to avoid shaking hands with too many people, and had kept my belongings within sight.

It was evening. I was sitting in my room reading my Bible. Suddenly, without warning, and for the second time in my life, I began sobbing from all the way inside, uncontrollably, inconsolably. For a long time I had no idea what the grief was about. And then there was a drumbeat in my distant imagination. *Boom, boom, boom, boom, boom.* I stepped out onto the balcony and cried even harder. *Boom, boom, boom, boom, boom.*

Now the drum seemed familiar, and it got more familiar until I recognized it as the beating of a broken heart—of an ancestor whose son had been kidnapped and shipped away forever. I had just known that broken heart myself, when my own children were taken from me. It didn't matter that I have no idea whether any of my relatives actually came from this land of Nigeria, where thousands and maybe millions of Africans had been taken. The feeling was bigger than that. I was connected by an invisible umbilical cord to this continent's soil. *I am back! I am back! I love your house, Grandpa. I love your kids,* a voice in me said. And yet, I hadn't eaten the African man's food, or shaken his hand, or sat in his presence.

Just like that, I went downstairs and took up residence in the lobby, my feet up on the furniture as if this whole country was my home. I struck up conversations with anyone walking by. Half of them I hugged. I greeted and hugged, and hugged and greeted, and the more I did, the warmer they became. On the street, I said hello to everyone. They said hello back. I ate everything put in front of me (and got diarrhea). I took part in the life of the city, visiting youth centers and hospitals and churches, and going fishing on Saturdays.

No one stole so much as a shoelace.

My U.S.I.A. adviser had told me, "These people will never accept you as a brother." But he was wrong. The people I spent the most time with began to seem like family, and accepted me as their family.

It was also true that, above all, I was an American. I could never live anywhere else but in the United States. But Africa was a life-changing experience. I'd already had a few of those, and there were a few yet to come.

Andrea had a new boyfriend. Felix. He wasn't the best influence on my children. Every time Freeda or Monk came to my house, they had a new bad habit or two I had to break them of. But that was all right. Monk grew more like me every day. It was right to have given him my nickname. He'd see me standing with my legs crossed and try to imitate the posture exactly. He cried to get his own boxing gloves and would wrap a belt around his waist, pretending it was a championship belt. He was George Foreman, the Baby. You didn't get him started unless you were prepared to finish—just like me as a kid—and he never finished till after you did. My sisters would buy him clothes that looked exactly like mine, even boots. If he saw me wearing something that he had too, he'd run and change. He slept with me, showered with me, worked with me. Whatever I did, he wanted to do. I loved that boy with all the love you can feel for a child.

If Monk was George Foreman as a boy, Freeda was me as a girl. Taller than the other eight-year-olds, she even looked like me from behind. She also had my sense of humor. Problem was, when the other kids were around, she didn't want me spending time with them. She'd get into trouble just to steal my attention, and just as often she'd do anything short of backflips to please me. It was hard for her, living half in her mother's secular world and half in my strictly religious one.

Sometimes I would hear her say to Joan, "You're in my daddy's bathroom," or, "You come out of my daddy's bedroom."

Freeda was confused by remembering Joan as the woman who'd baby-sat her for a few days at her mother's and then worked in the house for me. Now Joan was the mother, the mistress of the house.

Freeda was also confused by the different ways her mother and I responded to her appetite. I'd fix her a lobster dinner or anything she wanted, and afterward we'd exercise. Like her sister Michi, she leans a bit toward the heavy side; like a lot of people, she needs to burn calories. As long as she got on my treadmill, I let her eat what she pleased. That's how I believed it should be done. Her mother forced her to diet all the time.

Andrea's marriage to Felix meant I only had to pay child support, which was still a small fortune. They wanted to live in South Carolina, where Felix was from, but a move would have violated the judge's decision. If Andrea left Texas, the kids would be all mine. I was hoping she'd go, because I considered Freeda and Monk better off with Joan and me.

One Monday after Freeda had spent the weekend with me, I dropped her off at Andrea's; Monk was already there. When they didn't turn up after a few days, I called. The number had been changed and there was no answer at the new number. At first I panicked and thought she'd run away again with my kids. But I calmed myself: Andrea wouldn't risk flight again, not with that judge having been so emphatic. Besides, given the disorderly way Andrea kept to the schedule, this wasn't so much out of the ordinary.

Thursday passed, then Friday. It got harder to avoid the inevitable conclusion. Each time I thought of knocking on their door, I remembered Andrea's urging the soldiers in St. Lucia to shoot me; I wouldn't go by her house.

The following Monday, I received in the mail official notification from the Texas Department of Children's Protective Services: I'd been accused of abusing Freeda. Until the matter was resolved, I was prohibited from having contact with either Freeda or Monk. I immediately called the court-appointed social worker and court-appointed attorney I'd dealt with during the mess that had followed the St. Lucia caper. They said there was nothing they could do.

A few days later, notice arrived that I was being investigated for criminal child abuse. I visited my own attorney, Robert Lord, who looked over the complaint and declared it to be "a serious criminal matter." He consulted with two other criminal attorneys, and they informed me that I had to report to the police. A grand jury was going over the evidence and deciding whether to indict me. I got a sick feeling whenever I realized that people I knew, including these attorneys, might believe for even a second that I'd really done such terrible things.

Reporting to the police station in Humble was a dramatic experience. I knew the officers there; wanted men had turned themselves into me and I'd escorted them myself to the station. The chief of police, Leo Medley, was a friend. My children attended the private school run by his wife.

I sat alone with Leo in his office, where he told me something that made me cry. "Reporters come here every day and go through this list of people being served warrants," he said. "They're looking for news. I want you to know that when I saw your name in here, I took it out. I said, 'We're not going to do this to George.' "

A woman from Children's Protective Services soon came to interview me, Joan, Natalie, Michi, and Little George. She asked questions that were so far from the reality of our lives that I kept thinking it was like I was watching a horror movie.

My lawyers told me that the grand jury had studied a videotape of Freeda talking to a child-abuse expert, and that the testimony was "unconvincing"; it looked as though she was being led to say the "right" things. One member of the grand jury leaked word that they suspected an ulterior motive behind the charges. In fact, the judge assigned to the case wrote a report stating that he believed the charges resulted from an internal family squabble. What that family squabble was, he didn't know. But I did: Andrea hoped to move to South Carolina. She could do that with the children only if I agreed. And why did she want the children? For the child-support payments. That's what saddened me most. These kids were her paycheck.

Despite the flimsiness of the case, I knew that the news media would eventually get hold of the allegations and turn them into a tabloid scandal. I also knew they wouldn't print or broadcast the name of the child named in the complaint, which meant that all my children faced questions and queer glances from their friends and teachers: "Was it you he did it to?" I, who had been willing to die for these children, now wondered what impact my determination to clear my own name would have on the entire Foreman family.

I huddled with my other children and their mothers. They deserved to hear the story from me and no one else. Michi was thirteen then, Little George was twelve, and Georgetta was nine. They offered Dad their first advice as young adults: "Let those kids go." Freeda, they said, often invented things to get attention. "We know what she's capable of doing." Freeda apparently didn't understand that such matters don't blow over in a day, and that just being sorry doesn't necessarily repair damage.

The children's mothers agreed with them. "We like fighting with you too, George," one of them said. "But this is going too far." Out of this adversity, they became my friends. (Around the same time, Adrienne accompanied Michi to Houston to discuss with me some problems Michi was having. Because heavy rainfall prevented her from getting to her hotel, she spent the night in my spare bedroom. When she got back to Minneapolis, she told me, her boyfriend asked in a jealous tone if she'd been with me. "Yeah," she said, "and let me tell you something. I've been with a saint. Do you know that exists? He's a saint.")

I still hadn't decided what to do when I went to sleep that night. In a dream, I saw myself dressed in my then favorite suit, a gray silk Brooks Brothers that always made me feel like the chairman of all the boards—a serious suit worn only on serious occasions. Now here I was, wearing it in the boxing ring, ready to take on some giant. And I wasn't scared. So why then did I stop and back out of the ropes? Never in my life had I quit.

In the morning, I understood that the dream was a message from the Good Lord: Back off; don't fight.

"Look," I told the lawyers, "I did everything I could to get my children with me, to look after their lives. I tried to raise them in a right way. And I didn't do this thing I'm being accused of. But that doesn't matter. I'm not going to be the one to destroy them."

To illustrate my meaning, I recounted the biblical story of King Solomon, who decided a dispute between two women claiming to be the mother of the same infant. When no amount of questioning uncovered the truth, Solomon raised his sword. He said he was going to divide the baby in half, then split the halves between the two "mothers." When one of the women gasped and declared she would give her half to the other woman instead of seeing the child die, Solomon knew which was the real mother.

"I've got to let my kids live," I said. "I've got to save their name. If this gets in the newspapers, I will have destroyed them. They'll never again be able to lift their heads. Just let Andrea go. I love my children enough not to cut them in half."

When Andrea heard that I would not contest her leaving, the charges were instantly withdrawn. And they left—Freeda and Monk, with Andrea and Felix—almost as fast. Andrea wouldn't allow me to say good-bye.

I suffered for that loss, almost as though these children had died. I didn't even know where they lived exactly, because the child-support checks were sent to a welfare agency in Greenville, South Carolina. My tears would well up at any time, and with little warning. "I'll be back in a minute," I'd say to my wife. Then I'd lock myself in a room to cry. Later Joan told me she could hear my wails of grief. I'd get on my knees and say, "God, these are my children. Now they're gone from me."

Once again, my only comfort came from the Book of Job. Job was tested when all manner of tragedy befell him. But his faith in God survived them all, and because of that his wealth before the troubles began was doubled. In church, I explained that a true dairy farmer with sixteen cows can turn out more milk than a big corporate milk producer with eight times as many cows. The difference is that the farmer pulls the last drop out of each cow. That's what I did with the Book of Job. I milked every word and applied what I read to my own hard praying. Even when I reached my lowest, my faith survived and was strengthened.

Faith helped me to accept that Freeda had been dragged into something terrible she didn't understand. And faith helped me to reconcile myself to not seeing my Monk—that miniature George Foreman, my mirror. I'd understood everything about that boy, including how to reach him when it seemed like nothing could get through that skull. Losing him was like losing a limb.

I didn't see those two children from 1986 until 1991. Nearly five years had passed when Andrea called and admitted that she was sorry for what happened. She claimed that if she had it to do over again, she wouldn't do what she did.

"They need you, George," she said. "I've ruined their lives." She apologized for the damage done and told me in not so many words that I should blame her, not Freeda, for the problems Freeda was having.

I called my attorney for advice. He recommended that I get signed letters from Andrea and Freeda swearing that I never hurt or abused anyone, which I did.

When we were reunited, it took only a minute to see that Freeda was suffering terribly. We talked endlessly. She told me her problems and I passed on the benefit of what I knew. After a time I said, "You know, Freeda, you haven't ever told me you were sorry for all of that stuff. I think if you apologize, you'll find peace. Try to forgive and forget, and walk on, because you're always going to be my child."

"Dad," she said, "I'm sorry. I really am."

Andrea and I worked out an arrangement so the kids lived with their mother but spent vacations with me.

It had been five years since Monk had seen me—nearly his whole lifetime. All that he knew of me was whatever Andrea had told him. He didn't even recognize me. I said, "Hey, son. How ya' doin'?" He looked me over and over. When I grabbed him and hugged him, he went all stiff. He was still so much like me, hugging him was like hugging myself years ago. The strange thing is that he loved Joan right from the beginning, as though he remembered being a baby on her hip. He called me "George." Felix was "Daddy."

Monk and I spent more time together. In Marshall, I taught

him to ride horseback. We built the relationship slowly. It took a while before he got used to my hugging, though. I said, "Son, we have to make a deal here. We've got to embrace each other hello and good-bye. You don't mind, do you?"

"No, I don't mind."

He didn't know that I'd been thinking about the years I'd missed with Leroy Moorehead, but he went along with me anyway.

Soon he was visiting every vacation and holiday he could squeeze out of the calendar. Then every weekend. "Daddy, come get me," he'd say. He cried every time he had to go home. Andrea called once to say that he was still crying when she picked him up at the airport in South Carolina. But it wasn't until one day in 1994 when she said, "I hate to do it, but Monk wants to live with you. He wants to leave."

I'd dreamed about hearing those words, but I had to think more about what was best for my boy in the long run than about what I needed now. I got on the phone with him: "Son, you have to know that I want you to be with me more than anything in the world. But you're eleven years old now. You just can't desert your mother." Andrea had just divorced Felix, who'd taken their young child with him, and Freeda was a wild girl. "You've got to be your mom's hero now. You look after her, because I want my son to be like me."

I explained that the sum of who his father is began with my mother. Not in the womb, but in Fifth Ward. It was my mother who loved me enough to beat fear into me, and loved me enough to push me into the world that was best for me; then loved me enough to cry in secret when I was going to Oregon. From my mother, I learned how to get up and go to work. I learned to take my last dime and pay a bill. I learned to care. I learned to be a man.

"One of the main ingredients of George Foreman is the way I felt about my mother," I told him. "I was ashamed to be nothing for her. I had a commitment to her. That's why I became a boxer, to buy her a nice home and a life so she wouldn't break her back. That day I told her that she was through renting, that

I'd bought her a house, was one of the best days of my life. And I want you to have what I have, have that ingredient. You can only get it through your mom. You've got to look after her, son."

It was a tough call. And the right one. At the time I was thinking about Little George, who'd had an on-and-off relationship with his mother, Pamela, partly because she and I had had so little communication. He, too, had wanted to live with me full time. I hadn't allowed that, either.

In 1993 Little George accompanied me on a publicity tour. While we were in San Francisco, he left to visit his mother in nearby Sacramento. At the time, Pam was ill with cancer. When I called over the next day to see how they were doing, she told me that this nineteen-year-old standing there in a sport coat and tie had gladdened her heart beyond the telling. "I cannot believe it," she said. She was that far from crying. "You don't know how happy I felt. This is some young man you've given me. What a man you've given me." She repeated the sentence over and over.

After the tour Little George went off to his freshman year of college near Marshall. I called him up one day and asked him to come over.

"Son, sit down," I said. "I've got something to tell you."

How do you explain such a thing to your child? "She's dead, son. Your mother's dead." He got that look like he wanted to kill the world.

"But what—"

"There's nothing we can do about it. There it is."

I made him stay with me for a long while, holding him as he cried it out. "Just sit," I said. "Just sit. It's going to be okay." The words worked, only because he trusted me. But that was a terribly hard ordeal for Little George, and for me to see that boy's heart breaking. I knew that a part of him won't be there until he has a daughter.

I said no to Monk's living with me because I wanted to make sure that if his mother should die, he'd be prepared to say goodbye and make peace as well as Little George had. I think he will. He has a strong mind and strong body.

"Dad said I can't leave you," he told Andrea. "So we're going to Houston." He actually convinced her to move from South Carolina back to Houston. Then this eleven-year-old boy spent literally all night working alone to load a U-Haul van with their furniture and belongings.

"You don't know this child," Freeda said. "You just don't know. He's out there."

Monk's just beginning to have in him that desire to champion his mother and sister. But he loves Joan, too. He tells her about what's going on and everything that's gone wrong. When he said he wanted to play saxophone, I told him I'd buy him one if he showed he was serious with the one the school let him use. Now he spends hours with that thing strapped around his neck, practicing and waiting for me to call and ask him to play a tune. When he's here at the house, he follows me everywhere. He can drive me nuts because he's such a talker. He even boasts, the way I did as a kid.

"My name's George Edward Foreman, the same as my father," he told my friend Mort Sharnik. "My brothers and I all have the same name. But I'm the only one who has my father's nickname."

It's great to see how Monk and Natalie, who's fourteen, have become spiritual twins, more like brother and sister than even Monk and Freeda. Natalie was just a couple of years older but wanted to be responsible for him when he was a baby. When he'd wet his pants, she'd say, "You come on to the bathroom now." She'd disciplined him, too. "I can fix you bread and butter if you're hungry, but you've got to sit here at the table." That kind of thing.

Natalie is a determined young lady. She decided to be the best basketball player in the gym, but I told her no sports unless she kept her grades above ninety-six, even in her advanced classes. Easily accomplishing that, she set out to achieve her goal. I explained that if she expected to walk on the court and have the boys pass her the ball just because she was a girl, she was in for an awakening.

"If you want it," I said, "you have to take it. If you're going for

a rebound, you keep jumping until you grab it." Well, my relentless daughter has now taken over the gym. So when she says she
has her eye on Stanford Medical School, I believe that's where
she'll soon be.

Michi and I have a different relationship. She's at the stage
where she wants to be my parent, and doesn't like it when
Daddy tells her about life. What she doesn't realize yet is that
certain things come only with age. Michi's an artist, with the soul
of a poet and the brain of a comedian. Bette Midler reminds me
exactly of her. Same friendly look, same outrageous personality.

Georgetta's a serious girl, humble and intelligent. Of all my
children, she's the one I have the dearest relationship with right
now. What I like about her is her maturity. Come fall, she's going
off to college in California to study journalism. She has prepared
herself for feeling homesick at first, knowing that it's part of the
growing-up and breaking-away process. When I told her that I
wanted to buy a small place near her school so that I could visit
her anytime, she laid down the law: "I won't have time for you,
Daddy. I've got to be doing my thing."

In 1986 Joan and I had Leola, who's named for my favorite
aunt. Queen of the house, she acts as though she has royal blood.
She must have a lot of her mother in her, because people say the
same about Joan. It seems everyone defers to her. Or at least,
they respect her. When Leola meets adults for the first time, she
extends her hand and gives a firm shake that surprises them.

Big Wheel, the little man of the family, is a year younger than
Leola, but doesn't live in her shadow. He's the most independent
of my boys. I'm hoping he'll study law and then pursue a career
in politics, where he can do a lot of good for the country. That's
why I call him Big Wheel: People know when the big wheel rolls
into town. Of all my children, he's the only one who says "Yes,
ma'am" and "No, ma'am" to his mother, and "Yes, sir" and "No,
sir" to me. He won't tolerate foolishness. Where as a child Georgetta would disappear when the teasing began, Big Wheel puts
his foot down and says, "Enough!" He'll probably never spend a
day as a kid. His teacher told me that on the days when the class
visits children with disabilities or handicaps, he gets up without

being asked and takes over their care. Whenever I hear the line in the Blood, Sweat and Tears song "There'll be one child born in the world to carry on, to carry on," I think of Big Wheel. He'd be that child. This is one boy I'll never have to chase and say, "I love you." He knows who he is and where he stands.

Then there's the baby of the family. Some children are born old, like Big Wheel, and some are forever kids. That last applies to Red, my four-year-old. His name is short for "red light," because you constantly have to tell him to stop. There's no giving him an inch without him wanting the whole nine yards.

All my children are different, and I like it that way. As a young thug who had to know who was talking tough and who really was tough, I learned to peg character. I use that ability now to figure out what each of my kids needs in the way of discipline or freedom. Rather than try to fit each into the same mold, I try to mold my parenting to fit each of their personalities. I've seen children beaten by parents who wanted their kids to be all alike.

It's sad and too bad that my relationship with Freeda didn't heal the same way it did with Monk, and that she and I haven't been able to get back on a firm footing since that whole mess.

At seventeen, before finishing high school, Freeda married a man I'm not too fond of and don't believe is the type she needs. I bought her a nice car as soon as she turned sixteen, because I wanted her to know she was special. But I really think that's why this guy hoped to marry her. I'd brought her to live in my home, and I said, "You don't have to take anything off anybody." For Freeda, this love with him was different from what she felt for Mom there and Dad way over there. This was her own. It didn't matter that the young man was short on job prospects.

After the marriage I got her an apartment and my mother bought her furniture. Then she quit school. I gave her some money and urged her to go back. She took the money but refused the advice. We went up and down on the issue, and finally I threw up my hands and said, "Hey! Get your life together. I just can't support a woman and her husband. It's not natural."

I guess she decided I'd hadn't helped them enough. She called around to the tabloids and, for a promise of ten thousand dollars, repeated the allegations she made against me as a child. At the time I'd recently fought twice for the heavyweight title and was starring in an ABC television sitcom named for me.

My attorney in Beverly Hills, Henry Holmes, called one day to warn me about the tabloid reporters investigating Freeda's story. "Stay away from those people," he said. "They're mean. Don't even bother to try explaining yourself. Just don't talk to them."

I called Andrea to find out whether she had any idea of what had gotten into Freeda again. "I don't know what's happened to her," she said. "She's going to mess up her name. She thinks you hate me."

The poor girl had gotten one thought frozen in her mind and missed everything afterward.

Andrea and I launched a rescue mission. That was the moment when Andrea and I became friends. Maybe for the first time, we were on the same side. We had to team up to get our daughter out of trouble before the damage was too great. We snatched Freeda off the scene and bent her ear. Andrea said, "Don't you destroy your relationship with your father. It's way too important to treat it like that."

I said, "Freeda, you've got to understand. Your destiny is not to put a bridge between us forever. I can't let you do this. I can't have a daughter who's practically dead to me."

The girl hadn't weighed the consequences of her actions. In her mind, she'd get her money and everything would be right.

I said, "You cannot be in the world without a father. I'm not going to let you do it. I love you, and I want you to know that you have a father, and you always will." We hugged, and I thought she became my daughter again.

When the money arrived from the tabloid, Freeda returned it with a pledge to tell the real story. She also signed legal releases, admitting the false allegations.

We got closer and closer. I spoiled her with shopping sprees, because it was good to see her alive and smiling. But after a while she began demanding this and that. That's when I put a halt to the buying. She'd decided that my being nice to her came from the fear that she'd accuse me again.

"Hey," I said. "I love you. That's why I've been buying you things, not because I'm afraid you're going to tell some stories on me."

That ruptured the relationship.

Not long afterward I heard she was pregnant and that she had signed a deal with an author to write a book about me and her.

While I could never stop loving her, I try now not to bother with Freeda's life. I don't know how she and her husband support themselves. I do know that, as I write this, she hasn't yet given birth. When she does, I know that that child will be what we need to bridge the gulf between us.

After I fought for the world championship, Monk said that he and Freeda had watched the fight together. He said she rooted against me, yelling comments like, "Get him. Please don't let him win."

"That's your sister, boy," I told Monk. "You've got to find a way to love her."

"I do, Daddy," he said.

During the mid-1970s, my brother Roy had received a percentage of my boxing purses in exchange for taking care of my business affairs. By the time I retired in 1977, both he and my brother Sonny, who also worked for me, had earned a fair amount of money—but by the early 1980s, both were broke. In Roy's case, the reversal of fortune was due to poor investments. When I returned with the kids from my St. Lucia adventure in 1983, he and his wife had separated, and he was living at my mother's. Mom told me he was volunteering his time teaching kids how to box at a church gym. Roy hadn't really boxed himself, but from hanging around me all those years he knew enough about boxing to be an effective teacher.

I stopped by one day to see him and offer encouragement. The gym was a decrepit, flimsy place that the preacher had agreed to let Roy use on the condition that if he ever collected dues or fees from the kids or their parents, he would turn the money over to the church. When I got there, he was getting set to work with some of the kids in the ring. A few of the mothers were busy signing up their boys for the program. One young mother must have recognized me and thought that George Foreman, former champ, might really be able to help her son stay out of trouble; at least, that's what I saw on her face. But I wanted no part. I was a preacher now. My congregation couldn't think that I had any connection to boxing again. My opinion was that if she really wanted to keep her son out of trouble, she'd have sent him to church services instead.

About two months later, I ran into Roy somewhere. For some reason, I happened to ask about the kid whose mother had given me that look.

"That kid went to prison," he said.

"Prison?! Man, you've got to be kidding." I'd just seen that boy. He was standing near me from here to there.

"Yeah, he robbed a store with a friend. The storekeep shot his friend, so he shot the storekeep."

"Killed him?"

"No. Hurt him bad, though."

Turned out that the store he robbed was in Humble, not far from my home. I felt badly shaken and couldn't sleep. I was torn apart. I felt ashamed that I hadn't helped that boy when I could have. I'd let him slip through my fingers. If only I'd have grabbed him.

"Roy," I said, "we've got to do something."

Down the block from my church was a large warehouse that a building contractor had abandoned before completion. It was a perfect space and perfect location for the plan that had started to form in my head. Tapping my retirement fund that had been sapped by the St. Lucia trip, I formed a charitable foundation that bought the warehouse, refurbished it, and fitted it out with weights, a basketball court, boxing gloves, and the boxing ring from my ranch in Marshall. So began the George Foreman Youth and Community Center.

Roy and I erected a fence around the place, with a gate, to give it the look of a club. Soon busloads of kids were pulling up. That's how important it must have been.

We charged a dollar a year as dues, because I'm from that old school where you don't give kids anything for free. But we had some families that could barely afford even that. And some kids from these households had a lot of loving to get and a lot of growing up to do.

Charley, one of the baddest kids of the bunch, was just eight or so. But you could already peg him as a future Hell's Angel—tattoos on a Harley. I called him "Good Time Charley" to soften him up. He didn't get very soft at first, though. He reminded me of another belligerent young man I'd once known, fighting and raising Cain. I'd say, "Charley, be still" when he was disturbing the peace.

"Your mother—" he'd say.

Really a bad kid.

Finally it got to the point that Charley was making too much trouble for us to let him stay. "You can't come back here anymore," I told him.

Next afternoon his grandmother, who lived across the street from the center, brought him back. "I'm sorry," she said, "but Charley can't come home. My husband's sick, and Charley's mother doesn't finish work until late. We can't do anything with him. Please, you've got to keep him until his mother comes."

"This is a bad kid," I said.

She reached down to the ground and picked up a stick. "You've just got to use this on him," she said. That turned out to be unnecessary, because Charley sort of became my boy. I had him camped out by my side. When he talked, I listened. When he messed with other kids, I'd tell the other kids not to bother with Charley, then scold him. It wasn't long before you could see Charley with his chest a little farther out, picking fewer fights.

Another kid stood six feet tall at age thirteen. As you might imagine, Adrien had huge feet. Whenever I bought myself new sneakers, I bought him a pair, too. He told me that his daddy had been a basketball player. In fact, he was always talking about his six-foot, eight-inch-tall father who'd played power forward in college. He used to nag me constantly to take him to wrestling matches—Hulk Hogan and those guys. I said, "Man, why don't you ask your dad to take you sometime. He should do things like that with you. That's what dads are for."

Adrien looked down, then up. "I don't want to tell you this," he said, "but I don't know who my daddy is."

Stories like that made me a surrogate father to many of these boys. They'd follow me around. And more and more of them came from all over Houston. One group of about six spoke only Spanish, so I learned enough of the language to talk to them a bit.

My role was just to be there. I sat and watched them play basketball and lift weights and shadowbox. All they really wanted from me was my attention: "Hey, you blocked that shot"; "Keep your hands up in that ring"; "Man, that's a lot of weight."

There were no rules, except fair play and sportsmanship; those rules I enforced. Everything else was up to them. No set program.

I also had books if they wanted to read. All sorts of books— on history, art, writing, animals. Even Bibles. But I never gave sermons. No evangelizing. Still, in time, one kid after another would come to me with a confession and vow: He was giving up a bad habit or two, cleaning up his life.

It was a thrill to see these young men transform themselves in a matter of days and weeks. The most obvious were the boys who'd walk in one day frail and scared. After a few boxing lessons and some serious hanging out, they'd return a stare with confidence. Even better, they thought enough of themselves not to pick fights just for the fun of it. Showing self-respect was a bylaw of the center.

The boys grew so fast. It seemed that one day a kid would have peach fuzz on his cheeks, and the next day he'd have sprouted whiskers. A lot of my boys came from troubled homes, and some of them brought trouble home with them. Their parents might not speak to each other because the boy was confusing them so badly. We'd schedule the boy for a boxing match and invite the parents, who always ended up cheering for their son. Two or three months later, maybe Mom and Dad were partners again and in sync with their child. They were all together and no one was ashamed. So many fathers started coming that I began a six-week introductory boxing and boxing-appreciation class. In the final session, the guys would actually put on gloves and headgear and get in the ring to spar. And their boys would cheer for them, too.

That's the sort of stuff that can't be planned. But it happened often enough for me to understand how important the center had become. Sometimes you don't know what the need is until it's filled. The center was a haven, safe from the outside world. Someone once left a gold chain on a bench. A week later it was still there for him. Boys and men both would sit and relax, just do nothing. People often slept. This was a place where everyone got to be a giant in his own world.

One day Ed Wallaceson, my attorney who'd set up my financial affairs, came to me with news he knew I didn't want to hear. "George," he said, "it's great that you're trying to help people. But I have to tell you, you're going to be the saddest boxing story since Joe Louis began standing out there at Caesars Palace shaking hands. You can't afford to keep this place up. You're going to have to pull back."

Sometimes reality intrudes. I felt like crying, not just because what he said was true, but because I didn't want anybody, even him, to know what I already knew. That money my accountant had stolen was really setting me back now. One thing I didn't want to give up was my own children's college education money. But I had other obligations as well. These kids were jumping on buses every day to come to my center. If I didn't take care of them, who would? They didn't need to hear about my financial problems.

In late 1986, I received an invitation to speak from a church group in Minnesota that offered an honorarium, which I planned to apply to the center's operating costs. It occurred to me that as long as I had an adequate supply of speaking engagements, the honorariums would solve my center's financial problems. I called Roosevelt Grier, the former football player who'd become an evangelist. I said, "I hear that when you're invited to speak somewhere, people make donations."

He didn't seem to want to talk about it. He may have thought I was coming in the back door for a donation myself. That's exactly what I never wanted anyone to think, that I was an old boxer who'd run out of resources, lying that he's going to give the money he's asking for to underprivileged kids. *Yeah, right.*

I went to Minnesota and accepted the nine-hundred-dollar honorarium from the church deacon. I told him about my youth center and what I was trying to do. I said, "When you start trying to help people, it can get rough. You waste so many years helping yourself, you don't know that one day you're going to realize you need to help other people. And then you don't have it to give."

"I heard a story," he said, "a story about a man who didn't care about anyone but himself. His fields produced crops aplenty, but he kept all the food for himself. Then God spoke to him. God said that on this night the man was to put all the harvested crops under one roof. The man complained that he had so much, the barn was going to burst. 'I have to build new barns to hold everything.' And as he began to build, the Lord spoke to him again. The Lord said, 'On this night, thy soul is required.' "

The preacher stopped for a moment, then added, "On such a day we have everything, but nothing built up to God. And here you are, George, building up things for God without thought for yourself. He's not going to let you down."

I used eight hundred of the nine hundred dollars I'd earned to make the mortgage payment on the center and one hundred to buy ropes for the boxing ring. It seemed pretty easy to keep this place going, since I was getting at least one paying invitation a month. And for a few months, that's how it went. Then an invitation came to speak at a three-day evangelical conference in Georgia.

I agreed to speak all three days, but made it clear that I didn't want them passing the plate for me.

"Oh, no," the organizer said. "We'll give you a real honorarium."

For three days I spoke and met the people attending. These were just regular people, most of them poor. At the end of the conference the organizer rose and described the good work being done by the George Foreman Youth and Community Center. I smiled proudly until he turned the address into a request to dig deep for donations. "We're going to raise some money for George," he said. "He's helping these kids, our kids." I thought about becoming invisible. And it got worse. "Come on," he pleaded as the cash got passed forward. "You can give more money than that. You help George, for our kids' sake." They were looking at me, and I had to look back at them, and pretend I wasn't ashamed.

I vowed at that moment, sitting on a hard bench in front of those people, that as long as I lived I would never again be involved in a stunt like this. Yes, those kids needed me, and I wouldn't desert them. I'd just have to find another way to raise funds.

And then the thought struck me: *I know how to get money. I'm going to be heavyweight champ of the world. Again.*

Chapter Ten

SOME PEOPLE WOULD SAY (in fact, most people *did* say) that my returning to professional boxing at age thirty-seven after ten years away was as foolish as believing that Elvis (who gave up the ghost the year I hung up the gloves) was still alive. They said that I could never hope to get back in fighting shape (at 315 pounds, I was about a hundred pounds heavier than when I won the title from Joe Frazier fourteen years before), that the muscle memory I needed to throw a professional punch was lost forever, and that what I aimed to do couldn't be done because, well, it hadn't been done.

But I'd never approached boxing as a skill. I'd fought because I was good at it, and I saw no reason for that talent to desert me now. I'd left boxing; boxing hadn't left me. And now I wanted back because of the best reason. I couldn't allow fifteen-year-old boys to go on shooting people and ending up in jail. I had to help these kids. I wasn't an accountant or a welder or a golfer. Boxing was what I knew, and there was no time to learn anything else.

The problem I faced reentering boxing wasn't any of the usual concerns. I knew that, as a preacher, I'd no longer be able to use anger as a motivation in the ring; I just didn't have any. For me, boxing would have to become the gentlemen's sport that it was intended to be way back when, and I'd have to win my matches with an absence of rage and a minimum of violence.

After I left the conference in Georgia, I went jogging and thought about the decision from all viewpoints. Then, back in Humble, I broke the news to my wife.

"Guess what," I said, and told her my scheme.

"Uh-uh," she said. "Don't do it. Don't do it, George. You're going to get killed."

I wrote a letter to Barney Oldfield, my public relations friend at Litton, and asked for his opinion. He was mostly encouraging. I asked my friend and attorney Robert Lord what he thought. He said, "George, I don't think you should ask anybody else. They're bound to bring up negative stuff. If it's something you want to do, then do it."

I couldn't help asking Gil Clancy for his opinion. When I explained over the phone what I was planning, he said, "George, why don't I come down and take a look at you—let you know how you look; see what's going on. Then I can tell you what I think."

"I'll call you back," I said.

Robert had been right. Gil's answer was just the sort of thing I didn't want. Looking for a ringing endorsement, I heard anything less as negativity. There was no point in asking anyone else. Besides, only I knew what was in my heart and mind, and what I was capable of.

I called my older children together and explained my plans. I said, "We've all been through a lot. I've done everything I can to keep us together as a family. Everyone has suffered somehow. But now I want you to know that I think you're all old enough to make your own decisions. You're going to have to walk a line, because from now on you can't say, 'It's my mother's fault' or 'It's my father's fault.' Whatever decisions you make from now on are the ones you're going to be judged by."

And I told them one more thing: "I'm going to be heavyweight champ of the world."

The kids were great. "But Dad," one of them said. "You won't be able to go outside. People'll be asking you for autographs everywhere you go. We won't be able to go to restaurants and movies like we do now." I thought that was an interesting observation from kids who weren't old enough even to remember my first career.

That night I asked Joan to give me her honest opinion. "I'm not afraid of your getting hurt," she said. "I really don't think they'll kill you. I know you can do it if you put your mind to it. But I've seen publicity photos of you from before. I just don't want that kind of man in my life."

I promised my wife that she wouldn't lose her husband, and my kids that I'd still be the same dad.

To remove any of my own doubts, I submitted to a battery and a half of tests at the University of Texas's M. D. Anderson hospital—tests I doubt even the state athletic commissions knew about. Nothing like them had existed ten years before. They took pictures of my heart and lungs and circulatory system and brain, measured the stress on my heart after exertion, and checked my neurological functions. After two days, I was pronounced fit.

Unfortunately, my boxing trunks didn't. In fact, none of my boxing gear fit; not even my boots. I guess all the extra weight had made my feet larger, too. "Man, this stuff has shrunk," I said to my wife.

From my winning the gold medal until my retirement, companies like Everlast had sent me whatever I needed in the way of equipment and clothing. Now I had to go out and buy that stuff myself. One of my biggest surprises was finding that there were stores selling shorts and gloves and all the paraphernalia. But the biggest surprise was running shoes—they hadn't existed when I last fought.

"You mean," I said, "that there are shoes with a cushion on the bottom? And they're made just for running? Wow."

Joan acted as my first trainer, driving me five, eight, ten miles away, and dropping me off to run home. I found that I'd been blessed with another gift: willpower. Before, even as champ, I'd never run longer than three miles. Now, at age thirty-eight, I was running minimarathons. In fact, for the first time, I discovered what athletes meant when they talked about getting their "second wind." Forcing myself through the leg-dragging phase, I'd suddenly be refreshed, able to go as far as my willpower allowed, and that seemed like infinity.

One day I told my brother Sonny to hold the heavy bag for a half hour of nothing but right hands, one after another. He thought I was nuts, and wouldn't last more than ten minutes. After ten minutes I started thinking myself what a fool I was, that I didn't have to do this, that I was going to hurt my hand, that no trainer had ever pushed me this hard, and that I didn't have anything to prove. But I kept going anyway. By the end of the half hour, Sonny respected what he saw. He let go of the bag and began walking away. I called him back for a half hour of nothing but left hooks, then a half hour of jabs.

Soon I began skipping backward along the inside perimeter of the ring, first one way, then the other. I'd do it for the equivalent of ten rounds—ten three-minute stints with one minute in between. It's incredibly hard to do. Then I'd jump rope for two three-minute rounds.

When I didn't want to leave the family to train, I would take the pennies I'd been saving for years out onto the patio. For each lap I completed around the patio, either walking briskly or running the hundred-foot circumference, I'd drop a penny in a bucket until the bucket overflowed. One child would march with me until he got tired, then someone else would take his place to keep me company. Hundreds and hundreds, if not thousands, of laps.

Remembering the first time around all those years ago, Sonny marveled at how hard I was training. "Ten times harder than you used to," he said. This time around, I knew a thousand and one things I hadn't known then, one of them being that a returning fighter pushing age forty can't be ordinary; he has to be extraordinary. He can't be in good shape; he has to be in exceptional shape. Since it was the legs that would betray my age, the legs had to believe they were twenty years younger. I started using a treadmill so that I could supplement my daily runs outside with nighttime ones indoors.

But in spite of all the training, I couldn't get below 300 pounds for the longest time. That disappointed me, because I'd thought I'd get down to 220 in a month or two. Back when I weighed that, I never even worried about weight; my waist, yes, but not my weight. Nor had I concerned myself with muscles. I figured I had them—the evidence was the guys I'd knocked out. Now I was lifting weights and running hours at a time. The day the scale read 296 seemed like one of the happiest days of my life.

Then there was food. You could safely say that I hadn't kept up with the latest nutritional advances. My idea of a diet was the one I'd eaten in my boxing prime—lean steak and salad. After a few months I was reintroduced to a young man I'd known years before. Now he was trying to get into boxing promotion.

"George," he said, "don't you know the days of steak and salad are gone? There's a new day in boxing. Now people eat pasta. It's carbohydrates."

I switched. And in time, I got down to about 230 pounds.

I'd returned to boxing so that I could keep the youth center going by myself, but if I was going to take the training to its next level I'd need a trainer and sparring partners. That meant high expenses. Estimating that I needed to put together between $500,000 and $700,000, I tried to concoct a business deal with investors. In exchange for the upfront cash, I'd offer forty percent of all future boxing earnings.

"What are you going to do with the money?" they'd ask.

I'd explain that, instead of being at the mercy of promoters who'd have preferred to match me against guys I wasn't yet ready for, I intended to promote myself. I would travel around the country, fighting in small clubs against the right opponents to get myself in proper shape. Obviously, ticket prices would be reasonably priced.

"In time," I promised, "I'll be champ of the world."

Some guys snickered at that. Others flat out spoke what most people probably thought: "Too old. Can't take a chance on a guy who's so old."

"No, I really know how to do this," I'd say. "It's going to take some time, but you'll make a lot of money. A *lot* of money."

If they brought up Mike Tyson, who was champ then and considered unbeatable, I'd say, "Listen, Tyson's style is perfect for me. I can beat him, no problem."

I must not have been a very good salesman. I got no after no. Finally, when one guy refused, I said, "You had your chance.

You missed an opportunity to make millions of dollars. I'll take my own money and do it."

A few months before I'd gone to my bank to withdraw a few thousand dollars, to pay for the funeral of my mother's only brother, A. D. Nelson, who'd died almost penniless. Once again, I was breaking into my pension fund, which had stood at a couple of million dollars before the youth center and other expenses had reduced its worth.

"It's awful decent and honorable of you, George," the banker had said. "But you can't just keep doing that sort of thing for your family and friends. At the rate you're going, I'll give you two years before you're broke."

Even though he was only doing his job, I vowed then never to have another conversation with another banker over my financial affairs. So when I was planning to finance my own comeback, I didn't ask; I just took what was mine anyway. I had no doubts that I was going to replenish the capital ten times over.

What I lacked in funds, I made up for in experience. And in the boxing game especially, experience means wisdom.

As my trainer, I rehired Charley Shipes, who'd just gotten out of prison after serving several years (for "intent to distribute a controlled substance"). He didn't have a job, and his prospects weren't great, so it was a good opportunity for us both. His small salary now in exchange for a percentage of future earnings gave him the chance for some real money. I still remembered that night twenty years before when he was working my corner in a fight and he said, "I'm Sadler tonight," and I'd felt comforted.

It wasn't until I got in the ring and sparred that I knew my boxing antennae still worked. There was that invisible message telling the brain to move the body and head. As long as the antennae worked, I'd be fine. Without them, there was no point in going forward. Because without reception, even lightning reflexes are useless.

There was one problem. I couldn't get used to hitting people. By practicing only my defensive techniques, I was allowing my sparring partners to get right in on me and whale away. When my mom saw a welt over my eyebrow, she said, "Son, you know

I wasn't too happy about you getting back into boxing. But as long as you are, please, start hitting back."

Even then, I had trouble. After all, I wasn't a huge, tired guy; I was a huge, healthy guy. My sparring partners were men who weighed what I had ten years before. They seemed like matchsticks to me. If I wanted, I could bump them across the ring with my belly.

Apart from the hitting, having the gloves on again gave me unbelievable pleasure. I didn't know how much I'd missed the feeling until I returned. I was first to arrive at the center in the morning, and the last to leave at night. Most of that time, I was smiling. I wanted to spar all day. So when my paid partners left or were too exhausted, I took on the kids whom I'd tutored. (Obviously, I didn't hit them.)

The ten years off had been great. Now, with some maturity and perspective, I was able to truly appreciate the skills and talent God had given me. Boxing was what I'd been born to do. That's not always true of a boxer. Some guys, including champions, weren't necessarily made for the sport. Muhammad Ali, for example. Despite his remarkable accomplishments in the ring, he wasn't born to box; he was born to run. If he'd lived 150 years ago, before the modern rules made speed as important as punching power, he *couldn't* have survived as a boxer. Maybe he'd have been better off. (On the other hand, Muhammad would have made a terrific matinee idol. He was far and away the best-looking boxer I'd ever seen. He was right when he used to call himself "pretty.")

Every professional fighter has to be licensed by the state in which he's fighting. Some state athletic commissions are lenient about licensing. Others take the licensing job seriously, trying to make sure that physically or mentally unfit boxers don't climb into the ring. The most restrictive state commission is in California. That's why I decided to stage my comeback there. I figured that after California, getting licensed in any other state would be a formality.

As I'd predicted, the athletic commission initially refused to license me on the basis of my age, even though I'd passed their mandatory tests, which were much less severe than the ones I'd taken in Houston. At a hearing in San Diego, the commission's doctor insisted that, at my age, I could get seriously hurt boxing. He said the state didn't want my blood on its hands. There was no way he would reconsider, not even after seeing the results of my tests.

What turned the tide was a lawyer who represented the state attorney general's office. He asked why I wanted to fight again.

"Life, liberty, and the pursuit of happiness," I announced. That was the truth. Thomas Jefferson would have applauded my declaration of independence. My words left the attorney general's man no choice but to recommend licensing me.

"This man has satisfied all your requirements," he said. "So if there's nothing wrong with him, you should just go ahead and give him a license."

When I publicly announced my return, the people laughing loudest were sportswriters. I didn't mind. They could be excused for their ignorance. How were they to see what was in my heart, soul, and mind? Besides, they didn't know what to make of me anymore. Before my first fight was held in Sacramento in March of 1987, I spent two weeks making a dozen personal appearances, speaking at churches, schools, and hospitals. The local sportswriters and broadcasters following me around were obliged to report what I said in my speeches, so even these cynical, jaded guys ended up spreading good words. The closer we got to the fight, the more people would come to see my open sparring sessions. Beforehand, I'd talk to them about anything and everything, and as they left, they'd promise to bring their grandfathers and uncles and cousins to meet me tomorrow.

The fight itself, against Steve Zouski, was almost an anticlimax. But when the crowd gave me a standing ovation, I felt I'd come home, even if home was someplace new. Never before had I received a standing ovation in the ring. It was odd, too. Here I was, a preacher used to getting applause for spreading God's law. It was so odd, in fact, I actually stood there and deciphered what the applause was about.

I decided that, first, I was a novelty. Like a lot of fans, I was creeping up on middle age—or middle age was creeping up on me. We'd never before been on the best of terms, the fans and I, but we'd both matured. Maybe they were hoping that George could recapture some of their glory for them.

But these people weren't yelling for me to beat someone's brains in. They were simply acknowledging me. Ten and twenty years before, when they spoke of great boxers, they mentioned Louis and Dempsey and Marciano and Ali and Frazier—and me. And now, one of those names was back; they were being given a second chance to see history. I was that old well you don't miss until it runs dry. Suddenly, I was flowing again.

Then, too, I was that guy they'd seen in the 1960s who'd waved the flag around the ring when it wasn't fashionable. Now it wasn't unfashionable. They'd grown up and had kids, and wanted their kids to love America. So they appreciated me for what I'd done. At least, that's what I was thinking as the cheers increased.

I had butterflies before the bell rang. But what scared me most was taking off the robe and parading around the ring without my shirt. For most of the past decade I'd been seen only in proper slacks and long-sleeve shirts buttoned to the neck.

As the fight began, I was reluctant to hit Steve Zouski. Every time I did, I felt embarrassed, as though I were betraying myself. I knew there was no way I could go wild on a human being again; no way could I unleash a torrent of punches until the man crumpled to the mat. The ref kept ordering me to box. I used a new jab, one I'd been developing and never had before. When I hit him with it, I could see that it hurt. And if I used my right, it really hurt. So I'd stop for a while, and the ref would again order me to box.

"But he's hurt," I'd say.

"Just box, George," he'd reply.

I think the reason the ref stopped the fight in the fourth was that he got tired of arguing with me and knew the result wasn't in doubt. For my victory, I earned twenty-one thousand dollars.

In July, I fought Charles Hostetter in Oakland. Third-round K.O. In September Bobby Crabtree lasted six rounds in Springfield, Missouri. Then came a fourth-rounder in November against Tim Anderson in Orlando. These weren't ranked heavyweights, but they were all tough professionals with winning records. And the places we fought were little hitching posts. Still, the people came and stood for me, their applause filling the hall and my heart. I drank it in like a thirsty man. This was what I'd missed the first time out. No one ever appreciated it more than I. What's more, I think they saw I appreciated it, and saw how much I loved them back. That was a new experience for both of us.

With December and the Christmas shopping season coming up, finding a fight wouldn't be as easy as it had been. But I didn't want to lay off an extra month. I was in a hurry now. I had a goal, knew myself well enough to gauge progress, and understood exactly what it took to get there. I could almost see the path stretched out ahead of me, could anticipate the unpaved parts, like following a master plan. To watch people and other obstacles simply move out of the way without me having to honk was a sign.

Even though I didn't want to get involved yet with Las Vegas, I called Bob Arum. Bob's event-promotion company, Top Rank, is one of the must successful in the country.

"I need to fight," I said. "And no one will do anything over the holidays." I also told him that I didn't want to be on television, not right then. To do television right, you can't go and ask for television. You have to make television want you and come to you. It's simple: No one ever follows a water truck. But a fire truck, with sirens blaring, draws a crowd in a hurry; they'll come out of their houses. That's what I had to do—become a fire truck.

"Well, we've got a regular ESPN show," he said. "It goes on in December."

"Don't you have anything *off* the tube?" I really didn't want to be seen just yet, not even on cable.

"The ratings go down this time of year," he said. "Nobody comes to Vegas to see fights now. It'll be good for you."

Finally I agreed, but he said he couldn't pay more than $12,500—and wouldn't sign any three-fight deals. Word must have reached him that I'd been looking for investors, and he may have thought I was hitting him up.

"I don't want that anyway," I assured him.

Bob promoted my fight against Rocky Sekorski in a small banquet room at Bally's in Vegas. They brought in a lot of additional chairs to handle the crowd. With all the chairs filled and much of the aisle space, the fire marshal began turning people away.

I knocked Rocky out in the third round. Bob jumped into the ring as if I'd just won the title. Later he told me that the TV rating set a record for boxing shows. He said he wanted me to sign a three-fight deal.

"No."

But I did agree to fight Guido Trane, an Italian champ, in February. "You do this one for twenty-four thousand," he said. "I'm going to move you up each time. The one after will be for a hundred thousand."

A month later I knocked out Tom Trimm in the first round of a bout I set up myself in Orlando. Then I fought Trane, who figured to be my best test yet. He lasted five rounds. When I could see that he was hurt and could get more hurt, I asked him, "Are you okay?" I told the ref to stop the match. I had to do that. I wasn't just George Foreman now; I was the living symbol of the George Foreman Youth and Community Center. I stood for something. When I drew blood on a man's face, I'd yell, "He's cut" and point to it. Then, until the knockout, I'd hit only on the other side of the face from the cut.

Bob scheduled me in March to fight a tough young kid with a good reputation, Dwight Qawi. Before the fight, I dreamed that I told him, "Man, you're going to get killed." In the real ring, he ducked and dodged, tried to carry the fight into late rounds; it was like he'd watched a tape of the Ali fight. (He also hit me with some good shots early.) But he was no Ali, and I wasn't my 1974 model. One time I hit him with a wickedly hard right, then held him so he could recover. A while later, he just walked away and quit. Afterward, in the locker room, he told my brother Roy, "Man, I saw death. I wasn't going to die in that ring. That was death."

There were several sportwriters at the fight. While their stories about me had gotten a little more gracious, they now found a new angle: passivity. Instead of George Foreman being a brute, they wrote, he lacked the killer instinct. I knew then that there'd be no winning until I won it all.

Killer instinct or no, the crowds were loving me. They packed every hall I played. Seeing that, Bob Arum stepped in with plans to match me with this guy and that. Excited by potential, he had an architect's vision of my career. But I didn't like his plan and wouldn't go along with it. For one thing, he suggested firing Charley Shipes and hiring Gil Clancy as my trainer, then finding different sparring partners.

"I'm not going to do that," I said. "These guys are my friends. They understand what I'm trying to accomplish. And I want them to go along with me."

Bob also insisted that I sign a tough three-fight package. "You've got to do it," he insisted.

"No." I explained that I wasn't ready to fight top guys yet.

He got mad. He thought he knew what was better for me than I did.

"Listen," I said, "I didn't come back to make big money. I'm making enough now for what I set out to do. Anyway, I'm going to get the big money in time. I came back to be champ, and I'm going to do it my way."

That temporarily ended my association with Bob. He told some sportswriters that I should quit boxing. "He doesn't want to fight anyone," he said.

Reporters called me. "I don't care what Bob Arum said," I told them. "I didn't want to work the way he did. Besides, I don't need Top Rank. In fact, I don't need Don King. I made Don King. And I can make myself."

I was bold now, and starting to ballyhoo. The writers liked it, so I gave them more. "They say I'm old. But I'm going to show them that if you can dream, you can do anything. And I dreamed I was going to be heavyweight champ of the world. Nobody's going to stop me. I've got life, liberty, and the pursuit of happiness." I usually went on and on. The longer the better for the reporters. The guys who'd been there first time around were amazed by the change in me. And the young reporters who'd only heard about me were just as amused. They started coming to hear me talk, not to see me spar. One thing I never talked about to them was religion. On that subject, I let my actions speak for me.

This sort of ballyhooing was what Bob Arum apparently didn't understand. Ballyhooing seemed to be a lost art; it had died around the time I quit boxing, which coincided with the rise of television as the master. Ballyhooing was splattering a bus with posters and getting out on the road, beating guys you knew you could whip. They might look like he-men, but they had glass jaws that would shatter at the lightest touch. Glass jaws with muscles were everywhere. I could tell on film which guys fit the bill. Some guys who looked like palookas could take a punch better than Jack Dempsey, and some guys who looked like Dempsey fell at a sneeze. The art was to know which was which and match yourself properly against them. (Floyd Patterson, they said, had a glass jaw; his was just a lot harder to hit.) Arum had been bringing me films of guys with concrete chins and platinum reputations. I wasn't ready yet for them. I was trying to get some momentum going first. Building. Ballyhooing. He didn't understand my reasoning, which, in fairness, I didn't explain to him either. He kept talking about beating this guy and that guy and then getting Tyson. That's not how ballyhooing worked. I wasn't out to agonize my way up the ladder by beating every guy above me; I didn't have time for that. I wanted to win just enough battles to get everyone talking about George Foreman. Then, in order to meet Tyson, all I'd have to do was beat the guy right below him. Two battles, that's all. Dick Sadler had known about such things. I used to wonder why he'd match me with this or that particular guy. Eventually, I learned. And now, as my own manager, I had to watch out for my fighter. Me. What Arum misunderstood at the beginning was my reason for accepting the fights he brought to me. He believed I'd agreed because of the money he was offering. But I'd taken the fights because it just so happened he brought me the right fighters.

Working with promoter Ron Weathers, I ballyhooed, going almost anywhere for a fight. No, it wasn't for the kind of money Arum held in front of me. But using local promoters who owned licenses, we filled decent arenas in places like Anchorage, Marshall, Bakersfield, and Auburn Hills against top local talent—and the money got better and better. That year I fought in every month but April, July, and November. Most of the fights ended within three rounds. Only Qawi went seven.

The following year, 1989, I fought five times, the most memorable of them against Bert Cooper, who was a highly regarded puncher who'd beaten some excellent fighters and given others a hard time. I knocked him out in three rounds.

That attracted the attention of the USA Network. Now I was that fire truck roaring through the neighborhood.

Ron Weathers said he thought he could match me against Gerry Cooney, the big strong fighter who a lot of people had thought would be heavyweight champ some day. Ron went to Bob Arum to get some help from him. I laughed, feeling certain that if I'd listened to Bob two years before, I wouldn't have climbed so far. Now I was back in the hunt, and Arum was helping on my terms. I dreamed that I knocked out Gerry Cooney in the second round.

The fight, which took place in January of 1990, filled the convention center in Atlantic City and drew a huge pay-per-view audience as well. In the dressing room before the fight, I joined hands with my brother Sonny, Charley Shipes, and Mort Sharnik, who'd just begun handling my publicity. We prayed together.

All punches hurt. But if you feel the pain, you know you're okay. You can either rub the spot or run back to your corner after the round and cry for a minute. Some shots, however, are so ferocious they don't hurt. What they do is interrupt communications between the tower and the ground. Knees jiggle. You're looking at your opponent, but your legs are somewhere else. In my career, I remember two blows that taught me what it's like to be hit that hard. Neither Muhammad Ali nor Jimmy Young delivered them. One had been courtesy of Ron Lyle. The other came that night from Gerry Cooney. I'd heard about Cooney's famous left hook, but dismissed the talk as the hyped weapon every fighter of renown is supposed to have somewhere in his arsenal. Well, about thirty seconds into the first round he hit me with a left hook to the kisser that showed me, if nothing else, how durable I must be. Mort later told friends he thought the punch had broken me in two.

For some reason, Cooney didn't notice the damage he'd inflicted. If he had, I think he'd have entered his finishing mode and piled on the punishment until I went down. Instead, he kept looking for the one-punch knockout, and on wobbly legs I was somehow able to press forward until the round ended. Later, I saw on videotape the excitement in Cooney's corner between rounds. Gil Clancy, who was now working with Cooney, told him, "You really got him. You hurt him."

Inspired, Cooney came out for the second round punching the way he should have after his crushing blow in the first. But looking to finish me now was a major tactical error, because I'd gotten my legs back. I hit him some damaging shots—the best combinations I'd thrown in years—that put him down. When he rose at six, I threw a few more. Down and out he went. Just like the dream.

That told me my punching power had returned.

And it told other promoters that I was gold.

Punching power aside, the crowds at my fights and at home in their living rooms were rooting for a boxer as they hadn't since the glory days of Muhammad Ali. Why? Because all those years of preaching had taught me how to please an audience. In self-defense I'd had to learn persuasion: It had hurt to see people get up and leave my church or to watch them walk away from my street corner. Keeping them watching and listening is called "closing the door." Nobody leaves home and says, "I'm gonna watch a street-corner preacher." They have to be drawn to you by what you're saying.

People have told me I have charisma. I don't know what I've got. I only know that when I decided I'd have to close the door on these people, the Good Lord told me that he would give me the gift. And after I learned that closing the door may also mean making people laugh, the Lord spoke to me again. He said, "I hate to tell you this, but I'm going to have to make a comedian out of you."

Pretty soon, people did laugh. Either something I said or the way I said it, or both, made it hard for them to move from the pews or the sidewalk. It was a gift, being able to hold and amuse them in order to give them the Word.

Even when the word wasn't God's, I had to do the same thing now in front of cameras, microphones, and tape recorders that I'd been doing for ten years.

After not watching television for those ten years, I happened onto a video world in 1987 that was almost unrecognizable from the one I'd left in 1977. Suddenly, there were a hundred channels. As I sat there channel surfing with the remote in hand, I realized that what kept me stuck on a particular show was comedy—especially someone funny who didn't offend. I figured that what was true for me was probably true for most people. So if the ballyhoo was to be successful, I decided, I had to become a pure entertainer. That's why my job was to keep them laughing; never get serious; always have a joke; turn all dark questions into something funny. When a reporter asked me about brain damage in boxing, I said, "I already have that. I've been married four times." Asked what happened to all my money, I replied, "Fast women and slow horses." Questioned about when I should retire, I said, "I'm going to fight to pass a bill that would force a mandatory retirement age on boxers—sixty-five." Accused of fighting only guys on respirators, I said, "That's a lie. They've gotta be at least eight days off the respirator."

Sammy Davis, Jr., used to say, "Ya gotta make 'em love ya." It was the fan's gift to me that they did. And I loved them right back. Boy, did I love 'em back.

My popularity was measurable in the amount of endorsement offers I began receiving. I was reluctant to take them, however; it seemed somehow cheap. Out of the blue one day, Bill Cosby shocked me by calling to say hello. He said, "I like you, George. I heard you say once that when God told you to sit down, you didn't look for a chair. I liked that. You needed money for your youth center and your family, you didn't ask anybody for anything; you went to work. I admire that."

I mentioned the commercials and said, "I'm a preacher. I don't think I should be doing them."

"Now wait a minute," he said. "You're just like any other boy with dreams."

He was right. It hadn't occurred to me that I might like to see myself up there on television like Bill Cosby. That's when I began saying yes. And in time, I think I became the best salesman around, not because I'm a better actor, but because I'm not. What I do is fall in love with every product I sell. If I can't fall in love with it, I don't sell it. People can detect that in you. They know when you don't believe what you're saying, and they know when you do. That's what sells. Just like with preaching. Nobody doubts that I love God. And nobody seems to doubt that the George Foreman they see on the screen is the real George Foreman. Everyone thinks they know me. They do.

As the public, the press, the broadcast media, and I were spinning in this upward cycle, promoters chased me with offers. What rankled them was that I didn't play by the conventional rules. A large check dangling in front of my eyes didn't earn the usual reaction. After all, I wasn't just a boxer. I was the rainmaker for a charitable foundation. Every penny I made went into the George Foreman Community Center. Eventually, the mortgage note was paid off. But we still needed an endowment to fund the center in perpetuity—and to make improvements to the facilities.

One day when I was at the center, I spotted kids playing basketball on the blacktop and mud. A couple of them fell. Others complained about their knees. In fact, I'd hurt my knees on that court too. So when I accepted an offer to fight in England in September of 1990, my payment was the construction of an indoor court with a rubberized floor like the ones they had in the best gyms. (McDonald's had already donated a first-class scoreboard in exchange for my appearance in a commercial.)

The youth center had become a wonderful place. About the only thing it didn't have full time was George Foreman. Actually,

I spent as much time there as possible; that's where I trained. I tried not to travel for more than five days at a stretch, even for fights. In my presence or absence, my nephew Joey Steptoe managed, Mom acted as secretary, and Dad answered the phone. Everyone in the family did something or other.

The more I continued to win, the more inevitable became the Tyson-Foreman showdown. Then, in early 1990, came the boxing shock of many years: Mike Tyson lost to journeyman James "Buster" Douglas in Tokyo. That disappointed me terribly. But after fighting four more times that year, winning by knockouts in, respectively, the fourth, second, third, and first rounds, I signed to fight the new champ, Evander Holyfield, for the world championship on April 19, 1991, in the Atlantic City Convention Center.

"It's coming true," my wife said. "The dream's coming true for us."

In October, Holyfield had knocked out Douglas, who was making his first title defense. The reason Holyfield chose me was because I had enough fan support to guarantee him $20 million, and he thought this "old man" of forty-one (he was twenty-eight) would be easy pickings. According to experts, my beating Holyfield not only would be a much greater upset than Douglas's win over Tyson, but also would rank as maybe the greatest upset ever.

Sportswriters kept referring to the bout as a joke. They trotted out these tired old clichés about my weight to prove I was overmatched and unworthy of the shot. It was hard not to see that, sometime after 1977, writers became infatuated by these designer bodies they admired on guys like Sylvester Stallone and Mr. T. Some boxers went the same route. But a designer body is not necessarily a boxer's body. My body, now *that* is a boxer's body. I told that to one sportswriter and he laughed. Then I said, "You ever notice how the guys you see lying flat on their back and knocked out—the guys you have to pump back to life—all have ripples down their stomach? Boxing is physical fitness, man, not beauty. And I'm the most physically fit guy on the scene."

He and his colleagues either couldn't or didn't want to understand that I'd begun my comeback at well over 300, and now was down to a svelte 250; there was no way to explain that to them without their thinking that I was on the defensive. So instead of struggling against the tide, I swam in their direction. I began joking that my training camp was right next to Baskin-Robbins, that I'd gone on a cheeseburger diet, that I was the prodigal son of boxing looking for the fatted calf. "Yeah," I said. "I've got a strength coach. My wife. She gets big chains, and at night she puts them around the refrigerator. They're so strong, I can't break them."

Pretty soon, I was beating the sportswriters at their own game, and the snide comments slowed to a trickle.

Anyway, I'd learned not to take their game seriously. Hanging out at bookstores, I discovered stories written years and decades before about Joe Louis and Rocky Marciano, Jack Dempsey and Sugar Ray Robinson. These guys, too, had been reviled by sportswriters. In fact, just for fun, I substituted my own name for their names in these stories about how they were too old now, too slow, had only fought tomato cans. Sure enough, the old stories now read just like the new stories in my morning newspaper.

I was confident that I would beat Holyfield. My confidence came from knowing that I had finally perfected a world-class jab, which was something I'd lacked in my first life as a boxer. In fact, I decided that if the new George were somehow to meet the old George in the ring, the new George would win. New George's jab would keep Old George's right hand on ice. A good hard jab was the only weapon that could stop me from getting right up next to my opponent. (The toughest jab I ever faced was Sonny Liston's while we sparred. Muhammad Ali also had a great one that was hard to counter because it was so quick.)

Besides the jab, I'd also developed patience, something I had precious little of ten, fifteen, twenty years before. I'd become patient enough to jab, jab, jab for six rounds, then begin landing body shots. I'd learned to pace myself and set up the knockout with precision instead of brute strength.

What went wrong in my fight against Holyfield was that I'd campaigned and ballyhooed so long and so hard that, when the time came, I couldn't separate the ballyhoo from a haymaker. I didn't know how to turn off the entertainer in me. And despite how badly I wanted to win, I made the mistake of concentrating too much on not looking like something I wasn't anyway—an angry boxer out for the kill—than I did on winning.

A few days before the fight, cameras followed me into an Atlantic City church where I was preaching. "I don't want you to pray for me to win," I said, "but that I give God some glory."

The night before the fight, I went into the press room and spoke to the reporters. Fighters never do that so close to the opening bell. But I wanted to keep the ballyhoo going, to help establish a record breaker for pay-per-view. It worked, too, because the fight still holds the title for highest grossing pay-per-view event.

Just minutes before the fight, I entertained the likes of Donald Trump, Marla Maples, Kevin Costner, and Jesse Jackson in my dressing room. They basically just barged in, but I didn't want to be rude. The show must go on, and all that.

In the first round, Holyfield came out throwing his right. And I caught it. He threw it harder. And I caught it again. Then he tried to jab, and I beat him to the punch. This exchange confirmed to me that I was really the superior boxer. I was waiting for him to throw that little hook of his, which was the opening I needed for my jab.

In the second he came out jabbing. I moved out of range. Then he played with his hook but couldn't get it going because my jab was doing damage. One of them snapped his head way back and gave me the opportunity to throw a couple of heavy rights.

After that, the only times he scored well were when I made a mistake and tried to throw a power shot on top. He'd move out of the way and hit me back. It was a retaliation shot, but it still counted.

Near the end of the fifth round he attacked ferociously. I blocked, dodged, and landed a hook atop his head, then just missed with a right that I think would have put him down; another right pushed him into the ropes.

In the seventh, I landed a right that sent him reeling backward.

Then I went wild, a bit like the old George, throwing about thirty unanswered punches. He had just enough to deflect the best of them. I have to hand it to him, holding up under that barrage. Me, I was winded for a while afterward.

The next round he came back. Oh, did he come back. While I was catching my breath, he threw everything he had at me, and for a moment emptied himself out. Exhausted, he leaned against me. I didn't clinch. I just let him rest and collect himself.

For a few rounds I went back to the body and the jab. One shot was called a low blow. I'm still unconvinced. Anyway, I felt I was doing whatever I wanted to do, but in a way I was like a jazz musician who gets so proficient at playing his instrument, he forgets that there are people to entertain. In my mind I was defeating Evander Holyfield in so many ways, it didn't occur to me that the judges might not be seeing the same fight.

Charley Shipes told me to begin throwing the right hand more during the last few rounds. In the twelfth and final round, I threw a hard jab, then a quick right. He staggered. I repeated the combination, and he staggered again. I thought he was going down. When he grabbed me, I let him hold on. The ref told him to let go. He didn't until he had his legs. That's what I'll remember most about that fight, besides thinking, at the final bell, that I'd won.

The three judges scored a unanimous but close decision for Holyfield. I was disappointed and hurt. I'd missed at least one chance to win, and I felt that I'd let my wife down. Before the fight she told me that in a dream, the Lord had come to her and asked what she wanted. "I want for George to win the title again," she said. I consoled myself with knowing that between Joan's vision and mine, I'd someday have another crack at the title.

In my dressing room, I felt depressed. But I couldn't let the cameras catch me that way, because millions of kids were watching. I had to come up with a line. "Give me something to say," I told Jesse Jackson.

He said, "Tell them that we didn't retreat and we kept our dignity."

"Great," I said. "That's great."

That was all I needed. I jumped off the table with enthusiasm, and when they stuck the microphone in my face, I exclaimed, "We didn't retreat, and we kept our dignity. So everyone at home can take pride that, while we may not win *all* the points, we *made* a point. Everyone grab your Geritol, and let's toast. Hip-hip-hooray."

Besides the satisfaction of having gone the distance and winning in my own heart, my compensation was being the *people's* champion (and endowing fully the youth center with my purse). They saw in me things they liked, some of which may not even have been there. I thought back on the old George Foreman and felt sorry for him. He and I had so little in common. The modern me was less an updated version of the old than a completely new model, like a four-cylinder Volkswagen compared to a twelve-cylinder Jaguar. I'd been the guy you didn't want your daughter anywhere near. Now hundreds of people trusted their kids to me. When I was invited to speak somewhere out of town, my hosts insisted that I stay in their spare bedroom. There was no reason not to continue.

In Reno at the end of that year I fought a kid named Jimmy Ellis, who couldn't come out for the third round. Then in April of 1992, I took on a highly regarded puncher, Alex Stewart. After I knocked him down a few times, I began hitting him on the tip of the nose. When I asked the referee to stop the fight, he refused, so I backed up and Stewart began swinging shots at me. My face took some hard pops and swelled; my nose bled. While I still won a clear decision, some people in boxing claimed I should stop. Not only had I lost my killer instinct, but now I was taking beatings, too. I reminded myself that such speculation was part of the boxing game. It didn't matter as long as I knew what I was doing.

January the following year, I knocked out the highly regarded South African fighter Pierre Coetzer in the eighth. That led to a fight being set up in June against Tommy Morrison for the vacant World Boxing Organization title. Early in the match I did exactly what I wanted, and I figured I was way ahead. The last thing I wanted was to hurt him. Late in the fight, I didn't pull the trigger on a lights-out combination because I was afraid of doing permanent damage to him. And he'd gone too far in the fight to suffer the humiliation of a knockout. I respected his grit. Even so, I was the most surprised person in the arena when Morrison won the decision. Bob Arum, who'd promoted the fight, said publicly that I should quit. Sportswriters did too. They wrote that I looked lackadaisical. When used to describe a boxer, that word's code talk for "old."

The loss hurt for a few days, because I knew that I'd given away a win. I wasn't regretful, though. This was a young man of twenty-four. I was forty-four. That gave me a perspective from the inside that no one else had. I'd seen tough young talent like Tommy Morrison get their futures knocked out of them by a real beating, which was the only way he was going to go down. And my conscience wouldn't allow me to clean his clock thoroughly. So, yes, I guess in that sense, Arum and the columnists were right to say that I was "lackadaisical," if that meant I lacked the killer instinct. Since mercy wasn't a quality too often seen in the boxing ring, they confused it with lack of ability. What they didn't understand is that I still had the drive to excel, to be champ again. Circumstances got in the way.

After the Morrison fight I received word that a pilot I'd already shot for an ABC sitcom had been picked up as a series for the fall season. The former boxer–turned-actor, and now producer, Tony Danza, had approached me to star in this series about an ex-champ who has a large family and is involved in helping kids. It sounded like familiar territory. What other title could he give it but *George*? If nothing else, the show was confirmation of how far I'd risen in the public esteem.

Tony told me that the network had ordered eight shows, and if the ratings were good we'd go to thirteen, and then twenty-four. Because my experience in TV was shows like *Hollywood Squares*, which were taped five per day, I thought that we'd be done working in a few weeks and I'd return to the ring. When I heard that this was a minimum of a few months of work, and that I'd have to stay in Los Angeles, away from my family—and that my contract prohibited me from fighting all that time—I got a little discouraged. But I went ahead and did it. I lived those months at the Century Plaza hotel.

While walking through the hotel lobby one day, a man asked me to say a few words to his convention that was meeting there. I felt shy but went along with him. I said hello and a few other words, anything to let them see that the guy they thought they knew was really the guy I am. I had to. After all, these were people who loved me and prayed for me. And you can never have too many people loving you and praying for you.

It was a national convention of rabbis.

The novelty of starring in a television series never wore off. I worked at acting, which was in most ways harder than boxing. I'd take a day to memorize my lines, and by the next day most of them would be changed. The fun came from playing George, rather than being George. My family and friends were proud. They'd watch the show and tape it at the same time, and we'd all watch together again when I was in town. Everyone laughed in all the right places. I'd look at myself and think, *I'm famous now*. But not famous enough, I guess, because the show was canceled after the first eight episodes. Located in television's graveyard, Saturday night, *George* ranked too near the bottom of the ratings. I was less disappointed, I think, than Tony Danza. But as time went on, I began to realize how much I'd enjoyed the whole experience and would miss it. At least now I could put on my tombstone: PREACHER, BOXER, ACTOR.

Right below that, I'd put the epitaph everyone else had written for me: HE WAS TOO OLD.

Chapter Eleven

I N THE YEARS after I became a preacher, funeral homes from all over the Houston area would call and ask me to deliver eulogies. I considered it an honor to meet and comfort people in their time of grief. The family would paint a word portrait of the deceased for me, and I would try to focus my memorial comments on how the person had extended himself or herself to others. I'd also point out that at funerals we often grieve behind guilt, thinking about what we had wanted to do but never did for that person. And I'd tell them that when the sun comes up every day and we're still alive, we've been given a second chance to redeem ourselves. Ever since Puerto Rico, I've believed that, at any moment, I could be snatched from this world. I live in the shadow of that possibility. That's why I can never take a vacation, never rest on what I accomplished yesterday. There's too much good work yet to be done, and my feeling is that as long as I'm working, I'm here. If I pause to rest—who knows?

As a boxing commentator for HBO, I was at a press conference with the heavyweight champ Evander Holyfield in April of 1994, the day before he was to defend his title against Michael Moorer. In response to a question, Holyfield explained his future plans: beating Michael Moorer; fighting Lennox Lewis, who held the WBC belt, to unify the title; and then taking on Mike Tyson, who'd presumably be out of prison. He didn't mention my name. His plan would take at least two years. At the time I was already forty-five, and didn't want to fight any other boxers to reestablish myself as a leading contender. That day, I was a sad commentator. I thought my boxing career might have come to an end after all.

During their fight, it seemed to me that Moorer could have taken out Holyfield early, but he backed away. Later, it seemed to me that Holyfield couldn't finish off Moorer after knocking him down. When the judges gave the bout—and therefore the championship—to Moorer, I recognized the decision as a violation of the unwritten rule: to become the champ you've got to beat the champ by knocking him out or winning so clearly on points that there's no doubt in anyone's mind. I said into the microphone that something needed to be done about boxing's monkey-business scoring system, and that the Duvas (father Lou and son Dan run Main Events, a New Jersey–based event promotion, management, and boxing-training company) held too many fighters for the health of boxing. They controlled at least a part of both Holyfield and Moorer.

Well, a big brouhaha developed over those comments, so much so that in HBO's rebroadcast of the fight, they were edited out. The Duvas threatened to sue me. And I figured that I'd finally messed with the wrong guys. My boxing career, I decided, was definitely history.

Dejected and depressed while driving to Marshall for some R&R, I used my cellular phone to call Bob Arum at his Los Angeles home. We chatted for a while about nothing in particular. Then I asked if he'd heard my comments during the fight. He said he had and agreed with them. We talked a little more about fighting and the new champ.

"Hey George," he said, "I sense from the way you're talking that you want to fight Moorer."

"Boy, would I," I said.

Before he could respond, the static overpowered the phone; I was driving through a bad reception area. In a mile or so, when I saw a pay phone at a gas station, I stopped and called Bob back.

He said, "You really think you can beat the guy?"

"Bob, I'm positive I can beat him. His style's perfect for me."

"Okay, let me see what I can do."

I'd thought I could beat Michael Moorer because both Joan and I had dreamed of my winning the heavyweight championship again. And that first night in Marshall, I dreamed that I knocked out Michael Moorer.

Pretty soon Bob was reporting back that initial contact with the Moorer camp was going well. While Moorer wasn't in Bob's stable of fighters, he had some leverage because mine was the most recognizable name among heavyweights. Fans would come out to see me fight against almost anyone, and particularly for the heavyweight championship. That translated to money in Moorer's pocket.

The only monkey wrench was that the Duvas wanted to cut out Bob Arum and promote the fight themselves. Though I didn't have a signed contract with Arum, I wouldn't do that. He'd already worked hard to make this fight happen. When I refused to go ahead without Arum, the Moorer people said that they would put me on the undercard of Moorer's first title defense, and that if I won I'd get my shot. I refused that, too. For any other fighter, that would have ended negotiations. But Moorer, like everyone else in his camp, believed that I'd be an easy payday. They figured I was old and slow and that he could box my ears off. For him, this was a win-win situation: high reward and low risk.

In May, when Bob began negotiating in earnest, I insisted that I needed to fight more than I needed to get richer. There were to be no deal breakers—conditions that had to be met—and he was to give in whenever necessary. I'm sure that was painful for a born deal maker like Bob. The result was that I agreed to a guarantee that came to less money than any of my fights since Gerry Cooney. The fight was set for November 5 at the MGM Grand Garden, in Las Vegas.

Bob, my attorney Henry Holmes, and I were having lunch at Bob's house one afternoon when Bob said, "Now, George, are you serious about this fight? Are you going to get in shape? Or are we just going through the motions?"

"I want this championship more than anything," I said. "I'm going to get in shape. I promise you and Henry that, starting today, I'm going to train my hardest, and I promise you that I will win the heavyweight championship."

"That means going on a diet, George," Henry said.

My diet began with that meal. As Henry said at the press conference announcing the fight, "No more hot dogs and hamburgers until November sixth."

To train, I rented a house in Malibu Colony, next to Tom Hanks's house. Early each morning I'd run a few miles up the beach to Henry's house. Henry would always set out on his porch some celery and a glass of water to sustain me for the run back. "Henry, are you up?" I'd yell from the sand, knowing he wasn't but that he'd pretend to be. He and I would sit outside and talk for a while before I ran back.

One morning Henry looked unusually serious. "I just got word from Bob Arum," he said, "that the W.B.A. has refused to sanction the fight. They say you're too old, that you lost to Tommy Morrison, and that you're not a top contender—and the W.B.A. rules state Moorer has to face a top contender."

It took me a moment or so to swallow the news. I said softly, "These things go on in boxing."

"Well," Henry said, "let's both think about what we do here. I have a feeling that what's been done is not right."

I sensed this was my payback for the comment about the Duvas. They wanted another of their fighters in there against Moorer. The W.B.A. had informed Michael Moorer that if he fought me, they would strip him of his title. Moorer understandably replied that he wouldn't risk losing his belt, so he called off the fight.

A few mornings later I ran by Henry's again. "I feel so bad," I admitted. "I feel like people are going to think there's something wrong with me."

That afternoon I went to a meeting at Henry's office. Bob Arum was there, as were some other attorneys from Henry's firm, Michael Schenkman and Mike Bergman. Bob, who'd been an assistant United States attorney in the Kennedy administration, said he'd discovered some evidence that the W.B.A. hadn't always followed its own rules, which made its rules meaningless. Henry and his team recommended that I file a lawsuit against the W.B.A., the Moorer camp, and Nevada's athletic commission. The charge was that if the fight didn't go forward, my career would be irreparably damaged. Worse than the damage to my career, though, was the feeling that people would look at me as damaged goods. I told Henry that if there was any chance at all to win, I wanted to try.

After we filed suit, Pat English, an attorney for the Duvas, predicted that we had only a five percent chance of winning our case. That was five times more than I needed to press forward.

The hearing was held before a judge in Las Vegas on August 19th. So many lawyers were in the room, it looked like a Bar Association convention. Much of the talk before I took the stand was about W.B.A. procedural matters and whether or not a W.B.A. attorney had asked Moorer's management for a small piece of the action, possibly to help in getting the fight sanctioned. Asked if professional fighters have only a certain number of years in which to make a living, John Davimos, Moorer's manager, said, "Unless you're George Foreman."

When I was called to testify, Henry asked me to state my true age. At dinner the night before, he'd warned me that I would have to answer under oath, which means swearing on the Bible. Over the years my age has been a matter of some dispute, because the *Ring Record Book*, boxing's statistical bible, added a year to my age by printing an incorrect birthdate.

"I was born January tenth, 1949," I said. "I'm forty-five years old."

Henry later asked about the boxer that the W.B.A. wanted to fight Moorer instead of me. Joe Hipp seemed to me a silly replacement, and I said so, because he'd been knocked cold by Tommy Morrison—against whom I'd gone the distance. I then related the perfect results of another two days' worth of extensive medical testing I'd just undergone, including a retina exam by a "ban boxing" zealot who'd said my eyes showed no evidence of my having ever been in a fight.

"Now, George Foreman," Henry asked, "do you want this fight?"

"More than anything in the world," I said.

"Why?"

"I've wanted to be heavyweight champ of the world ever since I reentered the ring in 1987. It means more to me probably than anything else athletically in the world. I wanted to fight for the title to show the world not only that I can win this thing, but that age forty is truly not a deficit."

"What would you have done if you had failed any of those medical examinations?"

"More important than fighting is my health in general," I said. I was thinking of my responsibilities and obligations. My family and the families of the George Foreman Youth and Community Center needed me for more than my money.

At about eight o'clock that night, after another few hours of testimony from other witnesses, Judge Donald Mosley gave us his decision. "It might well be argued," he said, "that Mr. Foreman, if he can sit and listen to eleven hours of lawyers, would have no problem going ten rounds with anyone." He found that I was medically fit, and that the rules the W.B.A. claimed this fight was violating had been violated in the past by the W.B.A. itself.

I began training like a racehorse, practicing every move, working out harder and with more determination than I ever had. I even jumped rope, which I hadn't done since 1990. I knew that to win this bout, I couldn't avoid knocking my man out. But because my dream had foretold that Michael Moorer would be knocked out and not seriously hurt, I rested easy. I was having so much fun, I didn't want to leave the gym. My rage now wasn't to kill, but to win.

I went to Las Vegas about two weeks before the fight, to get accustomed to the desert air. Good thing, too, because it took me until three days before the fight to gain my wind.

Two days before the fight was the weigh-in, which turned out to be more like a George Foreman love-in. Hundreds of people crowded into one of the MGM Grand's big ballrooms to watch me and Michael Moorer stand on the scales. When I stepped up, the crowd exploded. I was surprised and excited. I could feel what they were feeling for me, and I wondered what Michael Moorer was thinking. No one seemed to be in his corner.

My fight plan was to win by the three-knockdown rule. Regulations said that if Moorer went down three times, the referee would have to stop the fight. I preferred to do it in the early rounds, which would save him from too much hurt. But about forty minutes before the bout, the ref, Joe Cortez, came into the locker room and explained that the three-knockdown rule had been waived.

All of a sudden, I was once again the forty-five-year-old compassionate preacher-boxer who faced a dilemma. I was almost in tears. To win now, I realized, I was going to have to punish Michael Moorer—rattle his brains until he went down and stayed down. He might get in three punches to my one, but each of mine would do a lot more damage, especially as they accumulated. Eventually, there'd be that one last punch to send him down and out. In my thinking, Moorer was probably going to win every round but the one in which the lights went out for him. I guessed the eighth or ninth round.

Well, there was no turning back now. I had planned, hoped, and prayed—even litigated—for this fight. I was exactly where I'd wanted to be. So I wasn't nervous. When an HBO camera caught me shadowboxing in the hallway outside the dressing room, I laughed. I didn't want anyone watching to think I was having anything but fun.

A while later, an HBO producer walked into the dressing room and asked if I had any special music to play as I entered the arena. This was the first time anyone had ever asked. I handed her the Sam Cooke tape I'd been jumping rope to during training, and thought about how wonderful it was going to be to run out there to my song. My intention was to explode into the ring—to look not like a guy who's just fighting, but like one who's actually happy to be given the chance to fight. I was pumped.

Soon "If I Had a Hammer" by Sam Cooke began playing over the P.A. system, bringing cheers and hand-clapping from the nearly fourteen thousand people at the MGM Grand Garden.

When I jogged down the aisle into view, wearing a sweatshirt with the hood up, the cheering became a deafening roar. By the time I climbed into the ring, everyone was standing; most were screaming, "George! George! George!"

A lot of these people, including some of those cheering loudest, probably believed in their hearts that what the "experts" said was true: George is too old, too fat, and too slow to have any real chance of winning the championship. For them, I was a symbol, the man who refused to accept middle age. Anyway, their reasons didn't matter to me. I just appreciated their love.

The cheering stopped and booing began when rap music came through the P.A. system. Michael Moorer was approaching the ring for his first title defense. The boos increased and lasted long after he climbed inside. Listening to the boos, I thought, *I know what you're going through, son,* and I almost felt sorry for him. The heavyweight champ of the world was not, on that night, the people's choice. Still, the boos had nothing to do with disliking him. It was just that the crowd wanted to give me home court advantage. I hoped he knew that.

Psychiatrists masquerading as sportswriters had been writing that retribution was what motivated George Foreman to fight Michael Moorer, a man young enough to be his son. As they pointed out, it had been twenty years and a few days since I'd lost my title to Muhammad Ali. They said that I was trying to recoup that loss. But they were wrong. What they wrote said much more about them than it did about me. The truth was, if I had known on that night of my loss to Muhammad what lay in both of our futures, I would have helped him to appreciate the beauty of his win.

When the fight began, I knew that if I knocked him down early, he'd run the rest of the fight, except for zinging me with his speed. It wouldn't matter that, between fighters, my one power shot was worth more than his three slaps. Those three slaps would tell the judges and commentators that he had a strategy. And especially if you're the champion, having that "strategy" impresses judges and wins fights.

Moorer was a lefty—in fact, the first southpaw heavyweight

champion in history. I decided that, whatever he would do, I'd counter it with a jab; and as soon as he finished his combinations, I'd close with a jab. He'd land more punches and look a lot prettier, but I knew my jabs were digging deeper than his; I was using his own momentum against him. Every time he leaned forward to throw a punch, I'd stick out the jab and touch it to the tip of his face. (What had happened by accident to the Russian boxer in the Olympic finals was what I was planning here.) Whatever he did, I threw the jab. So even if he landed that big left hook of his, he was still tasting punishment. My jab, if it hits you around the middle of the face, eventually weakens your legs, because it snaps your head back and interferes with nerve response. After four rounds, you're half the boxer you were. Yes, Moorer was landing jabs, too—probably more jabs than I. But he was throwing them because he'd been tutored to throw them, but didn't know why he was. Mine were thrown with particular intent. While it may seem odd that a jab thrown with intent to weaken is more powerful than one thrown without intent, I know from experience that the marriage of mind and body makes the sum more powerful than the individual parts.

As the fight went on, with Moorer landing so many shots, I felt like a lion carrying off a gazelle. The lion just shuts his eyes, because he knows he's going to get kicked before he eats his meal. If their contest were on the point system, the gazelle would win. But it's not.

About the only times I threw my right were when he went to his straight left. As soon as he did it—*boom!* With his body crossing over toward me, my right would be that much more effective. The harder he threw his left, the more punishing was my right. Few people watching would notice, being too caught up in the speed and grace of Moorer's punching; to them, it looked like he was getting the better of me—and I have to admit that some of his shots hurt. But Moorer knew the real score. These exchanges were telling him that he maybe ought to be jabbing more and throwing that left less.

By the third round, Moorer was bleeding in the nose and mouth. Around then is when I got him into a little boxing match, where he jabbed me and I moved out of the way to counter him. He smiled. I understood that smile. It meant that I wasn't supposed to be able to do that. It meant that I'd gotten him thinking; he wanted to show old George what he could do. It meant that he was abandoning his original fight plan.

Between rounds, I didn't sit on a stool. I'd stopped sitting on stools years before, early in my second career. That one minute had begun to seem like an hour; I got bored. Besides, the way I trained—sparring against one partner, who'd be replaced immediately by another, sometimes for seventeen rounds' worth— was without rest. And since I wasn't using any of my real punching power in the ring, I wasn't drained of energy. After each round I'd listen to what my cornermen Charley Shipes and Angelo Dundee had to say, then turn slowly around to see what was going on in Moorer's corner. I wanted to study his body posture, how he held his arms, whether his shoulders were slumping. With each round, I could see that the jab was increasingly taking its toll. It didn't matter that I was throwing fewer punches with each round, as long as I made each one count.

Here and there, Moorer landed some hard punches. One uppercut might have put me on the mat if I weren't so much taller than he, or if I'd been leaning down. But by the time it got to my chin, it had lost most of its force.

In the eighth, I could clearly see that he was slowing down. That's when I threw a left hook that caught him under the right armpit. I don't know what the judges thought of that punch; on TV, the commentators ignored it. But I do know what kind of damage it did. Moorer's hands dropped a little lower, to protect his side. And his reaction time wasn't what it had been earlier, because of the constant jabbing. Body shots are money in the bank. They sap whatever strength is left in the legs after the constant jabbing, so that after the knockout punch, while the arms want to get up, and the chest wants to get up, and the stomach wants to get up, the legs say "Uh-uh."

In the ninth, I did what you're never supposed to do against a southpaw—moved to my right, in front of his power. Southpaws practice trying to get guys into that position, and here I was doing it for nothing. It was like giving him too much ice cream; he didn't know how to handle it. I was daring him, you see. That made him suspicious. In my corner, Charley and Angelo were going crazy, thinking that *I* was crazy. But there was a method to my madness. I was thinking about my watermelon patch in Marshall, which used to be destroyed each year by wolves until someone told me to paint a few of the melons white—every other one, then every fifth one; a random sampling. When the wolves would show up, they'd see the white watermelons, get suspicious, and go away. They were thinking too much to relax and enjoy the fruit. I'd used their brains against them.

Same with Moorer. As an intelligent man, he had to be wondering what George was up to. Right before the bell, as he was contemplating the free gift, I landed a hard blow to his midsection, one of the first body shots I'd thrown with any power behind it. That got him thinking some more.

The tenth. With his attention on the body, I threw a few jabs to his face. When he reached to throw a right, I countered with a left hook that was supposed to hit him in the same spot underneath the armpit. But because of his position after following through on that right, my shot caught him on the back. The ref issued a warning, which actually supported my strategy, because it confirmed Moorer's suspicions that I'd begun targeting his body. Now was the time to show him power in the face.

I touched him twice with my right hand, then threw a left hook with all my might that caught him on the ear. I've been hit with those before. You hear ringing. After landing the same three punches again, I saw an opening and loaded up a big roundhouse hook. When I missed, it must have looked like I was swinging at a knuckleball. *Okay, now, George, settle down,* I told myself.

I threw a sharp left jab, then a strong right that caught him on the forehead and made my hand hurt. I could feel it swell almost immediately. Still, seeing him stopped in his tracks, I knew he was far more hurt than my hand was. I expected him to go down. When he didn't, I gave him credit for being tougher than I thought.

Not wanting to whale on him until he fell, I decided to bring the shot a little lower. So after another quick left jab, I followed with a short right from the hip that landed at ground zero on the chin. He crashed to the mat.

I knew before the ref started counting that he wasn't getting up. Anyway, I hoped he wasn't. Despite my dream, I would have had a serious dilemma over whether to hit him again.

"Three, four, five," the ref said. He wasn't up yet. "Six, seven." Now I knew for sure he was down for the count. "Eight, nine, ten." It was over.

I looked up to heaven. *Can You believe it?* I thought. *We did it.* I prepared to get down on my knees and give thanks. I'd already told God, when I left the hotel before the fight, that if I won, I would for the first time say a prayer in public. And as I knelt in the closest corner that's exactly what I did. "Thank you, Jesus," I said. "Thank you for helping me out, and for helping my wife to go through what she's gone through. Thank you for my winning this. I just want you to know I appreciate all the help you've given me." I was just as thankful for not having to hit Michael Moorer anymore.

On my feet again, I looked around at mayhem in the ring. My brother Roy had fainted from excitement. Out in the auditorium, I never saw so many obviously happy people in one place. It was a joyful noise they made. The victory belonged to them all. That was something you could feel. There was Henry Holmes, crying happiness. There was Dane Issenman, the man who'd built my home, jumping up and down, hugging strangers. Everybody was doing it. They acted like children at their best. For a moment, they were free. Something I'd done had given them freedom. I hope I never do anything to unfreeze that moment in time for anyone who watched and felt that way.

A month or so after the fight I was on the treadmill in my exercise room, thinking about how you can't ever be an expert on God. You have to wake up each morning and tell yourself, "I've got faith." I guess that's why it's called faith, not science.

As I prayed right there on the treadmill, I gave thanks for all the goodness that's come my way for forty-six years. As vividly as if it happened the day before, I remembered the look on Mrs. Moon's face that first time I passed through the lunch line at the Oregon Job Corps center. She smiled at me. That was the moment I decided I was special.

"God," I said, "This is some kind of life you've given me."